THE SOUL AFTER DEATH

The twenty stations of the aerial toll-houses.
Detail of a 16th-century Novgorod icon,
Hann Collection, Pittsburgh, Pennsylvania.

HIEROMONK SERAPHIM ROSE
1934–1982

THE SOUL AFTER DEATH

CONTEMPORARY "AFTER-DEATH" EXPERIENCES
IN THE LIGHT OF THE ORTHODOX
TEACHING ON THE AFTERLIFE

BY FR. SERAPHIM ROSE

ST. HERMAN OF ALASKA BROTHERHOOD
2022

First Printing, 1980
Second Printing, Second Edition, 1982
Third Printing, 1987
Fourth Printing, Third Edition, 1993
Fifth Printing, 1995
Sixth Printing, 1998
Seventh Printing, Fourth Edition, 2004
Eighth Printing, Fourth Edition, 2009
Ninth Printing, Fifth Edition, 2015
Tenth Printing, Fifth Edition, 2020
Eleventh Printing, Fifth Edition, 2022

Printed in the United States of America

Front cover: Russian icon of the Last Judgment. Courtesy of A. Dean McKenzie, John F. Waggaman, and the Timken Art Gallery.
Back cover: Fr. Seraphim Rose in front of the Holy Doors at the St. Herman of Alaska Monastery, Platina, California, 1977.

Publishers Cataloging-in-Publication

Rose, Hieromonk Seraphim, 1934–1982.
      The soul after death: contemporary "after-death" experiences in the light of the Orthodox teaching on the afterlife / by Fr. Seraphim Rose.—5th ed.
      p.   cm.
      Includes bibliographical references and index.
      ISBN: 0–938635–14–X
      1. Future life—Orthodox Eastern Church. 2. Orthodox Eastern Church—Doctrines. 3. Near-death experiences—Religious aspects—Orthodox Eastern Church.   I. Title

BX323.R67 2004
236/.2—dc22   93–085175

THERE WAS a certain rich man, which was clothed in purple and fine linen, and fared sumptuously every day; and there was a certain beggar named Lazarus, which was laid at his gate, full of sores, and desiring to be fed with the crumbs which fell from the rich man's table; moreover, the dogs came and licked his sores. And it came to pass, that the beggar died, and was carried by the angels into Abraham's bosom; the rich man also died, and was buried, and in hell he lifted up his eyes, being in torments, and seeth Abraham afar off, and Lazarus in his bosom. And he cried and said, Father Abraham, have mercy on me, and send Lazarus, that he may dip the tip of his finger in water, and cool my tongue; for I am tormented in this flame. But Abraham said, Son, remember that thou in thy lifetime receivedst thy good things, and likewise Lazarus evil things; but now he is comforted, and thou art tormented. And beside all this, between us and you there is a great gulf fixed, so that they which would pass from hence to you cannot; neither can they pass to us, that would come from thence. Then he said, I pray thee therefore, father, that thou wouldest send him to my father's house: for I have five brethren, that he may testify unto them, lest they also come into this place of torment. Abraham saith unto him, They have Moses and the prophets; let them hear them. And he said, Nay, father Abraham: but if one went unto them from the dead, they will repent. And he said unto him, If they hear not Moses and the prophets, neither will they be persuaded, though one rose from the dead. —Luke 16:19–31

An angel carrying the soul of St. Artemius of Verkola to heaven.
*Detail of a 17th-century icon from Moscow/Yaroslavl, depicting
St. Artemius with scenes from his life.*

Contents

Contents

CONTENTS

CONTENTS

Preface

THE AIM of the present book is two-fold: first, to give an explanation, in terms of the Orthodox Christian doctrine of life after death, of the present-day "after-death" experiences that have caused such interest in some religious and scientific circles; and second, to present the basic sources and texts which contain the Orthodox teaching on life after death. If the Orthodox teaching is so little understood today, it is largely because these texts have been so neglected and have become so "unfashionable" in our "enlightened" times; and our attempt has been to make these texts more understandable and accessible to present-day readers. Needless to say, they constitute a reading material infinitely more profound and more profitable than the popular "after-death" books of our day, which, even when they are not merely sensational, simply cannot go much below the spectacular surface of today's experiences for want of a coherent and true teaching on the whole subject of life after death.

The Orthodox teaching presented in this book will doubtless be criticized by some as being too "simple" or even "naive" for a 20th-century man to believe. It should therefore be emphasized that this teaching is not that of a few isolated or untypical teachers in the Orthodox Church, but is the teaching which the Orthodox Church of Christ has handed down from her very beginning, which is expressed in countless Patristic writings and Lives of Saints and in the Divine services of the

Orthodox Church, and which has been taught uninterruptedly in the Church even down to our own day. The "simplicity" of this teaching is the simplicity of truth itself, which—whether it is expressed in this or in other teachings of the Church—comes as a refreshing fountain of clarity in the midst of the dark confusion caused in modern minds by the various errors and empty speculations of recent centuries. Each chapter of this book attempts to point to the Patristic and hagiographical sources which contain this teaching.

The chief inspiration for the writing of this book has been a 19th-century Russian Orthodox Father, Bishop Ignatius Brianchaninov, who was perhaps the first great Orthodox theologian to face squarely the very problem which has become so acute in our own days: how to preserve the authentic Christian tradition and teaching in a world that has become entirely foreign to Orthodoxy and strives either to overthrow and dismiss it or else "reinterpret" it so that it can be made compatible with a worldly way of life and thinking. Acutely aware of the Roman Catholic and other Western influences which were striving to "modernize" Orthodoxy even in his days, Bishop Ignatius prepared for the defense of Orthodoxy both by delving deeply into the authentic Orthodox sources (whose teaching he absorbed in some of the best Orthodox monastic centers of his time) and by familiarizing himself also with the scientific and literary culture of his century (he attended an engineering school, not a theological seminary). Armed thus with a knowledge both of Orthodox theology and of secular knowledge, he devoted his life to the defense of authentic Orthodoxy and to an exposure of the modern deviation from it. It is no exaggeration to say that no other Orthodox country in the 19th century possessed such a defender of Orthodoxy against the temptations and errors of modern times; his only rival, perhaps, was his fellow-countryman, Bishop Theophan the Recluse, who did much the same thing on a less "sophisticated" level.

One volume of Bishop Ignatius' Collected Works (Volume III) was devoted specifically to the question of the Church's teaching on life after death, which he defended against the Roman Catholic and other modern distortions of it. It is chiefly from this volume that we have borrowed our own discussion in the present book on subjects like toll-houses and the apparitions of spirits—teachings which, for some reason, the "modern" mind finds it impossible to accept in a simple way, but insists on "reinterpreting" them or rejecting them altogether. Bishop Theophan also, of course, taught the same teaching, and we have also made use of his words; and in our own century another great Russian Orthodox theologian, Archbishop John Maximovitch of blessed memory, repeated this teaching so clearly and simply that we have used his words to form most of the conclusion of the present book. That the Orthodox doctrine on life after death has been taught so explicitly and clearly by great Orthodox teachers in modern times, right down to our own day, is an immense help to us who are striving today to preserve the true Orthodoxy of the past, not merely in its correctly transmitted words, but even more in the authentically Orthodox interpretation of these words.

In this book, in addition to the Orthodox sources and interpretations mentioned above, we have made considerable use of today's non-Orthodox "after-death" literature, as well as of some occult texts on this subject. In this we have followed Bishop Ignatius' example in presenting a false teaching as fully and fairly as needed to expose its falsity so that Orthodox Christians will not be tempted by it; and we have also found, like him, that non-Orthodox texts, when it is a matter of actual *experiences* that are being described (and not mere opinions and

interpretations), often provide striking confirmations of Orthodox truths. Our chief aim in this book has been to present as
detailed a *contrast* as necessary to point out the full difference
that exists between the Orthodox teaching and the experience
of Orthodox saints on the one hand, and the occult teaching
and modern experiences on the other. If we had merely presented the Orthodox teaching without this contrast, it would
have been convincing to few save the already-convinced; but
now, perhaps, some even of those who have been involved in
the modern experiences will be awakened to the vast difference
between their experience and genuine spiritual experience.

However, the very fact that a good part of this book
discusses *experiences,* both Christian and non-Christian, also
means that not everything here is a simple presentation of the
Church's teaching on life after death, but also contains the
author's interpretations of these various experiences. Concerning these interpretations, of course, there is room for a legiti-
mate difference of opinion among Orthodox Christians. We
have tried as far as possible to present these interpretations in a
provisional way, without trying to "define" such matters of
experience in the same way that the Church's general teaching
on life after death can be defined. Specifically, regarding occult
"out-of-body" experiences and the "astral plane," we have simply presented these as they have been described by participants
in them, and compared them to similar manifestations in
Orthodox literature, without trying to define the precise nature
of such experiences; but we have accepted them as real experiences wherein actual demonic forces are contacted, and not as
mere hallucinations. Let the reader judge for himself how
adequate this approach has been.

It should be obvious that this book has by no means
exhausted the Orthodox teaching on life after death; it is only

an introduction to it. In reality, however, there is no "complete teaching" on this subject, and there are no Orthodox "experts" on it. We who live on earth can hardly even begin to understand the reality of the spiritual world until we ourselves come to dwell in it. This is a process that begins now, in this life, but ends only in eternity, when we will behold "face to face" what we now see only "through a glass, darkly" (I Cor. 13:12). But the Orthodox sources to which we have pointed in this book give us a basic outline of this teaching, and this is sufficient to inspire us, not to acquire a precise knowledge of something which is, after all, beyond us, but to begin to struggle to attain the Heavenly Kingdom which is the goal of our Christian life, and to avoid the demonic pitfalls which are spread everywhere in the way of Christian strugglers by the enemy of our salvation. The other world is *realer* and *closer* than we usually think; and the path to it is right here in front of us, in the life of spiritual discipline and prayer which the Church has handed down to us as the way to salvation. This book is dedicated and addressed to those who wish to lead such a life.

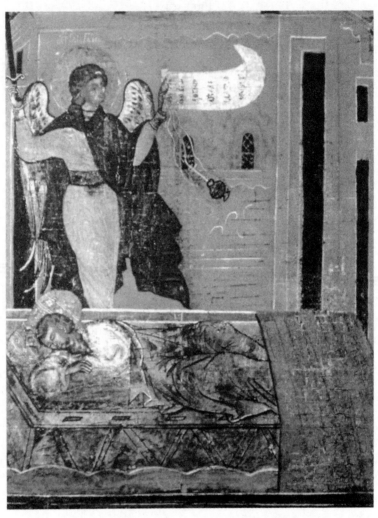

A Guardian Angel meeting a soul at death.
Detail of a 17th-century Russian icon.

CHAPTER ONE

Some Aspects of Today's Experiences

THE SUBJECT of life after death, quite suddenly, has become one of widespread popular interest in the Western world. In particular, a number of books purporting to describe "after-death" experiences have been published in the past two years, and reputable scientists and physicians have either authored such books themselves or given them their wholehearted endorsement. One of these, the world-renowned physician and "expert" on problems of death and dying, Elizabeth Kubler-Ross, finds that these researches into after-death experiences "will enlighten many and will confirm what we have been taught for two thousand years—that there is life after death."

All this, of course, is an abrupt departure from the hitherto-prevailing atmosphere in medical and scientific circles, which in general have viewed death as a "taboo" subject and relegated any idea of after-death survival as belonging to the realm of fantasy or superstition, or at best as a matter of private belief for which there is no objective evidence.

The outward cause of this sudden change of opinion is a simple one: new techniques of resuscitating the "clinically dead" (in particular, by stimulation of the heart when it has stopped beating) have come into widespread use in recent years. Thus, people who have been technically "dead" (without pulse or heartbeat) have been restored to life in large numbers, and many of these people (once the "taboo" on this subject and the fear of being considered "crazy" had worn off) are now speaking about it openly.

But it is the *inward* cause of this change, as well as its "ideology," that are most interesting to us: why should this phenomenon have become suddenly so immensely popular, and in terms of what religious or philosophical view is it being generally understood? It has already become one of the "signs of the times," a symptom of the religious interest of our day; what, then, is its significance? We shall return to these questions after a closer examination of the phenomenon itself.

But first we must ask: on what basis are we to judge this phenomenon? Those who describe it themselves have no clear interpretation of it; often they are searching for such an interpretation in occultist or spiritistic texts. Some religious people (as well as scientists), sensing a danger to their established beliefs, simply deny the experiences as they are described, relegating them usually to the realm of "hallucinations." This has been done by some Protestants who are committed to the opinion either that the soul is in a state of unconsciousness after death, or that it goes immediately to be "with Christ"; likewise, doctrinaire unbelievers reject the idea that the soul survives at all, no matter what evidence is presented to them. But such experiences cannot be explained merely by denying them; they must be properly understood, both in themselves and in the whole context of what we know concerning the fate of the soul after death.

Unfortunately, some Orthodox Christians also, under the

influence of modern materialistic ideas (as filtered through Protestantism and Roman Catholicism), have come to have rather vague and indefinite ideas of the afterlife. The author of one of the new books on after-death experiences (David R. Wheeler, *Journey to the Other Side,* Ace Books, New York, 1977) made a point of asking the opinions of various "sects" on the state of the soul after death. Thus, he called a priest of the Greek Orthodox Archdiocese and was given a very general opinion of the existence of heaven and hell, but was told that Orthodoxy does not have "any specific idea of what the hereafter would be like." The author could only conclude that "the Greek Orthodox view of the hereafter is not clear" (p. 130).

On the contrary, of course, Orthodox Christianity has a quite precise doctrine and view of life after death, beginning from the very moment of death itself. This doctrine is contained in the Holy Scripture (interpreted in the whole context of Christian doctrine), in writings of the Holy Fathers, and (especially as regards the specific experiences of the soul after death) in many Lives of Saints and anthologies of personal experiences of this sort. The entire fourth book of the *Dialogues* of St. Gregory the Great, Pope of Rome (†604), for example, is devoted to this subject. In our own days an anthology of these experiences, taken both from ancient Lives of Saints and more recent accounts, has appeared in English (*Eternal Mysteries Beyond the Grave,* Jordanville, N.Y., 1968). And just recently there was reprinted an English translation of a remarkable text written in the late 19th century by someone who returned to life after being dead for 36 hours (K. Uekskuell, "Unbelievable for Many but Actually a True Occurrence," *Orthodox Life,* July-August, 1976). The Orthodox Christian thus has a whole wealth of literature at his disposal, by means of which it is possible to understand the new "after-death" experiences and evaluate them in the light of the whole Christian doctrine of life after death.

The book that has kindled the contemporary interest in this subject was published in November, 1975, and was written by a young psychiatrist in the southern United States (Dr. Raymond A. Moody, Jr., *Life After Life,* Mockingbird Books, Atlanta, 1975). He was not then aware of any other studies or literature on this subject, but even as the book was being printed it became evident that there was already great interest in this subject and much had already been written about it. The overwhelming success of Dr. Moody's book (with over two million copies sold) brought the experiences of the dying into the light of widespread publicity, and in the four years since then a number of books and articles on these experiences have appeared in print. Among the most important are the articles (and forthcoming book) of Dr. Elizabeth Kubler-Ross, whose findings duplicate those of Dr. Moody, and the scientific studies of Drs. Osis and Haraldsson. Dr. Moody himself has written a sequel to his book (*Reflections on Life after Life,* A Bantam-Mockingbird Book, 1977) with supplementary material and further reflections on the subject. The findings of these and other new books (all of which are in basic agreement concerning the phenomena in question) will be discussed below. As a starting point, we will examine Dr. Moody's first book, which is a fairly objective and systematic approach to the whole subject.

Dr. Moody, in the past ten years, has collected the personal testimonies of some 150 persons who have had actual death or near-death experiences, or who have related to him the experiences of others as they were dying; out of these he has concentrated on some fifty persons with whom he has conducted detailed interviews. He attempts to be objective in presenting this evidence, although he admits that the book "naturally reflects the background, opinions and prejudices of its author" (p. 9) who by religious affiliation is a Methodist of rather liberal views. And in fact there are some drawbacks to the book as an objective study of "after-death" phenomena.

First, the author does not give a single *entire* "death" experience from start to finish, but gives only excerpts (usually very brief) from each of fifteen separate elements which form his "model" of the "complete" experience of death. But in actual fact the experiences of the dying as described in this and other recent books are often so different in details one from the other that it seems to be at best premature to try to include them all in one "model." Dr. Moody's "model" seems in places artificial and contrived, although this, of course, does not lessen the value of the actual testimonies which he gives.

Second, the author has joined together two rather different experiences: actual experiences of "clinical death," and "near-death" experiences. The author admits the difference between them, but claims that they form a "continuum" (p. 20) and should be studied together. In cases where experiences which begin before death end in the experience of death itself (whether or not the person is revived), there is indeed a "continuum" of experience; but several of the experiences which he describes (the recalling of the events of one's life in rapid order when one is in danger of drowning; the experience of entering a "tunnel" when one is administered an anesthetic like ether) are fairly commonly experienced by people who have never experienced "clinical death," and so they perhaps belong to the "model" of some more general experience and may be only incidental to the experience of dying. Some of the books now appearing are even less discriminating in their selection of experiences to record, including "out-of-body" experiences in general together with the actual experiences of death and dying.

Third, the very fact that the author approaches these phenomena "scientifically," with no clear conception in advance of what the soul actually undergoes at death, lays him open to numerous confusions and misconceptions about this experience, which can never be removed by a mere collection of descriptions of it; those who describe it themselves inevitably add their own interpretations to it. The author himself admits that it is actually impossible to study this question "scientifically," and in fact he turns for an explanation of it to parallel experiences in such occult writings as those of Swedenborg and the *Tibetan Book of the Dead,* noting that he intends now to look more closely at "the vast literature on paranormal and occult phenomena" to increase his understanding of the events he has studied (p. 9).

All of these factors will lead us not to expect too much from this book and other similar books; they will not give us a complete and coherent account of what happens to the soul after death. Still, there is a sufficient residue of actual experiences of clinical death in this and other new books to merit one's serious attention, especially in view of the fact that some people are already interpreting these experiences in a way hostile to the traditional Christian view of the afterlife, as though they "disproved" the existence either of heaven or (especially) of hell. How, then, are we to understand these experiences?

The fifteen elements Dr. Moody describes as belonging to the "complete" experience of dying may be reduced, for purposes of discussion, to several main characteristics of the experience, which we shall here present and compare with the Orthodox literature on this subject.

1. The "Out-of-Body" Experience.

The first thing that happens to a person who has died, according to these accounts, is that he leaves his body and exists entirely separate from it, without once losing consciousness. He is often able to observe everything around him, including his own dead body and the resuscitation attempts on it; he feels himself to be in a state of painless warmth and ease, rather as if he were "floating"; he is totally unable to affect his environment by speech or touch, and thus often feels a great "loneliness"; his thought processes usually become much quicker than they had been in the body. Here are some brief excerpts from these experiences:

"The day was bitterly cold, yet while I was in that blackness all I felt was warmth and the most extreme comfort I have ever experienced.... I remember thinking, 'I must be dead' " (p. 27).

"I began to experience the most wonderful feelings. I couldn't feel a thing in the world except peace, comfort, ease— just quietness" (p. 27).

"I saw them resuscitating me. It was really strange. I wasn't very high; it was almost like I was on a pedestal, but not above them to any great extent; just maybe looking over them. I tried talking to them, but nobody could hear me, nobody would listen to me" (p. 37).

"People were walking up from all directions to get to the wreck.... As they came real close, I would try to turn around, to get out of their way, but they would just walk *through* me" (p. 37).

"I was unable to touch anything, unable to communicate with any of the people around. It is an awesome, lonely feeling, a feeling of complete isolation. I knew that I was completely alone, by myself" (p. 43).

Occasionally there is striking "objective proof" that a person is actually outside the body at this time, as when people are able to relate conversations or give precise details of events that occurred, even in adjoining rooms or farther away, while they were "dead." Among other examples like this, Dr. Kubler-Ross mentions one remarkable case where a blind person "saw" and later described everything clearly in the room where she "died," although when she came back to life she was once again blind—a striking evidence that it is not the eye that sees (nor the brain that thinks, for the mental faculties become quicker after death), but rather the *soul* that performs these actions *through* the physical organs as long as the body is alive, but *by its own power* when the body is dead. (Dr. Elizabeth Kubler-Ross, "Death Does Not Exist," *The Co-Evolution Quarterly*, Summer, 1977, pp. 103–4.)

None of this should sound very strange to an Orthodox Christian; the experience here described is what Christians know as the separation of the soul from the body at the moment of death. It is characteristic of our times of unbelief that these people seldom use the Christian vocabulary or realize that it is their *soul* that has been set free from the body and now experiences everything; they are usually simply puzzled at the new state they find themselves in.

The account of an after-death experience entitled "Unbelievable for Many but Actually a True Occurrence" was written by just such a person: a baptized Orthodox Christian who, in the spirit of the late 19th century, remained indifferent to the truths of his own Faith and even disbelieved in life after death. His experience of some eighty years ago is of great value to us today, and seems even providential in view of the new after-death experiences of today, because it is a single whole experience of what happens to the soul after death (going far beyond

8

the brief and fragmentary experiences described in the new books), made by a sensitive individual who began from the modern state of unbelief and ended by recognizing the truths of Orthodox Christianity—to such an extent that he ended his days as a monk. This little book actually may serve as a "test-case" against which to judge the new experiences. It was approved, as containing nothing opposed to the Orthodox teaching on life after death, by one of the leading Orthodox missionary-printers at the turn of the century, Archbishop Nikon of Vologda.

After describing the final agony of his physical death and the terrible weight pressing him down to earth, the author of this account relates that:

"Suddenly I felt a calm within myself. I opened my eyes, and everything that I saw in the course of that minute, down to the slightest details, registered in my memory with complete clarity.

"I saw that I was standing alone within a room; to the right of me, standing about something in a semi-circle, the whole medical staff was crowded together.... This group struck me with surprise: at the place where they were standing there was a bed. What was it that drew the attention of these people, what were they looking at, when I already was not there, when I was standing in the midst of the room?

"I moved forward and looked where they all were looking: *there on the bed I was lying.*

"I do not have any recollection of experiencing anything like fear when seeing my double; I only was perplexed: how can this be? I feel myself here, and at the same time I am there also....

"I wanted to touch myself, to take the left hand by the right: my hand went right through my body as through empty

9

space.... I called the doctor, but the atmosphere in which I was found turned out to be entirely unfit for me; it did not receive and transmit the sounds of my voice, and I understood myself to be in a state of utter dissociation from all that was about me. I understood my strange state of solitude, and a feeling of panic came over me. There really was something inexpressibly horrible in this extraordinary solitude....

"I glanced, and here only for the first time the thought emerged: is it possible that that which has happened to me, in our language, in the language of living people, is defined by the word 'death'? This occurred to me because the body lying on the bed had all the appearance of a corpse....

"With our understanding of the word 'death' there is inextricably bound the idea of some kind of destruction, a cessation of life; how could I think that I died when I did not lose self-consciousness for one moment, when I felt myself just as alive, hearing all, seeing all, conscious of all, capable of movement, thought, speech?...

"The dissociation from everything around me, the split in my personality more than anything could have made me understand that which had taken place, if I should have believed in the existence of a soul, if I were religious; but this was not the case and I was guided solely by that which I felt, and the sensation of life was so clear that I was only perplexed with the strange phenomenon, being completely unable to link my feelings with the traditional conception of death, that is to say, while sensing and being conscious of myself, to think that I do not exist....

"Afterwards, in recalling and thinking over my state of being at the time, I noticed only that my mental capacities functioned with striking energy and swiftness" (pp. 16–21).

The state of the soul in the first minutes after death is not described in such detail in the Christian literature of antiquity; there the whole emphasis is always on the much more striking experiences that come later. It is probably only in modern times, when the identification of "life" with "life in the body" has become so complete and pervasive, that we should expect to see such attention paid to those first few minutes when the expectations of most modern men are turned so thoroughly upside down, with the realization: death is not the end, life continues, a whole new state opens up for the soul!

There is certainly nothing in this experience that contradicts the Orthodox teaching on the state of the soul immediately after death. Some, in criticizing this experience, have raised doubts that a person is actually dead if he is revived in a few minutes; but this is only a technical question (which we will comment on in due time). The fact remains that in these few minutes (sometimes in the minutes before death also) there are often experiences that cannot be explained as mere "hallucinations." Our task here is to discover how we are to understand these experiences.

2. The Meeting with Others

The soul remains in its initial state of solitude after death for a very short time. Dr. Moody quotes several cases of people who, even before dying, suddenly saw already-dead relatives and friends.

"The doctor gave me up, and told my relatives that I was dying.... I realized that all these people were there, almost in multitudes it seems, hovering around the ceiling of the room. They were all people I had known in my past life, but who had passed on before. I recognized my grandmother and a girl I had known when I was in school, and many other relatives and friends.... It was a very happy occasion, and I felt that they had come to protect or to guide me" (p. 44).

This experience of meeting deceased friends and relatives at death is by no means a new discovery, even among modern scientists. Over fifty years ago it was made the subject of a small book by a pioneer in modern "parapsychology" or psychical research, Sir William Barrett (*Death-Bed Visions,* Methuen, London, 1926). After the appearance of Dr. Moody's first book, a much more detailed account of this experience, inspired by Sir William's book, was published, and it turned out that the two authors of this book had been doing systematic research on the experiences of the dying for many years. Here we should say a word about the findings of this new book (Karlis Osis and Erlendur Haraldsson, *At the Hour of Death,* Avon Books, New York, 1977).

This book is the first thoroughly "scientific" one to appear on the experiences of the dying. It is based on the results of detailed questionnaires and interviews with a randomly selected group of doctors and nurses in the eastern United States and northern India (the latter country being chosen for maximum objectivity, so as to test the differences in experience that might arise from the difference in nationality, psychology, and religion). The material thus obtained includes over a thousand cases of apparitions and visions occurring to the dying (and to a few who returned after being clinically dead). The authors find that in general Dr. Moody's findings are in harmony with theirs (p. 24). They find that apparitions of dead relatives and friends (and, in India, many apparitions of Hindu "gods") occur to the dying, often within an hour and usually within a day before death. In about half as many cases there is a vision of some other-worldly, "heaven"-like environment, which produces the same feelings (this "heaven" experience will be discussed below). This study is of special value in that it carefully distinguishes rambling, this-worldly hallucinations from clearly seen other-worldly apparitions and visions, and statistically analyzes the presence of factors such as use of hallucinogenic drugs, high temperatures, and diseases and impairment of the brain, all of which could produce mere hallucinations rather than actual experiences of something outside the patient's own mind. Very significantly, the authors find that the most coherent and clearly other-worldly experiences occur to the patients who are the most in contact with this-worldly reality and least likely to hallucinate; in particular, those who see apparitions of the dead or spiritual beings are usually in full possession of the mental faculties and see these beings with full awareness of their hospital surroundings. Further, they find that those who hallucinate usually see *living* persons, whereas the genuine apparitions of the dying seem rather to be of *dead* persons. The authors, while cautious in their conclusions, find themselves inclined to "acceptance of the after-life hypothesis as the most tenable explanation of our data" (p. 194). This book thus complements the findings of Dr. Moody, and impressively confirms the experience of meeting with the dead and with spiritual beings at the time of death. Whether these beings are actually those whom the dying take them to be is a question that will be discussed below.

Such findings, of course, are somewhat startling when they come from the background of agnosticism and unbelief that has so long characterized the assumptions of modern science. For an Orthodox Christian, on the other hand, there is nothing surprising in them; we know death to be only a transition to another form of existence, and are familiar with many apparitions and visions which occur to the dying, both saints and ordinary sinners. St. Gregory the Great, in describing many of these experiences in his *Dialogues,* explains this phenomenon of meeting others: "It frequently happens that a soul on the point of death recognizes those with whom it is to share the same eternal dwelling for equal blame or reward" (*Dialogues,* IV, 36). And specifically with regard to those who have led a righteous life, St. Gregory notes that "it often happens that the saints of heaven appear to the righteous at the hour of death in order to reassure them. And, with the vision of the heavenly company before their minds, they die without experiencing any fear or agony" (*Dialogues,* IV, 12). He gives examples when angels, martyrs, the Apostle Peter, the Mother of God, and Christ Himself have appeared to the dying (IV, 13–18).

Dr. Moody gives one example of a dying person's encounter, not with any relative or spiritual being, but with a total stranger: "One woman told of seeing during her out-of-body experience not only her own transparent spiritual body but also another one, that of another person who had died very recently. She did not know who this person was" (*Life After Life,* p. 45). St. Gregory describes a similar phenomenon in the *Dialogues:* he relates several incidents when a dying man calls out the name of someone who is dying at the same time in another place. And this is not at all a matter of clairvoyance experienced only by saints, for St. Gregory describes how one ordinary sinner, apparently destined for hell, sends for a certain Stephen, who unknown to him is to die at the same time, to tell him that "our ship is ready to take us to Sicily" (Sicily being a place of much volcanic activity, reminiscent of hell) (*Dialogues,* IV, 36). Evidently this is a matter of what is now called "extra-sensory perception" (ESP), which becomes particularly acute in many just before death, and of course continues after death when the soul is outside the realm of the physical senses entirely.

Thus, this particular "discovery" of modern psychical research only confirms what the reader of ancient Christian literature already knows concerning encounters at the time of death. These encounters, while they do not seem by any means to occur to everyone before death, still can be called universal in the sense that they occur without regard to nationality, religion, or holiness of life.

The experience of a Christian saint, on the other hand, while sharing the general characteristics which seemingly anyone can experience, has about it another dimension entirely—one that is not subject to definition by psychic researchers. In this experience special signs of God's favor often are manifest, and the vision from the other world is often visible to all or many who are near, not just to the dying person. Let us quote just one such example, from the same *Dialogues* of St. Gregory.

"While they stood around Romula's bed at midnight, a light suddenly shone down from heaven, flooding the entire room. Its splendor and brilliance struck fear and dread into their hearts.... Then they heard the sound of an immense throng. The door of the room was thrown wide open, as if a great number of persons were pushing their way in. Those who stood round the bed had the impression that the room was being crowded with people, but because of their excessive fear and extreme brightness they were unable to see. Fear paralyzed them and the brilliant light dazzled their eyes. Just then a delightful odor filled the air and with its fragrance calmed their souls which were still terrified by the sudden light.... Looking at her spiritual mother Redempta, she said in a pleasant voice, 'Do not fear, mother, I shall not die yet.' " For three days the fragrance remained, and on "the fourth night Romula again called her mistress and asked to receive Holy Communion. Scarcely had Redempta and her other disciple left the bedside when they saw two choirs of singers standing in the square in front of the convent.... The soul of Romula was set free from the body to be conducted directly to heaven. And as the choirs escorted her soul, rising higher and higher, the sound of their singing gradually diminished until finally the music of the psalms and the sweetness of the odor vanished altogether" (*Dialogues*, IV, 17). Orthodox Christians will remember similar incidents in the lives of many saints (St. Sisoes, St. Thais, Blessed Theophilus of Kiev, etc.).

As we advance further in this study of the experiences of dying and death we should keep well in mind the great differences that exist between the *general* experience of dying which is now arousing so much interest, and the grace-given experience of death which occurs to righteous Orthodox Christians. This will help us the better to understand some of the puzzling aspects of the death experiences that are now occurring and are being described.

An awareness of this distinction, for example, can help us to identify the apparitions which the dying see. Do relatives and friends actually come from the realm of the dead in order to appear to the dying? And are these apparitions themselves different from the appearances of saints to righteous Christians at their death?

To answer the first of these questions, let us remember that Drs. Osis and Haraldsson report that many dying Hindus see the "gods" of their Hindu Pantheon (Krishna, Shiva, Kali, etc.) rather than those close relatives and friends commonly reported in America. Yet, as St. Paul so clearly teaches, these "gods" are nothing in reality (I Cor. 8:4–5); any *real* experience of "gods" involves demons (I Cor. 10:20). Who, then, do these dying Hindus actually see? Drs. Osis and Haraldsson believe that the *identification* of the beings who are encountered is largely the product of subjective interpretation based on religious, cultural and personal background; and this seems indeed a reasonable judgment that will fit most cases. In the American cases also, it must be that the dead relatives who are seen are not actually "present" as the dying believe them to be. St. Gregory the Great says only that the dying man "recognizes" people, whereas to the righteous "the saints of heaven *appear*"—a distinction which not merely indicates the different experience of the righteous and ordinary sinners when they die, but also is directly bound up with the different afterlife state of the saints and ordinary sinners. The saints have great freedom to intercede for the living and to come to their aid, whereas deceased sinners, save in very special cases, have no contact with the living.

This distinction is set forth quite clearly by Blessed Augustine, the 5th-century Latin Father, in the treatise which he wrote at the request of St. Paulinus of Nola concerning the "care of the dead," where he tries to reconcile the undoubted fact that saints such as the Martyr Felix of Nola have clearly appeared to believers, with the equally undoubted fact that the dead as a general rule do *not* appear to the living.

After giving the Orthodox teaching, based on Holy Scripture, that "the souls of the dead are in a place where they do not see the things which go on and transpire in this mortal life" (ch. 13), and his opinion that cases of the seeming manifestations of the dead to the living are usually either through "the workings of angels" or are "false visions" through the working of devils who have in mind such purposes as leading men into a false teaching of the afterlife (ch. 10), Blessed Augustine proceeds to distinguish between the *seeming* manifestations of the dead, and the *true* manifestations of saints:

"How do the martyrs by their very benefactions, which are given to those who seek, indicate that they are interested in human affairs, if the dead do not know what the living are doing? For, not alone by the operations of his benefactions, but even to the very eyes of men, did Felix the Confessor appear, when Nola was being besieged by the barbarians. You (Bishop Paulinus) take pious delight in this appearance of his. We heard of this not by uncertain rumors, but from trustworthy witnesses. In truth, things are divinely shown which are different from the usual order nature has given to the separate kinds of created things. Just because our Lord, when He wished, suddenly turned water into wine is no excuse for us not to understand the proper value of water as water. This is a rare, in fact, an isolated instance of such divine operation. Again, the fact that Lazarus rose from the dead does not mean that every dead person rises when he wishes, or that a lifeless person is called back by a living one just as a sleeping person is aroused by one who is awake. Some events are characteristic of human action; others manifest the signs of divine power. Some things happen naturally; others are done in a miraculous manner, although God is present in the natural process, and nature accompanies the miraculous. One must not think, then, that any of the dead can intervene in the affairs of the living merely because the martyrs are present for the healing or the aiding of certain ones. Rather, one should think this: The martyrs through divine power take part in the affairs of the living, but the dead of themselves have no power to intervene in the affairs of the living" ("Care for the Dead," ch. 16, in Saint Augustine, *Treatises on Marriage and Other Subjects,* The Fathers of the Church, vol. 27, New York, 1955, p. 378).

Indeed, to take one example, Holy Fathers of recent times, such as Elder Ambrose of Optina, teach that the beings contacted at spiritistic seances are demons rather than the spirits of the dead; and those who have thoroughly investigated the phenomena of spiritism, if they have any Christian standard of judgment at all, have come to the same conclusion (see, for example, Simon A. Blackmore, S.J., *Spiritism: Facts and Frauds,* Benziger Bros., New York, 1924).

Thus, we need not doubt that the saints actually appear to the righteous at death, as is described in many Lives of Saints. To ordinary sinners, on the other hand, there are often apparitions of relatives, friends, or "gods" which correspond to what the dying either expect or are prepared to see. The exact nature of these latter apparitions it is probably impossible to define; they are certainly not mere hallucinations, but seem to be a part of the natural experience of death, a sign to the dying person (as it were) that he is about to enter a new realm where the laws of ordinary material reality no longer hold. There is nothing very extraordinary about this experience, which seems to hold constant for different times, places, and religions.

The experience of "meeting with others" commonly occurs just before death, and is not to be confused with the rather different meeting we will now describe: that with the "being of light."

3. The "Being of Light"

This experience Dr. Moody describes as "perhaps the most incredible common element in the accounts I have studied, and certainly the element which has the most profound effect upon the individual" (*Life After Life,* p. 45). Most people describe this experience as the appearance of a light which rapidly increases in brightness; and all recognize it as some kind of personal being, filled with warmth and love, to whom the newly-deceased is drawn by a kind of magnetic attraction. The identification of this being seems to depend on one's religious background; in itself it has no recognizable form. Some call it

"Christ," others call it an "angel"; all seem to understand that it is a being sent from somewhere to guide them. Here are some accounts of this experience:

"I heard the doctors say that I was dead, and that's when I began to feel as though I were tumbling, actually kind of floating.... Everything was black, except that, way off from me, I could see this light. It was a very, very brilliant light, but not too large at first. It grew larger as I came nearer and nearer to it" (p. 48).

After another person died he felt himself floating "up into this pure crystal clear light.... It's not any kind of light you can describe on earth. I didn't actually see a person in this light, and yet it has a special identity, it definitely does. It is a light of perfect understanding and perfect love" (p. 48).

"I was out of my body, there's no doubt about it, because I could see my own body there on the operating room table. My soul was out! All this made me feel very bad at first, but then, this really bright light came. It did seem that it was a little dim at first, but then it was this huge beam.... At first, when the light came, I wasn't sure what was happening, but then it asked, it kind of asked me if I was ready to die" (p. 48).

Almost always this being begins to communicate with the newly-deceased (more by a kind of "thought-transference" than by spoken words); what he "says" to them is always the same thing, which is interpreted by those who experience it as "Are you prepared to die?" or "What have you done with your life to show me?" (p. 47). Sometimes also, in connection with this being, the dying person sees a kind of flashback of the past events of his life. All emphasize, however, that this being in no way offers any "judgment" of their lives or actions; he merely provokes them to reflect on their lives.

Drs. Osis and Haraldsson have also noted some experiences of such a being in their studies, remarking that the experience of light is "a typical quality of other-worldly visitors" (p. 38) and preferring to follow Dr. Moody in calling the beings seen or felt in this light simply as "figures of light" rather than the spiritual beings and deities the dying often identify them as.

Who—or what—are these "beings of light"?

Many call these beings "angels," and point to their positive qualities: they are beings of "light," are full of "love and understanding," and inculcate the idea of "responsibility" for one's life. But the angels known to Orthodox Christian experience are very much more definite, both in appearance and in function, than these "beings of light." In order to understand this, and to begin to see what these "beings of light" may be, it will be necessary here to set forth the Orthodox Christian doctrine of angels, and then to examine, in particular, the nature of the guiding angels of the afterlife.

CHAPTER TWO

The Orthodox Doctrine of Angels

W E KNOW from the words of Christ Himself that the soul is met at death by angels. *And it came to pass that the beggar died, and that he was carried away by the angels into Abraham's bosom* (Luke 16:22).

Concerning the *form* in which angels appear, we know also from the Gospel: *An angel of the Lord (whose) appearance was as lightning, and his raiment white as snow* (Matt. 28:2–3); *a young man arrayed in a white robe* (Mark 16:5); *two men in dazzling apparel* (Luke 24:4); *two angels in white* (John 20:12). Throughout Christian history, the manifestations of angels have always been in this same form of *dazzling youths arrayed in white*. The iconographic tradition of the appearance of angels has also been consistent throughout the centuries, depicting just such dazzling youths (often with wings, which of course are a symbolic feature not usually seen in angelic apparitions); and the Seventh Ecumenical Council in 787 decreed that angels should always be portrayed only in this way, as men. The "cupids" of the Western art of the Renaissance and later periods are pagan in inspiration and have nothing to do with true angels.

Indeed, not only with regard to the artistic depiction of angels, but in the whole doctrine of spiritual beings, the modern

22

Roman Catholic (and Protestant) West has gone far astray from the teaching of the Scripture and of ancient Christian tradition. An understanding of this error is essential to us if we are to understand the true Christian doctrine of the fate of the soul after death.

Bishop Ignatius Brianchaninov (†1867), one of the great Fathers of recent times, noticed this error and devoted a whole volume of his collected works to exposing it and setting forth the true Orthodox doctrine on this subject (vol. III in the Tuzov edition, St. Petersburg, 1886). In criticizing the views of a standard Roman Catholic theological work of the 19th century (Abbé Bergier, *Dictionnaire de Théologie*), Bishop Ignatius devotes a large part of this volume (pp. 185–302) to combatting the modern idea, based on the 17th-century philosophy of Descartes, that everything outside the material realm belongs simply to the realm of "pure spirit." Such an idea, in effect, places the infinite God on the same level as various finite spirits (angels, demons, souls of the departed). This idea has become extremely widespread today (although those who hold it do not see its full consequences) and accounts for much of the confusion of the contemporary world regarding "spiritual" things: great interest is shown in everything that is outside the material world, with little distinction often made between what is Divine, angelic, demonic, or simply the result of extraordinary human powers or of the imagination.

Abbé Bergier taught that angels, demons, and the souls of the departed are "perfectly spiritual"; thus they are not subject to laws of time and space, we can speak of their "form" or "movement" only as metaphors, and "they have need to be clothed in a subtle body whenever God permits them to act on bodies" (Bishop Ignatius, vol. III, pp. 193–5). Even an otherwise knowledgeable 20th-century Roman Catholic work on modern spiritism repeats this teaching, stating, for example, that both angels and demons "can borrow the material required (for becoming visible to men) from a lower nature either animate or inanimate" (Blackmore, *Spiritism: Facts and Frauds,* p. 522). Spiritists and occultists themselves have absorbed these ideas from modern philosophy. One sophisticated apologist for supernatural Christianity, C. S. Lewis (an Anglican), properly criticizes the modern "conception of heaven as *merely* a state of mind," but he still seems himself to be at least in part caught up in the modern opinion "that the body, and locality and locomotion and time, now feel irrelevant to the highest reaches of the spiritual life" (C. S. Lewis, *Miracles,* The Macmillan Company, New York, 1967, pp. 164–5). Such views are the result of an over-simplification of spiritual reality under the influence of modern materialism and owing to a loss of contact with authentic Christian doctrine and spiritual experience.

To understand the Orthodox doctrine of angels and other spirits, one must first unlearn the over-simplified modern dichotomy of "matter-spirit"; the truth is more complex than that, and at the same time so "simple" that those who are still capable of believing it will probably be widely regarded as "naive literalists." Bishop Ignatius writes (emphasis added by us): "When God opens the (spiritual) eyes of a man, he is capable of seeing spirits *in their own form*" (p. 216). "Angels, in appearing to men, have always appeared in the form of men" (p. 227). Likewise, "from the Scripture it is clear with all apparentness that the human soul has the form of a man in the body, just like the other created spirits" (p. 233). He cites a multitude of Patristic sources to prove this point. Let us, then, look at the Patristic teaching for ourselves.

St. Basil the Great, in his book on the Holy Spirit, states that "in the heavenly powers their nature is that of an aerial spirit—if one may so speak—or an immaterial fire.... For this reason, they are limited by place, and become visible, appearing to those who are worthy, in the form of their own bodies." Again, "we believe that each (of the heavenly powers) is in a definite place. For the angel who stood before Cornelius was not at the same time with Philip (Acts 10:3; 8:26); and the angel who spoke with Zachariah near the altar of incense (Luke 1:11) did not at the same time occupy his own place in heaven" (chs. 16, 23; Works of St. Basil, Russian edition of Soikin, St. Petersburg, 1911, vol. 1, pp. 608, 622).

Likewise, St. Gregory the Theologian teaches: "Secondary lights after the Trinity, having a royal glory, are the brilliant, invisible angels. They freely go around the great Throne, because they are swiftly moving minds, a flame, and divine spirits which swiftly transport themselves through the air" (Homily 6, "On the Noetic Beings," in Works of St. Gregory the Theologian, in Russian, Soikin edition, St. Petersburg, vol. 2, p. 29).

Thus, angels, while being "spirits" and "a flame of fire" (Ps. 103:5, Heb. 1:7) and dwelling in a realm where earthly laws of time and space do not hold true, still are limited by time and space and act in such "material" ways (if one may so speak) that some Fathers do not hesitate to refer to the "aerial bodies" of angels. St. John Damascene, in summing up in the 8th century the teaching of the Fathers before him, states: "Compared with us, the angel is said to be incorporeal and immaterial, although in comparison with God, Who alone is incomparable, everything proves to be gross and material—for only the Divinity is truly immaterial and incorporeal." Again, he teaches: "The angels are circumscribed, because when they are in heaven they are not on earth, and when they are sent to earth by God they do not remain in heaven. However, they are not confined by walls or doors or bars or seals, because they are unbounded. I say that they are unbounded, because they do not appear exactly as they are to the just and to them to whom God wills them to appear. On the contrary, they appear under such a different form as can be seen by those who behold them" (*Exact Exposition of the Orthodox Faith,* II, 3, in The Fathers of the Church, New York, 1958, vol. 37, pp. 205–6).

In saying that angels "do not appear exactly as they are," St. Damascene does not, of course, contradict St. Basil, who teaches that angels appear "in the form of their own bodies." Both of these statements are true, as may be clearly seen in numerous manifestations of angels in the Old Testament. Thus, the Archangel Raphael was the travelling companion of Tobias for many weeks without it once being suspected that he was not a man. Yet, when the Archangel revealed himself in the end, he said: *All these days I was visible to you, but I did not eat and drink, but it only seemed thus to you* (Tobit 12:19). The three angels who appeared to Abraham also gave the appearance of eating and were thought to be men (Genesis, chs. 18 and 19). Likewise, St. Cyril of Jerusalem, in his *Catechetical Lectures,* instructs us concerning the angel who appeared to Daniel, that "Daniel at the sight of Gabriel shuddered and fell on his face and, prophet as he was, dared not answer him until the angel transformed himself into the likeness of a son of man" (*Catechetical Lectures* IX, 1, Eerdmans Nicene and Post-Nicene Fathers, vol. VII, p. 51). Yet, in the book of Daniel (Ch. 10) we read that even in his first dazzling appearance, the angel was also in the form of a man, only with such brightness (*his face like the appearance of lightning, his eyes like flaming torches, his arms and legs like the gleam of burnished bronze)* as not to be endured by human eyes. Thus, the appearance of an angel is the same as the appearance of a man; but because the angelic "body" is not material and the very sight of its fiery, shining appearance is enough to dumbfound any man still in the flesh, angelic apparitions must of necessity be adapted to the human viewers of them, appearing as less shining and awe-inspiring than they are in reality.

With regard to the human soul also, Blessed Augustine teaches that when the soul is separated from the body, "the man himself who is in such a state, though it be in spirit only, not in body, yet sees himself so like to his own body that he cannot discern any difference whatever" (*City of God,* Book XXI, 10; Modern Library edition, New York, 1955, p. 781). This truth has now been amply confirmed in the personal experiences of perhaps thousands of resuscitated people in our own times.

But if we speak of the "bodies" of angels and other spirits, we must be careful not to ascribe any crudely material characteristics to them. Ultimately, St. John Damascene teaches, "the form and definition of this substance only the Creator understands" (*Exact Exposition,* p. 205). In the West, Blessed Augustine wrote that it is all the same whether we prefer to speak of the "aerial bodies" of demons and other spirits, or simply call them "bodiless" (*City of God,* XXI, 10, p. 781).

Bishop Ignatius himself was perhaps a little too interested in explaining the "bodies" of angels in terms of the 19th-century scientific knowledge of gasses; for this reason a minor dispute arose between him and Bishop Theophan the Recluse, who thought it necessary to emphasize the uncompound nature of spirits (who, of course, are not composed of elemental molecules as are all gasses). On the basic point, however—the "subtle covering" which all spirits possess—he was in agreement with Bishop Ignatius (see Fr. Georges Florovsky, *Ways of Russian Theology,* in Russian, Paris, 1937, pp. 394–5). Perhaps some similar misunderstanding on a secondary point or question of terminology was responsible for the opposition which arose in the West in the 5th century when the Latin Father, St. Faustus of Lerins, taught this same doctrine of the relative "materiality" of the soul, based on the teaching of the Eastern Fathers.

If the precise definition of the angelic nature is known to God alone, an understanding of angelic activity (at least in this world) is accessible to everyone, for of this there are many testimonies both in Scripture and in Patristic writings, as well as in the Lives of Saints. To fully understand the manifestations that occur to the dying, we shall have to know in particular how the *fallen* angels (demons) appear. True angels always appear in their own forms (only less dazzling than they are in reality), and they act solely in order to carry out the will and commandments of God. Fallen angels, on the other hand, although they appear sometimes in their own form (which St. Seraphim of Sarov described, from his own experience, as "hideous"), usually assume various appearances and perform numerous "miracles" with the powers they have in submission to *the prince of the power of the air* (Eph. 2:2). Their special habitat is the air, and their chief function is to tempt or frighten men and thus drag them to perdition with themselves. It is against them that the struggle of the Christian is directed: *Our wrestling is not against flesh and blood, but against the principalities, against the powers, against the world-rulers of this darkness, against the spiritual hosts of wickedness under the heavens* (Eph. 6:12).

Blessed Augustine, in his little-known treatise "The Divination of Demons," written when he was asked to explain some of the many demonic manifestations of the ancient pagan world, gives a good general view of the activities of demons:

"The nature of demons is such that, through the sense perception belonging to the aerial body, they readily surpass the perception possessed by earthly bodies, and in speed, too, because of the superior mobility of the aerial body, they incomparably excel not only the movements of men and of beasts but even the flight of birds. Endowed with these two faculties, in so far as they are the properties of the aerial body, namely, with keenness of perception and speed of movement, they foretell and declare many things that they have recognized far in advance. At this, because of the sluggishness of earthly perception, men wonder. The demons too, through the long period into which their life is extended, have gained a far greater experience in events than accrues to men because of the brief span of their lives. Through these faculties, which the nature of the aerial body has allotted, demons not only foretell many things that will occur, but also perform many miraculous acts" ("The Divination of Demons," ch. 3, in The Fathers of the Church, vol. 27, p. 426).

Many of the "miracles" and spectacles of the demons are described in the long discourse of St. Anthony the Great contained in St. Athanasius' Life of him; here also the "lighter bodies" of the demons are mentioned (ch. 11, edition of Eastern Orthodox Books, Willits, Calif., 1976, pp. 19–29). The Life of St. Cyprian the former sorcerer also contains numerous descriptions of demonic transformations and miracles as related by an actual participant in them (see *The Orthodox Word*, 1976, no. 5).

A classic description of demonic activity is contained in the seventh and eighth *Conferences* of St. John Cassian, the great 5th-century Father of Gaul who first transmitted the full teaching of Eastern monasticism in the West. St. Cassian writes: "Such a multitude of evil spirits fills this air which is spread out between heaven and earth and in which they fly in disturbance and not idly, that the Divine Providence for our benefit has hidden and removed them from the gaze of men; otherwise, from fear of their attack, or of the frightful spectacle of the faces into which they are transformed and changed by their own will, whenever they wish, men would be struck with unbearable terror and ready for collapse....

"And of the fact that the unclean spirits are governed by the more evil powers and are subject to them, we are instructed, not only by the witness of Holy Scripture, which we read in the description of the Lord's reply to the Pharisees who slandered Him: *"If I cast out demons by Beelzebub, the prince of demons"* (Matt. 12:27)—but also by clear visions and many experiences of saints.

"When one of our brethren was travelling in this desert, having found a certain cave after nightfall, he stopped there and wished to perform the evening prayer in it. While he was singing psalms according to custom, the time passed and it was already after midnight. After finishing the rule of prayer, desiring to rest his exhausted body a little, he lay down and suddenly began to see innumerable hordes of demons coming together from all directions; coming in an endless file and a very long row, some preceded their chief, while others followed him. Finally came the prince, who was both taller than all in size and more frightful in appearance. After a throne had been placed, he sat down upon an elevated tribunal and with careful investigation began to examine the activity of each one. Those who said that they had not yet been able to seduce their antagonists he ordered to be banished from his sight with reproof and abuse, as inactive and careless, reproaching them with a roar of rage that they had wasted so much time and labor for nothing. But those who declared that they had seduced those assigned to them he let go with great honors, to the enthusiasm and acclaim of all, as most courageous warriors, glorified as an example for all.

"One most evil spirit from among their number stepped forth and reported with evil joy, as of an illustrious victory, that he had finally conquered a well-known monk, whose name he gave, after fifteen years of ceaselessly tempting him, having enticed him this very night into fornication.... At this report there was extraordinary hilarity among everyone, and he departed, exalted by the high praises of the prince of darkness and crowned with glory. With the approach of dawn, all this multitude of demons vanished from sight." Later the brother who witnessed this spectacle learned that the report of the fallen monk was indeed true (*Conferences* VIII, 12, 16; Russian translation of Bishop Peter, Moscow, 1892, pp. 313, 315).

Such experiences have occurred to Orthodox Christians right down to the present century. They are clearly not dreams or visions, but waking experiences of the demons as they are in themselves—but only, of course, after one's spiritual eyes have been opened to see these beings who are normally invisible to human eyes. Until quite recently it was perhaps only a few "old-fashioned" or "simple-minded" Orthodox Christians who could still believe in the "literal truth" of such accounts; even now some Orthodox find them hard to accept, so pervasive has been the modern belief that angels and demons are "pure spirits" and do not act in such "material" ways. Only with the greatly increased demonic activity of recent years do these accounts once again begin to seem at least plausible. Now also the widespread "after-death" experiences have opened up the realm of non-material reality to many ordinary people who have had no contact with the occult, and a coherent and true explanation of this realm and its beings has become one of the needs of the times. Only Orthodox Christianity can supply this explanation, having preserved the authentic Christian doctrine to our own days.

Now let us see more specifically how angels (and demons) appear at the moment of death.

CHAPTER THREE

Appearances of Angels and Demons at the Hour of Death

IN these experiences the newly-deceased is usually met by two angels. This is how the author of "Unbelievable for Many" describes them: "Hardly had the old nurse uttered these words ('May he inherit the Kingdom of Heaven!'), than two angels appeared at my side; for some reason in one of them I recognized my Guardian Angel, but the other was unknown to me" (p. 22). (Later a pious wanderer told him that this was the "meeting angel.") St. Theodora, whose journey after death through the aerial "toll-houses" is related in the Life of St. Basil the New (10th century, March 26), related that "when I was at the end of my strength, I suddenly saw two radiant angels of God, who were like splendid youths of inexpressible beauty. Their faces were brighter than the sun, their gaze was full of love, the hair of their head was white like snow, around their head a golden radiance was poured out, their garments glistened like lightning and were girded about the chest with golden sashes in cross-form" (see translation in *Eternal Mysteries Beyond the Grave*, p. 70). The 6th-century bishop of Gaul, St. Salvius, thus describes his own death experience: "When my cell shook four days ago, and you saw me lying dead, I was raised up by two angels and carried to the highest peak of heaven" (St. Gregory of Tours, *History of the Franks,* VII, 1; see the life of St. Salvius in *The Orthodox Word,* 1977, no. 5).

The mission of these angels is to take the soul of the newly-reposed on its journey into the afterlife. There is nothing vague about them, either in appearance or action; having a human appearance, they firmly grasp the "subtle body" of the soul and conduct it away. "The light-bearing angels immediately took my soul in their arms" (St. Theodora, see *Eternal Mysteries,* p. 71). "Having taken me by the arms, the angels carried me right through the wall of the ward ..." ("Unbelievable for Many," p. 22). St. Salvius was "raised up by two angels." Such examples could be multiplied.

It cannot be asserted, therefore, that the "being of light" in today's experiences—who has no visible form, who does not conduct the soul anywhere, who stops to engage the soul in dialogue and shows "flashbacks" of one's past life—is a guiding angel of the afterlife. Not every being that *appears* as an angel is such in fact, for *even Satan fashioneth himself into an angel of light* (II Cor. 11:14); and so these beings without even the *appearance* of angels can certainly not be identified as such. Unmistakable encounters with angels seem almost never to occur in today's "after-death" experiences—for a reason we shall attempt to explain below.

Is it possible, then, that the "being of light" is actually a demon masquerading as a formless "angel of light" in order to tempt the dying even at the moment when the soul is leaving the body? Dr. Moody (*Life after Life,* pp. 107–8; *Reflections,* pp. 58–60) and other investigators actually raise this question, only to dismiss the possibility as not in harmony with the "good" results the apparition produces in the dying. To be sure, the views of "evil" of such investigators are naive in the extreme; Dr.

Moody thinks that "Satan would presumably tell his servants to follow a course of hate and destruction" (*Life after Life,* p. 108) and seems to be totally unaware of the Christian literature which describes the actual nature of demonic temptations, which invariably are presented to their victims as something "good."

What, then, is the Orthodox teaching about demonic temptations at the hour of death? St. Basil the Great, in his interpretation of the words of the Psalm, *Save me from them that persecute me, and do Thou deliver me lest at any time like a lion he seize my soul* (Ps. 7:1–2), offers this explanation: "I think that the noble athletes of God who have wrestled considerably with the invisible enemies during the whole of their lives, after they have escaped all of their persecutions and reached the end of their life, are examined by the prince of this world in order that, if they are found to have wounds from wrestling or any stains or effects of sin, they may be detained. But, if they are found unwounded and sinless, they may be brought by Christ into their rest as being unconquered and free. Therefore, the Prophet prays both for his life here and for his future life. Here he says: *Save me from them that persecute me,* and there, at the time of trial: *Deliver me, lest at any time like a lion he seize my soul.* And this you can learn from the Lord Himself, Who before His suffering said: *Now the prince of this world cometh, and he hath nothing in Me* (John 14:30)" (St. Basil, *Exegetic Homilies,* Catholic University of America Press, 1963, pp. 167–168).*

Indeed, it is not only Christian strugglers who have to face the testing by demons at the hour of death. St. John Chrysos-

---

* This passage probably refers more particularly to the toll-houses which are encountered after death; in Chapter Six below there is a detailed discussion of the experience of demonic trials and temptations undergone by the soul both before and after death.

tom, in his Homilies on the Gospel of St. Matthew, vividly describes what often happens to ordinary sinners at their death. "Most persons may be then heard relating horrors, and fearful visions, the spectacle of which the dying are unable to endure, but often shake their very bed with great power, gaze fearfully on the bystanders, the soul urging itself inwards, unwilling to be torn away from the body, and unable to bear the sight of the approaching angels. If human beings that are frightful strike terror into us beholding them, when we see angels threatening, and stern powers, among our visitors, what shall we not suffer, the soul being forced from the body, and dragged away, and bewailing much, all in vain?" (Homily 53 on St. Matthew, Nicene and Post-Nicene Fathers, Eerdmans edition, 1973, vol. 10, pp. 331–32.)

The Orthodox Lives of Saints have numerous accounts of such demonic spectacles which appear at the moment of death, usually with the aim of frightening the dying person and making him despair over his salvation. St. Gregory in his *Dialogues,* for example, tells of a certain rich man who was a slave to numerous passions: "A short time before he died, he saw hideous spirits standing before him, threatening fiercely to carry him to the depths of hell.... The entire family gathered round, weeping and lamenting. Though they could not actually see the evil spirits and their horrible attacks, they could tell from the sick man's own declarations, from the pallor on his face and from this trembling body, that the evil spirits were present. In mortal terror of these horrible images, he kept tossing from side to side on his bed.... And now, nearly worn out and despairing of any relief, he shouted, 'Give me time until morning! Hold off at least until morning!' With that his life was snatched away" (*Dialogues* IV, 40, pp. 245–6). St. Gregory reports other similar incidents, as does Bede in his *History of the English Church and*

People (Book V, Chs. 13, 15). Even in 19th-century America such experiences were not at all uncommon; a recent anthology contains numerous 19th-century death-bed visions of unrepentant sinners with such titles as "I am in the flames—pull me out!", "Oh save me! They drag me down!", "I am going to hell!", and "The devil is coming to drag my soul down to hell!" (John Myers, *Voices from the Edge of Eternity*, Spire Books, Old Tappan, N.J., 1973, pp. 71, 109, 167, 196, etc.)

Dr. Moody however, records nothing whatsoever like this: virtually all the experiences of the dying in his book (with the notable exception of suicides, see pp. 127–8) are pleasant ones, whether the people are Christian or non-Christian, religious or not. Drs. Osis and Haraldsson, on the other hand, found something not too far from this experience in their studies.

These researchers found, in their American study, the same results as Dr. Moody: the apparition of other-worldly visitors is seen to be something positive, the patient accepts death, the experience is pleasant, causing serenity or elation and often the cessation of pain before dying. In the Indian study, however, fully one-third of the patients who saw apparitions have an experience of fear, depression and anxiety resulting from the apparition of the "yamdoots" (Hindu messengers of death) or other beings; these Indians resist and try to escape the other-worldly messengers. Thus in one experience, an Indian clerical worker related as he was dying: " 'Someone is standing there! He has a cart with him so he must be a yamdoot! He must be taking someone with him. He is teasing me that he is going to take me! ... Please hold me; I am not going.' His pain increased and he died" (*At the Hour of Death*, p. 90). One dying Hindu "suddenly said: 'Yamdoot is coming to take me away. Take me down from the bed so that Yamdoot does not find me.' He pointed outwards and upwards. 'There he is.' This hospital room was on a ground floor. Outside, at the wall of the building, there was a large tree with a great number of crows sitting on its branches. Just as the patient had his vision, all the crows suddenly flew away from the tree with much noise, as if someone had fired a gun. We were very surprised by this and ran outside through an open door in the room, but we saw nothing that might have disturbed the crows. They were usually peaceful, so it was very memorable to all of us present when the crows flew away with a great uproar, exactly at the time the patient had his vision. It was as if they, too, had become aware of something terrible. As this happened, the patient fell into a coma and expired a few minutes later" (pp. 41–2). Some "yamdoots" have a fearful appearance and cause even more consternation in the dying.

This is the most striking difference between the American and the Indian experience of dying in the study of Drs. Osis and Haraldsson, but the authors can give no explanation for it. One naturally wonders: Why is the modern American experience almost totally lacking in an element—the fear produced by frightful other-worldly apparitions—so common both in the Christian experience of the past and the present-day Indian experience?

It is not necessary for us to define precisely the nature of the apparitions of the dying in order to see that they depend to some extent, as we have already seen on what the dying person *expects* or is *prepared* to see. Thus, Christians of past centuries who had a lively belief in hell, and whose conscience accused them in the end, often saw demons at death; Indians of today, who are certainly more "primitive" than Americans in their beliefs and understanding, often see beings that correspond to their still very real fears about the afterlife; while contemporary Americans, with their "enlightened" views, see apparitions in harmony with their "comfortable" life and beliefs, which in general do not include a very realistic fear of hell or awareness of demons.

On the objective side, the demons themselves offer temptations which accord with the spiritual state or expectations of those being tempted. For those who fear hell, the demons may appear in terrible forms in order to make a person die in a state of despair; but for those who do not believe in hell (or for Protestants who believe they are infallibly "saved" and therefore need not fear hell) the demons would naturally offer temptations in some other form that would not so clearly expose their evil intent. Likewise, even to a Christian struggler who has already suffered much, the demons may appear in such a way as to *seduce* him rather than frighten him.

The demonic temptations that beset St. Maura, the 3rd-century martyr, as she was dying, offer a good example of this latter kind of temptation at the hour of death. After being crucified for nine days together with her husband, St. Timothy, she was tempted by the devil. The Life of these saints tells how St. Maura herself related her temptations to her husband and fellow-martyr:

"Take courage, my brother, and banish sleep from yourself. Be vigilant and know what I have seen; it seemed to me that before me, when I was in a kind of ecstasy, was a man who had in his hand a cup filled with milk and honey. This man said to me 'Take this and drink.' But I said to him: 'Who are you?' And he replied: 'I am an angel of God.' Then I said to him: 'Let us pray to the Lord.' Then he said to me: 'I have come to you in order to ease your sufferings. I saw that you greatly desired to eat and drink, since until this moment you have not eaten any food.' Then I said to him: 'Who inspired you to show me this mercy? And what do my patience and fasting matter to you? Do you not know that God is mighty to do what is impossible to men?' When I prayed, I saw that this man turned his face away toward the west. From this I understood that this was a satanic deception; Satan wished to tempt us even on the cross. Soon after this the vision vanished.

"Then another man came up to me, and it seemed to me that he brought me to a river flowing with milk and honey, and he said to me: 'Drink.' But I replied: 'I have already told you that I will not drink either water or any other earthly drink until I shall drink the cup of death for Christ my Lord, which He Himself will mix for me with the salvation and immortality of eternal life.' When I had said this, that man drank from the river, and suddenly he himself and the river with him disappeared" (Lives of Saints, in Russian, May 3; see English translation in J. A. M. Fastre, S.J., *The Acts of the Early Martyrs,* Fifth Series, Philadelphia, 1878, pp. 227–8). The third apparition to St. Maura, that of a true angel, will be quoted later in this study; but here already it is clear what caution true Christians have in accepting "revelations" at the time of death.

The hour of death, then, is indeed a time of demonic temptation, and the "spiritual experiences" which people have at this time (even if they seem to be "after" death—a point yet to be discussed below) are to be subjected to the same standard of Christian teaching as are any other "spiritual experiences." Likewise, the "spirits" who may be encountered at this time are to be subjected to the universal test which the Apostle John expresses in the words: *Test the spirits, whether they are of God, because many false prophets are gone out into the world* (I John 4:1).

Some critics of today's "after-death" experiences have already pointed out the similarity of the "being of light" to the "spirit guides" and "spirit friends" of mediumistic spiritism. Let us therefore look briefly at the spiritistic teaching where it talks about "beings of light" and their messages. One standard spiritistic text (J. Arthur Hill, *Spiritualism, Its History, Phenomena and Doctrine,* George H. Doran Co., New York, 1919), notes that "the spirits' teaching is always or practically always in line with high moral standards; in the matter of belief it is always theistic, always reverent, but not much concerned with intellectual niceties such as occupied the minds of Bishops in Church Councils" (p. 235). Further, this book states that *love* is the "key-note" and "central doctrine" of spiritistic teaching (p. 283); that "glorious knowledge" is received from the spirits, causing spiritists to undertake the missionary labor of spreading "the knowledge that life after death is a certainty" (pp. 185–6); and that the "advanced" spirits lose the "limitations" of personality and become more like "influences" than persons, becoming more and more full of "light" (pp. 300–1). Indeed, spiritists in their hymns literally invoke "beings of light":

"Holy ministers of light!

Hidden from our mortal sight ...

Send thy messengers of light

To unseal our inward sight" (pp. 186–7).

All of this is enough to make one quite suspicious of the "being of light" who is now appearing to people who are quite unaware of the nature and subtlety of the workings of demons. Our suspicion is only increased when we hear Dr. Moody report that some describe this being as "a fun person" with "a sense of humor" who gives the dying person "a good time" and "fun" (*Life After Life*, pp. 49, 51). *Such* a being, with his message of "love and understanding," does indeed sound remarkably like the trivial and often good-humored "spirits" at seances, who are unquestionably demons (when the seance itself is not fraudulent).

This fact has led some to condemn the whole "after-death" experience now being reported as a demonic deception. One book, by evangelical Protestants, declares that "we feel that there are certain new and unfamiliar dangers to this whole life-after-death deception. Believing even vaguely in the reported clinical experiences, we feel, can have serious consequences for Bible-believing people. More than one sincere Christian has totally bought the fact that the Being of Light is none other than Jesus Christ and, unfortunately, these people are in a perfect position to be fooled" (John Weldon and Zola Levitt, *Is There Life After Death?* Harvest House Publishers, Irvine, Calif. 1977, p. 76). To back up this point, the authors of this book cite some remarkable parallels between some of today's "after-death" experiences and the experiences of mediums and occultists in recent times, in addition to pointing out the undoubted fact that a number of researchers in "after-death" experiences are also interested in the occult and even have had contact with mediums (pp. 64–70).

There is, of course, much truth in these observations. Unfortunately, without the *full* Christian teaching on life after death, even the most well-meaning "Bible-believing people" go astray, dismissing the true experiences of the soul after death together with experiences that may indeed be demonic deceptions. Such people themselves are open to the acceptance of misleading "after-death" experiences, as we shall see.

Drs. Osis and Haraldsson, who both have had "extensive firsthand experience with mediums," note some similarity between the apparitions of the dying and the experiences of spiritism. However, they note a basic "glaring discrepancy" between these two kinds of experience: "Instead of a continuation of the mundane sort of life (which mediums describe), postmortem survival appears to plunge into a radically new mode of existence and way of experiencing" (*At the Hour of Death,* p. 200). Indeed, the realm of "after-death" experiences does seem on the whole to be quite distinct from the realm of ordinary mediumism and spiritism; but it is still a realm in which demonic deceptions and suggestions are not only possible, but are positively to be expected, especially in the latter days in which we live, when we are already seeing ever newer and more subtle spiritual temptations, even *great signs and wonders, so as to seduce, if possible, even the elect* (Matt. 24:24).

It befits us, therefore, to be very suspicious (at the least) of the "beings of light" who seem to appear in the moment of death. They seem very much like demons posing as "angels of light" in order to seduce, not only the dying person himself, but even more those to whom he will later tell this tale if he is resuscitated (concerning the chances of which, of course, the demons are well aware).

Ultimately, however, our judgment of this and the other "after-death" phenomena will have to rest on the *doctrine* which emerges from them, whether given by some "spiritual being" seen in the moment of death, or simply implied by or deduced from the phenomena. We shall approach the question of this judgment after our examination of the phenomena themselves is finished.

Some people who have "died" and returned—usually those who are or become the most "religious"—have identified the "being of light" which they encounter not as an angel, but as the invisible "presence" of Christ Himself. In such people this experience is often bound up with another phenomenon which for Orthodox Christians is perhaps, at first glance, the most puzzling one to be encountered in today's "after-death" experience: the vision of "heaven."

CHAPTER FOUR

The Contemporary Experience of "Heaven"

In *Life After Life* Dr. Moody remarks that the people he has interviewed do not seem to have experienced anything like "the mythological picture of what lies hereafter" and even tend to disbelieve in the usual view of heaven and hell and the whole "reward-punishment model of the afterlife" (p. 70).

In *Reflections on Life After Life,* however, he states that his later interviews have indeed revealed widespread after-death experiences of "other realms of being which might well be termed 'heavenly'" (p. 15). One man found himself in "a countryside with streams, grass, and trees, mountains" (p. 16); one woman was in a similar "beautiful place," and "off in the distance ... I could see a city. There were buildings—separate buildings. They were gleaming, bright. People were happy in there. There was sparkling water, fountains ... a city of light I guess would be the way to say it" (p. 17).

In actual fact, as some of the other new books reveal, this experience is a rather common one. The Protestant authors mentioned above believe that this experience (at least when its imagery is distinctively Biblical) is a *Christian* one and is to be sharply distinguished from most of the other "after-death" experiences, which they believe to be demonic deceptions. "Unbelievers seem to experience false doctrine of a kind specifically attributed to Satan in the Bible; believers experience doctrinally accurate events, which might come right out of the scriptures" (Levitt and Weldon, *Is There Life After Death?*, p. 116). Is this actually true, or are the experiences of believers and unbelievers really much closer than these authors imagine?

The experience which these authors cite as an authentic "Christian" one is that of Betty Malz, who has published a book describing her 28-minute "out-of-the-body" experience while being "clinically dead." After death she found herself immediately "walking up a beautiful green hill ... I was walking on grass, the most vivid shade of green I have ever seen." She was accompanied by another walking figure, "a tall, masculine-looking figure in a robe. I wondered if he were an angel.... As we walked together I saw no sun—but light was everywhere. Off to the left there were multi-colored flowers blooming. Also trees, shrubs ... We came upon a magnificent silver structure. It was like a palace except there were no towers. As we walked toward it, I heard voices. They were melodious, harmonious, blending in chorus and I heard the word, 'Jesus.'... The angel stepped forward and put the palm of his hand upon a gate which I had not noticed before. About twelve feet high, the gate was a solid sheet of pearl." When the gate opened, "inside I saw what appeared to be a street of a golden color with an overlay of glass or water. The yellow light that appeared was dazzling. There is no way to describe it. I saw no figure, yet I was conscious of a Person. Suddenly I knew that the light was Jesus." On being invited to enter the gate, she remembered her father who was praying for her, the gates closed, and she returned down the hill, noticing the sun rising above the jeweled wall—

which soon was turned into sunrise over the city of Terre Haute, where she returned to her body in the hospital in what was commonly acknowledged as a miracle (Betty Malz, *My Glimpse of Eternity*, Chosen Books, Waco, Texas, pp. 84–89).

Is this experience really different in kind from most of those that Dr. Moody relates? Is this actually a Christian vision of heaven? (Mrs. Malz is Protestant in belief, and her faith was strengthened by this experience.) The Orthodox Christian reader is not, of course, as convinced of this as are the Protestant authors quoted above. Quite apart from whatever knowledge we may have of how the soul approaches heaven after death, and what it goes through to get there (these will be discussed later)—this experience does not really seem to us to be so very different from the "secular" after-death experiences now being written about. Apart from the "Christian" coloration naturally given to this experience by a believing Protestant (the angel, the hymn, the presence of Jesus), there are several elements in common with the "secular" experiences: the feeling of comfort and peace (which she describes as being in sharp contrast to her months of painful illness), the "being of light" (which others also identify as "Jesus"), the approach to some kind of different realm which lies beyond some kind of "border." And it is a little strange that she should see the this-worldly sun rise over the jewelled walls, if this is really heaven.... How are we to interpret this experience?

In some of the other new books there are a number of similar experiences, a brief examination of which will give us a much better idea of what is involved.

One book has recently been compiled of "Christian" (mostly Protestant) dying and "after-death" experiences (John Myers, *Voices from the Edge of Eternity*, Spire Books, Old Tappan, N.J., 1973). In one experience related in this book, a woman "died," was freed from her body and came to a place of great light looking through a "window of heaven." "What I saw there made all earthly joys pale into insignificance. I longed to join the merry throng of children singing and frolicking in the apple orchard.... There were both fragrant blossoms and ripe red fruits on the trees. As I sat there drinking in the beauty, gradually I became aware of a Presence; a Presence of joy, harmony and compassion. My heart yearned to become a part of this beauty." After she returned to her body, after being "dead" for fifteen minutes, "the rest of that day and the next, that other world was far more real to me than the one to which I had returned" (pp. 228–231, reprinted from *Guideposts Magazine*, 1963). This experience produced a seeming "spiritual" joy comparable to that of Mrs. Malz, and likewise gave a new religious dimension to the person's life after the experience; but the image of "heaven" that was seen was quite different.

A vivid "after-death" experience was had by a Virginia physician, Dr. George C. Ritchie, Jr. A brief account of it was published in *Guideposts Magazine* in 1963, and a longer version has been published in book form by Chosen Books with the title *Return from Tomorrow*. In this account, after a long adventure of being separated from his body (which was pronounced dead), the young George Ritchie returned to the small room where his body lay, and only then did he realize that he was "dead," whereupon a great light filled the room, which he felt to be Christ, "a presence so comforting, so joyous and all-satisfying, that I wanted to lose myself forever in the wonder of it." After seeing flashbacks of his life, in answer to the question "What did you do with your time on earth?" he saw three visions. The first two seemed to be of "a very different world occupying the same space" as this earth, but still with many earthly images (streets and countrysides, universities, libraries, laboratories). "Of the final world I had only a glimpse. Now we no longer seemed to be on earth, but immensely far away, out of all relation to it. And there, still at a great distance, I saw a city—but a city, if such a thing is conceivable, constructed out of light ... in which the walls, houses, streets, seemed to give off light, while moving among them were beings as blindingly bright as the One who stood beside me. This was only a moment's vision, for the next instant the walls of the little room closed around me, the dazzling light faded, and a strange sleep stole over me." Before this, he had not read anything about life after death; after the experience, he became very active in Protestant church work (*Voices from the Edge of Eternity,* pp. 56–61).

This striking experience occurred in 1943, and as it turns out, such experiences are not at all unique to the "resuscitation" experiences of the past few years. The Protestant minister Norman Vincent Peale records some similar experiences and has this comment: "Hallucination, a dream, a vision—I do not believe so. I have spent too many years talking to people who have come to the edge of 'something' and had a look across, who unanimously have reported beauty, light and peace, to have any doubt in my own mind" (Norman Vincent Peale, *The Power of Positive Thinking,* Prentice-Hall, Inc, New York, 1953, p. 256). *Voices from the Edge of Eternity* takes numerous examples from three 19th-century anthologies of death-bed visions and near-death experiences; although none of these examples is as detailed as some of the more recent testimonies, they offer abundant proof that the vision of other-worldly apparitions and scenes has been a fairly common occurrence to the dying. In these experiences, those who feel themselves to be Christians and prepared for death have feelings of peace, joy, light, angels, heaven, while unbelievers (in the more fundamentalistic America of the 19th-century!) often see demons and hell.

Having established the *fact* of these visions, we must now ask the question: what is their nature? Is the vision of heaven really so common among those who, while dying as Christians in the best way they know, are still outside the Church of Christ, the Orthodox Church?

In judging the nature and value of such experiences, we shall begin by repeating our approach to the question of the "meeting with others." Let us examine the dying experiences of *non-Christians* in order to see if they are markedly different from those of professed Christians. If non-Christians also commonly see "heaven" while dying or after "death," then we will have to understand this experience as something natural that may occur to anyone, and not as something specifically Christian. The book of Drs. Osis and Haraldsson has abundant evidence on this point.

These researchers report some 75 cases of "visions of another world" among dying patients. Some people describe unbelievably beautiful meadows and gardens; others see gates opening up to a beautiful countryside or city; many hear other-worldly music. Often a rather worldly imagery is mixed in, as with the American woman who went to a beautiful garden in a taxi, or the Indian woman who rode a cow to her "heaven" (*At the Hour of Death,* p. 163), or the New Yorker who entered a lush green field, his soul full of "love and happiness"—and could see the buildings of Manhattan and an amusement park in the distance (David Wheeler, *Journey to the Other Side,* pp. 100–105).

Significantly, Hindus see "heaven" as often as Christians in the Osis-Haraldsson study, and while the latter often see "Jesus" and "angels," the former just as often see Hindu temples and gods (p. 177). Even more significantly, the depth of the patients' commitment to or involvement in religion seems to have no effect whatever on their ability to see other-worldly visions; "deeply involved patients saw gardens, gates, and heaven no more often than those of lesser or no involvement" (p. 173). Indeed, one member of the Indian Communist Party, an atheist and materialist, was transported while dying to "a beautiful place, not of this earth.... He heard music and also some singing in the background. When he recognized that he was alive, he was sorry that he had to leave this beautiful place" (p. 179). One person attempted suicide, and while dying reported "I am in heaven. There are so many houses around me, so many streets with big trees bearing sweet fruit and small birds singing in the trees" (p. 178). Most of those who have such experiences feel a great joy, peace, serenity, and acceptance of death; few wish to come back to this life (p. 182).

Thus, it is clear that we must be extremely cautious in interpreting the "visions of heaven" that are seen by dying and "dead" people. As above, when discussing the "meeting with others" in chapter 1, so now also we must clearly distinguish between genuine, grace-given visions of the other world, and a merely natural experience which, even though it may be outside the normal limits of human experience, is not in the least spiritual and tells us nothing about the actual reality of either the heaven or the hell of authentic Christian teaching.

The most important part of our investigation of "after-death" and dying experiences now lies before us: the measuring and judging of them by the yardstick of the authentic Christian teaching and experience of life after death, and a definition of their meaning and their significance for our times. It is already possible here, however, to give a preliminary evaluation of the "heaven" experience so commonly reported today: most, perhaps indeed all, of these experiences have little in common with the Christian vision of heaven. These visions are not spiritual, but *worldly*. They are so quick, so easily attained, so common, so earthly in their imagery, that there can be no serious comparison of them with the true Christian visions of heaven in the past (some of which will be described below). Even the most "spiritual" thing about some of them—the feeling of the "presence" of Christ—persuades one more of the spiritual immaturity of those who experience it than of anything else. Rather than producing the profound awe, fear of God, and repentance which the authentic experience of God's presence has evoked in Christian saints (of which St. Paul's experience on the road to Damascus may be taken as a model—Acts 9:3–9), the present-day experiences produce something much more akin to the "comfort" and "peace" of the modern spiritistic and pentecostal movements.

Nevertheless, it cannot be doubted that these experiences are extraordinary; many of them cannot be reduced to mere hallucinations, and they seem to occur outside the limits of earthly life as generally understood, in a realm somewhere between life and death, as it were.

What is this realm? This is the question to which we now turn. In order to answer it, we shall look first of all to authentic Christian testimony, and then—as Dr. Moody and many other writers on this subject are doing—to the writings of modern occultists and others who claim to have travelled in this realm. This latter source, if properly understood, provides a surprising corroboration of Christian truth.

To begin with, then, let us ask the question: what is the realm, in Christian teaching, which the soul first enters after death?

CHAPTER FIVE

The Aerial Realm of Spirits

I N order to understand what is the realm into which the soul enters at death, we must look at it in the whole context of man's nature. We shall have to know of man's nature before his fall, the changes it underwent after the fall, and the capabilities man has for entering into contact with spiritual beings.

Perhaps the most concise Orthodox discussion of these subjects is to be found in the same book of Bishop Ignatius Brianchaninov which we have already quoted concerning the Orthodox doctrine of angels (Vol. III of his collected works). Bishop Ignatius devoted one chapter of this book to a discussion of "the sensuous perception of spirits"—that is, angelic and demonic apparitions to men. In what follows we shall quote this chapter, which gives the Orthodox Patristic teaching, soberly and precisely handed down by one of the great Orthodox Fathers of modern times. (Titles added by translator.)

1. Man's Original Nature

"Before the fall of man, his body was immortal, a stranger to infirmities, a stranger to its present crudeness and heaviness, a stranger to the sinful and fleshly feelings that are now natural to it (St. Macarius the Great, Homily 4). His senses were incomparably more subtle, their activity was incomparably broader and totally free. Being clothed with such a body, with such organs of sense, man was capable of the sensuous perception of spirits, to which rank he himself belonged in soul; he was capable of communion with them, of that Divine vision and communion with God which is natural to holy spirits. The holy body of man did not serve as a hindrance to this, did not separate man from the world of spirits. Man, clothed in a body, was capable of dwelling in paradise, in which now only saints, and only in their souls, are capable of remaining, into which the bodies of the saints also will ascend after the resurrection. Then these bodies will leave in the grave the crudeness which they assumed after the fall; then they will become spiritual, even spirits, in the expression of St. Macarius the Great (Homily 6, ch. 13), and will manifest in themselves those qualities which were given them at their creation.* Then men will again enter the rank of the holy spirits and will be in open communion with them. We may see an example of the body that will be at the same time both body and spirit in the body of our Lord Jesus Christ after His resurrection.

2. The Fall of Man

"By the fall both the soul and body of man were changed. In the strict sense the fall was for them also a death. That which we see and call death is in essence only the separation of the soul from the body, both of which had already before this been put to death by an eternal death! The infirmities of our body, its

---

* There is, however, a distinction in subtlety between the body of man in paradise before his fall, and his body in heaven after the resurrection. See Homily 45, ch. 5, of St. Symeon the New Theologian, in *The Orthodox Word*, no. 76 and *The Sin of Adam*, St. Herman Monastery Press, 1979. *(Ed. note.)*

subjection to the hostile influence of various substances from the material world, its crudeness—these are a consequence of the fall. By reason of the fall our body entered into the same rank as the bodies of animals; it exists with an animal life, the life of its fallen nature. It serves for the soul as a prison and tomb.

"These expressions we have used are strong. But even so they do not adequately express the descent of our body from the height of the spiritual condition to the fleshly condition. One must cleanse oneself by careful repentance, one must feel at least to some degree the freedom and height of the spiritual condition, in order to acquire an understanding of the miserable condition of our body, the condition of its deadness caused by estrangement from God.

"In this condition of deadness, by reason of their extreme crudeness and coarseness, the bodily senses are incapable of communion with spirits, they do not see them, do not hear them, do not sense them. Thus the blunted axe is no longer capable of being used according to its purpose. The holy spirits avoid communion with men who are unworthy of such communion; while the fallen spirits, who have drawn us into their fall, have mingled with us and, so as the more easily to hold us in captivity, strive to make both themselves and their chains unnoticeable to us. And if they do reveal themselves, they do it in order to strengthen their dominion over us.

"All of us who are in slavery to sin must understand that communion with holy angels is unnatural to us by reason of our estrangement from them by the fall; that what is natural to us, for the same reason, is communion with the fallen spirits, to whose rank we belong in soul; that the spirits who appear sensuously to men who are in a state of sinfulness and fall, are demons and not in the least holy angels. 'A filthy soul,' said St.

Isaac the Syrian, 'does not enter the pure realm and is not joined to holy spirits' (Homily 74). Holy angels appear only to holy men who have restored communion with God and with them by a holy life.*

3. Contact with Fallen Spirits

"Although the demons, in appearing to men, usually assume the appearance of bright angels in order to deceive the more easily; although they also strive sometimes to convince men that they are human souls and not demons (this manner of deception at the present time is in special *fashion* among demons, due to the particular disposition of contemporary men to believe it); even though they sometimes foretell the future; even though they reveal mysteries—still one must not trust them in any way whatsoever. With them truth is mixed with falsehood; truth is used at times only for a more convenient deception. *Satan is transformed into an angel of light, and his ministers as the servants of righteousness,* said the Apostle Paul (II Cor. 11:14,15)" (Bishop Ignatius, *Collected Works,* vol. III, pp. 7–9).

"A general rule for all men is by no means to trust the spirits when they appear in sensuous form, not to enter into conversation with them, not to pay any attention to them, to acknowledge their appearance as a great and most dangerous temptation. At the time of this temptation one should direct one's mind and heart to God with a prayer for mercy and for deliverance from temptation. The desire to see spirits, curiosity to find out anything about them and from them, is a sign of the

---

* However, in rare cases, for some special purpose of God, holy angels do appear to sinful men and even to animals, as Bishop Ignatius notes below. (*Ed. note.*)

greatest foolishness and total ignorance of the Orthodox Church's traditions concerning moral and active life. Knowledge of spirits is acquired quite differently than is supposed by the inexperienced and careless experimenter. Open communion with spirits for the inexperienced is the greatest misfortune, or serves as a source of the greatest misfortunes.

"The Divinely-inspired writer of the book of Genesis says that after the fall of the first men, God, in pronouncing sentence on them before banishing them from paradise, *made for them garments of skins, and clothed them* (Gen. 3:20). The garments of skins, in the explanation of the Holy Fathers (St. John Damascene, *Exact Exposition of the Orthodox Faith*, Book 3, ch.1), signify our coarse flesh which, at the fall, was altered: it lost its subtlety and spiritual nature and received its present crudeness. Although the original reason for this change was the fall, still the change occurred under the influence of the Almighty Creator, in His unutterable mercy towards us, and for our great good. Among the other consequences, profitable for us, which come from the condition in which our body now is, we should indicate this one: through the crudeness of our body we have become incapable of the sensuous perception of the spirits into whose realm we have fallen.... The wisdom and goodness of God have placed an obstacle between men, cast down to earth from paradise, and the spirits who had been cast down to earth from heaven; this obstacle is the coarse materiality of the human body. Thus do earthly rulers separate evil-doers from human society by a prison wall, lest they harm this society according to their own desire and corrupt other men. (St. John Cassian, Conference 8, ch. 12.) The fallen spirits act on men, bringing them sinful thoughts and feelings; but very few men attain to the sensuous perception of spirits" (Bishop Ignatius, pp. 11–12).

"The soul, clothed in a body, closed off and separated by it from the world of spirits, gradually trains itself by the study of God's law, or, what is the same thing, by the study of Christianity, and acquires the capability to distinguish good from evil (Heb. 5:14). Then the spiritual perception of spirits is granted to it, and, if this is in conformity with the purposes of God Who guides it, the sensuous perception of them also, since delusion and deception are for it now much less dangerous, while experience and knowledge are profitable.

"At the separation of the soul from the body by visible death, we again enter into the rank and society of spirits. From this it is evident that for a successful entry into the world of spirits it is essential to train oneself in good time in the law of God, that it is precisely for this instruction that there has been furnished us a certain amount of time, determined for each person by God for his pilgrimage on earth. This pilgrimage is called earthly life.

4. The Opening of the Senses

"Men become capable of seeing spirits by a certain alteration of the senses, which is accomplished in a way that is unnoticeable and inexplicable to a man. He only notes in himself that he has suddenly begun to see what before this he had not seen and what others do not see, and to hear what before this he had not heard. For those who experience in themselves such an alteration of the senses, it is very simple and natural, even though not explainable to oneself and others; for those who have not experienced it, it is strange and not understandable. In the same way, it is known to all that men are capable of being immersed in sleep; but what kind of phenomenon sleep is, and in what way, unnoticed to oneself, we pass over from a condition of wakefulness to a condition of sleep and self-forgetfulness—this remains a mystery for us.

"The alteration of the senses by which a man enters into sensuous communion with the beings of the invisible world is called in Sacred Scripture the *opening of the senses*. The Scripture says: *Then the Lord opened the eyes of Balaam, and he saw the angel of the Lord standing in the way, with his drawn sword in his hand* (Numbers 22:31). Being surrounded by enemies, the Prophet Elisha, in order to calm his frightened servant, *prayed and said: Lord, open his eyes that he may see. And the Lord opened the eyes of the young man, and he saw; and behold, the mountain was full of horses and chariots of fire round about Elisha* (IV Kings 6:17–18)." (See also Luke 24:16–31.)

"From the quoted places of Sacred Scripture it is clear that the bodily organs serve as it were as doors and gates into the inner chamber where the soul is, and that these gates are opened and closed at the command of God. Most wisely and mercifully, these gates remain constantly closed in fallen men, lest our sworn enemies, the fallen spirits, burst in upon us and bring about our perdition. This measure is all the more essential in that we, after the fall, find ourselves in the realm of *fallen* spirits, surrounded by them, enslaved by them. Having no possibility to break in on us, they make themselves known to us from outside, causing various sinful thoughts and fantasies, and by them enticing the credulous soul into communion with them. It is not permitted for a man to remove the supervision of God and by his own means (by God's allowance but not by His will) to open his own senses and enter into visible communion with spirits. But this does happen. It is obvious that by one's own means one can attain communion only with fallen spirits. It is not characteristic of holy angels to take part in something not in agreement with the will of God, something not pleasing to God....

"What attracts men into entering into open communion with spirits? Those who are light-minded and ignorant of Christianity in action are attracted by curiosity, by ignorance, by unbelief, without understanding that by entering into such communion they can cause themselves the greatest harm" (pp. 13–14).

"The idea that there is anything especially important in the sensuous perception of spirits is a mistaken one. Sensuous perception without spiritual perception does not provide a proper understanding of spirits; it provides only a superficial understanding of them. Very easily it can provide the most mistaken conceptions, and this indeed is what is most often provided to the inexperienced and to those infected with vainglory and self-esteem. The spiritual perception of spirits is attained only by true Christians, whereas men of the most depraved life are the most capable of the sensuous perception of them.... A very few people are capable of this by their natural constitution,* and to a very few the spirits appear because of some special circumstance in life. In the latter two cases a man is not subject to blame, but he must make every effort to get out of this condition, which is very dangerous. In our time many allow themselves to enter into communion with fallen spirits by means of magnetism (spiritism), in which the fallen spirits usually appear in the form of bright angels and deceive and delude by means of various interesting tales, mixing together truth with falsehood; they always cause an extreme disorder to the soul and even to the mind" (p. 19).

"Those who see spirits, even holy angels, sensuously

---

* I.e., by a mediumistic talent which can be inherited (*Ed. note.*)

should not have any fancies about themselves: this perception alone, in itself, is no testimony whatever of the merit of the perceivers; not only depraved men are capable of this, but even irrational animals (Numbers 22:23)" (p. 21).

5. The Danger of Contact with Spirits

"The perception of spirits with the eyes of sense always brings harm, sometimes greater and sometimes less, to men who do not have spiritual perception. Here on earth images of truth are mixed together with images of falsehood (St. Isaac the Syrian, Homily 2), as in a land in which good is mixed together with evil, as in the land of banishment of fallen angels and fallen men" (p. 23).

"One who perceives spirits sensuously can easily be deceived to his own harm and perdition. If, on perceiving spirits, he shows trust or credulity towards them, he will unfailingly be deceived, he will unfailingly be attracted, he will unfailingly be sealed with the seal of deception, not understandable to the inexperienced, the seal of a frightful injury in his spirit; and further, the possibility of correction and salvation is often lost. This has happened with many, very many. It has happened not only with pagans, whose priests were for the most part in open communion with demons; it has happened not only with many Christians who do not know the mysteries of Christianity and out of some circumstance or other have entered into communion with spirits; it has happened with many strugglers and monks who have perceived spirits sensuously without acquiring spiritual perception of them.

"The correct, lawful entry into the world of spirits is provided only by the doctrine and practice of Christian struggle. All other means are unlawful and must be renounced as worthless and ruinous. It is God Himself Who leads the true struggler of Christ into perception (of spirits). When God is guiding, the phantoms of truth, in which falsehood clothes itself, are separated from truth itself; then the struggler is given, first of all, the spiritual perception of spirits, revealing to him in detail and with precision the qualities of these spirits. Only after this are certain ascetics granted the sensuous perception of spirits, by which the knowledge of them attained by spiritual perception is completed" (p. 24).

6. Some Practical Advice

Bishop Ignatius takes from the discourse of St. Anthony, in St. Athanasius' Life of him (already mentioned above as a chief source of our knowledge of the activity of demons), practical advice for Christian strugglers on how to behave with regard to sensuous perceptions of spirits if they should happen to occur to one. This is of extreme value to all who wish to lead a true Christian spiritual life in our own days, when (for reasons we shall try to explain below) the sensuous perception of spirits has become much more common than heretofore. St. Anthony teaches:

"You must know the following for your protection. When any kind of vision presents itself, do not become frightened, but no matter what kind of vision it might be, manfully ask it first of all: 'Who are you, and where do you come from?' If it is a manifestation of saints, they will calm you and will turn your fear into joy. But if it is a demonic apparition, when it encounters firmness in your soul it will immediately waver, because the question serves as a sign of a brave soul. By asking such a question, Joshua son of Nun became convinced of the truth (Joshua 5:13), and the enemy did not hide from Daniel (Daniel

10:20)" (Bishop Ignatius, pp. 43–44; *Life of St. Anthony,* English edition of Eastern Orthodox Books, p. 29).

After relating how even St. Symeon the Stylite was once almost deceived by a demon who appeared to him in the form of an angel in a fiery chariot (Lives of Saints, Sept. 1), Bishop Ignatius warns the Orthodox Christians of today: "If the saints have been in such danger of being deceived by evil spirits, this danger is even more frightful for us. If the saints have not always recognized demons who appeared to them in the form of saints and Christ Himself, how is it possible for us to think of ourselves that we will recognize them without mistake? The sole means of salvation from these spirits is absolutely to refuse perception of them and communion with them, acknowledging ourselves as unfit for such perception and communion.

"The holy instructors of Christian struggle ... command pious strugglers not to trust any kind of image or vision if they should suddenly appear, not to enter into conversation with them, not to pay any attention to them. They command that during such apparitions one should guard oneself with the sign of the Cross, close one's eyes, and in resolute awareness of one's unworthiness and unfitness for seeing holy spirits, to entreat God that He might protect us from all nets and deceptions which are cunningly set out for men by the spirits of malice" (pp. 45–6).

Further, Bishop Ignatius quotes St. Gregory the Sinaite: "By no means accept it if you see anything sensuously or with the mind, inside or outside of you, whether it be an image of Christ or an angel or some saint, or if a light should be fancied or depicted by the imagination in the mind. For by nature it is characteristic of the mind itself to indulge in fantasies, and it easily forms the images it desires; this is usual in those who do not pay strict attention to themselves, and by this they do harm to themselves" (pp. 47–49).

Conclusion

In conclusion, Bishop Ignatius teaches: "The only correct entrance into the world of spirits is the doctrine and practice of Christian struggle. The only correct entrance into the sensuous perception of spirits is Christian advancement and perfection" (p. 53).

"When the time comes which is assigned by the one God and is known to Him alone, we will unfailingly enter the world of spirits ourselves. This time is not far from each of us! May the all-good God grant us to spend earthly life in such a way that during it we might break off communion with fallen spirits, and might enter into communion with holy spirits so that, on this foundation, having put off the body, we might be numbered with the holy spirits and not the fallen spirits!" (p. 67).

This teaching of Bishop Ignatius Brianchaninov, written over a hundred years ago, could well have been written today, so accurately does it describe the spiritual temptations of our own times, when the "doors of perception" (to use the phrase popularized by one experimenter in this realm, Aldous Huxley) have been opened in men to a degree undreamed of in Bishop Ignatius' day.

These words scarcely need any commentary. The perceptive reader may already have begun to apply them to the "after-death" experiences we have been describing in these pages and thereby have begun to realize the frightful danger for the human soul which these experiences represent. One who is aware of this Orthodox teaching cannot but look in amazement and horror at the ease with which contemporary "Christians" trust the visions and apparitions which are now becoming so common. The reason for this credulity is clear: Roman Catholicism and Protestantism, cut off for centuries now from the Orthodox doctrine and practice of spiritual life, have lost all capability for clear discernment in the realm of spirits. The absolutely essential Christian quality of distrust of one's "good" ideas and feelings has become totally foreign to them. As a result, "spiritual" experiences and apparitions of spirits have become perhaps more common today than at any other time in the Christian era, and a gullible mankind is prepared to accept a theory of a "new age" of spiritual wonders, or a "new outpouring of the Holy Spirit," in order to explain this fact. So spiritually impoverished has mankind become, imagining itself to be "Christian" even while preparing for the age of demonic "miracles" that is a sign of the last times (Apocalypse 16:14).

Orthodox Christians themselves, it should be added, while theoretically being in possession of the true Christian teaching, are seldom aware of it, and often are as easily deceived as the non-Orthodox. It is time for this teaching to be recovered by those whose birthright it is!

Those who are now describing their "after-death" experiences reveal themselves to be as trusting of their experiences as any who have been led astray in the past; in all the contemporary literature on this subject, there are extremely few cases where a person seriously stops to question whether at least part of the experience might be from the devil. The Orthodox reader, of course, will ask this question and try to understand these experiences in the light of the spiritual teaching of the Orthodox Fathers and Saints.

Now we must go on and see what specifically happens to the soul, according to Orthodox teaching, when it leaves the body at death and enters into the realm of spirits.

CHAPTER SIX

The Aerial Toll-Houses

THE particular place which the demons inhabit in this fallen world, and the place where the newly departing souls of men encounter them—is the *air*. Bishop Ignatius further describes this realm, which must be clearly understood before today's "after-death" experiences become fully understandable.

"The word of God and the Spirit which acts together with it reveal to us, through its chosen vessels, that the space between heaven and earth, the whole azure expanse of the air which is visible to us under the heavens, serves as the dwelling for the fallen angels who have been cast down from heaven.... The holy Apostle Paul calls the fallen angels the *spirits of wickedness under the heavens* (Eph. 6:12), and their chief *the prince of the powers of the air* (Eph. 2:2). The fallen angels are dispersed in a multitude throughout the entire transparent immensity which we see above us. They do not cease to disturb all human societies and every person separately; there is no evil deed, no crime, of which they might not be instigators and participants; they incline and instruct men towards sin by all possible means. *Your adversary the devil*, says the holy Apostle Peter, *walketh about like a roaring lion, seeking whom he may devour* (I Peter 5:8), both during our earthly life and after the separation of the soul from the body. When the soul of a Christian, leaving its earthly dwelling, begins to strive through the aerial spaces towards the homeland on high, the demons stop it, strive to find in it a kinship with themselves, their sinfulness, their fall, and to drag it down to the hell *prepared for the devil and his angels* (Matt. 25:41). They act thus by the right which they have acquired" (Bishop Ignatius, *Collected Works,* vol. III, pp. 132–133).

After the fall of Adam, Bishop Ignatius continues, when paradise was closed to man and a cherubim with a flaming sword was set to guard it (Gen. 3:24), the chief of the fallen angels, satan, together with the hordes of spirits subject to him, "stood on the path from earth to paradise, and from that time to the saving suffering and life-giving death of Christ he did not allow on this path a single human soul when it departed from the body. The gates of heaven were closed to men forever. Both the righteous and sinners descended to hell (after death). The eternal gates and the impassable way were opened (only) for our Lord Jesus Christ" (pp. 134–135). After our redemption by Jesus Christ, "all who have openly rejected the Redeemer comprise the inheritance of satan: their souls, after the separation from the body, descend straight to hell. But Christians who are inclined to sin are also unworthy of being immediately translated from earthly life to blessed eternity. Justice itself demands that these inclinations to sin, these betrayals of the Redeemer should be weighed and evaluated. A judging and distinguishing are required in order to define the degree of a Christian soul's inclination to sin, in order to define what predominates in it—eternal life or eternal death. The unhypocritical Judgment of God awaits every Christian soul after its departure from the body, as the holy Apostle Paul has said: *It is appointed unto men once to die, and after this the judgment* (Heb. 9:27).

"For the testing of souls as they pass through the spaces of the air there have been established by the dark powers separate judgment places and guards in a remarkable order. In the layers of the under-heaven, from earth to heaven itself, stand guarding legions of fallen spirits. Each division is in charge of a special form of sin and tests the soul in it when the soul reaches this division. The aerial demonic guards and judgment places are called in the Patristic writings the *toll-houses,* and the spirits who serve in them are called the *tax-collectors"* (vol. III, p. 136).

1. How to Understand the Toll-Houses

Perhaps no aspect of Orthodox eschatology has been so misunderstood as this phenomenon of the aerial toll-houses. Many graduates of today's modernist Orthodox seminaries are inclined to dismiss the whole phenomenon as some kind of "later addition" to Orthodox teaching, or as some kind of "imaginary" realm without foundation in Scriptural or Patristic texts or in spiritual reality. Such students are the victims of a rationalistic education which is lacking in a refined awareness of the different levels of reality which are often described in Orthodox texts, as well as of the different levels of meaning often present in Scriptural and Patristic writings. The modern rationalistic over-emphasis on the "literal" meaning of texts and a "realistic" or this-worldly understanding of the events de-scribed in Scripture and in Lives of Saints—have tended to obscure or even blot out entirely the spiritual meanings and spiritual experiences which are often primary in Orthodox sources. Therefore, Bishop Ignatius—who on the one hand was a "sophisticated" modern intellectual, and on the other a true and simple child of the Church—can well serve as a bridge on which today's Orthodox intellectuals might find their way back to the true tradition of Orthodoxy.

Before presenting further Bishop Ignatius' teaching on the aerial toll-houses, let us make note of the cautions of two Orthodox thinkers, one modern and one ancient, for those who enter upon the investigation of other-worldly reality.

In the 19th century, Metropolitan Macarius of Moscow, in his discussion of the state of souls after death, writes: "One must note that, just as in general in the depictions of the objects of the spiritual world for us who are clothed in flesh, certain features that are more or less sensuous and anthropomorphic are unavoidable—so in particular these features are unavoidably present also in the detailed teaching of the toll-houses which the human soul passes through after the separation from the body. And therefore one must firmly remember the instruction which the angel made to St. Macarius of Alexandria when he had just begun telling him of the toll-houses: 'Accept earthly things here as the weakest kind of depiction of heavenly things.' One must picture the toll-houses not in a sense that is crude and sensuous, but—as far as possible for us—in a spiritual sense, and not be tied down to details which, in the various writers and various accounts of the Church herself, are presented in various ways, even though the basic idea of the toll-houses is one and the same."*

Some specific examples of such details which are not to be interpreted in a "crude and sensuous" way are given by St. Gregory the Dialogist in the Fourth Book of his *Dialogues* which, as we have already seen, is devoted specifically to the question of life after death.

Thus, when describing the after-death vision of a certain Reparatus, who saw a sinful priest being burned atop a huge

---

* Metropolitan Macarius of Moscow, *Orthodox Dogmatic Theology* (in Russian), St. Petersburg, 1883, vol. 2, p. 538.

pyre, St. Gregory notes: "The pyre of wood which Reparatus saw does not mean that wood is burned in hell. It was meant, rather, to give him a vivid picture of the fires of hell, so that, in describing them to the people, they might learn to fear eternal fire through their experience with natural fire" (*Dialogues,* IV, 32, pp. 229–230).

Again, after St. Gregory has described how one man was sent back after death because of a "mistake"—someone else with the same name being the one who was actually called out of life (this has occurred also in today's "after-death" experiences)—St. Gregory adds, "Whenever this occurs, a careful consideration will reveal that it was not an error, but a warning. In His unbounded mercy, the good God allows some souls to return to their bodies shortly after death, so that the sight of hell might at last teach them to fear the eternal punishments in which words alone could not make them believe" (*Dialogues,* IV, 37, p. 237).

And when one person in an after-death vision saw dwellings of gold in paradise, St. Gregory comments: "Surely, no one with common sense will take the phrase literally.... Since the reward of eternal glory is won by generosity in almsgiving, it seems quite possible to build an eternal dwelling with gold" (*Dialogues,* IV, 37, p. 241).

Later we shall have some more to say on the difference between *visions* of the other world and actual "out-of-body" experiences there (the experiences of the toll-houses, and many of today's "after-death" experiences, clearly belong to the latter category); but for now it is sufficient for us to be aware that we must have a cautious and sober approach to all experiences of the other world. No one aware of Orthodox teaching would say that the toll-houses are not "real," are not actually *experienced* by the soul after death. But we must keep in mind that these experiences occur not in our crudely material world; that both time and space, while obviously present, are quite different from our earthly concepts of time and space; and that accounts of these experiences in earthly language invariably fall short of the reality. Anyone who is at home in the kind of Orthodox literature which describes after-death reality will normally know how to distinguish between the spiritual realities described there and the incidental details which may sometimes be expressed in symbolic or imaginative language. Thus, of course, there are no visible "houses" or "booths" in the air where "taxes" are collected, and where there is mention of "scrolls" or writing implements whereby sins are recorded, or "scales" by which virtues are weighed, or "gold" by which "debts" are paid—in all such cases we may properly understand these images to be figurative or interpretive devices used to express the spiritual reality which the soul faces at that time. Whether the soul actually *sees* these images at the time, due to its lifelong habit of seeing spiritual reality only through bodily forms, or later can *remember* the experience only by use of such images, or simply finds it impossible to *express* what it has experienced in any other way—this is all a very secondary question which does not seem to have been important to the Holy Fathers and writers of saints' lives who have recorded such experiences. What is certain is that there *is* a testing by demons, who appear in a frightful but human form, accuse the newly-departed of sins and literally try to seize the subtle body of the soul, which is grasped firmly by angels; and all this occurs in the air above us and can be seen by those whose eyes are open to spiritual reality.

Now let us return to Bishop Ignatius' exposition of the Orthodox teaching of the aerial toll-houses:

2. Patristic Testimony of the Toll-Houses

"The teaching of the toll-houses is the teaching of the Church. *There is no doubt whatever* (emphasis in the original) that the holy Apostle Paul is speaking of them when he declares that Christians must do battle with the spirits of wickedness under the heavens (Eph. 6:12). We find this teaching in the most ancient Church tradition and in Church prayers" (vol. III, p. 138).

Bishop Ignatius quotes many Holy Fathers who teach concerning the toll-houses. Here we shall quote just a few.

St Athanasius the Great, in his famous Life of St. Anthony the Great, describes how once St. Anthony, "at the approach of the ninth hour, after beginning to pray before eating food, was suddenly seized by the Spirit and raised up by angels into the heights. The aerial demons opposed his progress: the angels, disputing with them, demanded that the reasons of their opposition be set forth, because Anthony had no sins at all. The demons strove to set forth the sins committed by him from his very birth; but the angels closed the mouths of the slanderers, telling them that they should not count the sins from his birth which had already been blotted out by the grace of Christ; but let them present—if they have any—the sins he committed after he entered into monasticism and dedicated himself to God. In their accusation the demons uttered many brazen lies; but since their slanders were wanting in proof, a free path was opened for Anthony. Immediately he came to himself and saw that he was standing in the same place where he had stood up for prayer. Forgetting about food, he spent the whole night in tears and groanings, reflecting on the multitude of man's enemies, on the battle against such an army, on the difficulty of the path to heaven through the air, and on the words of the Apostle, who said: *Our wrestling is not against flesh and blood, but against the principalities and powers of this air* (Eph. 6:12; Eph. 2:2). The Apostle, knowing that the aerial powers are seeking only one thing, are concerned over it with all fervor, exert themselves and strive to deprive us of a free passage to heaven, exhorts: *Take up the whole armor of God, that ye may be able to withstand in the evil day* (Eph. 6:13), *that the adversary may be put to shame, having no evil thing to say of us* (Titus 2:8)."*

St. John Chrysostom, describing the hour of death, teaches: "Then we will need many prayers, many helpers, many good deeds, a great intercession from angels on the journey through the spaces of the air. If when travelling in a foreign land or a strange city we are in need of a guide, how much more necessary for us are guides and helpers to guide us past the invisible dignities and powers and world-rulers of this air, who are called persecutors and publicans and tax-collectors."**

St. Macarius the Great writes: "When you hear that there are rivers of dragons, and mouths of lions, and the dark powers under the heavens, and fire that burns and crackles in the members, you think nothing of it, not knowing that unless you receive *the earnest of the Holy Spirit* (II Cor. 1:22), they hold your soul as it departs from the body, and do not suffer you to rise to heaven"***

St. Isaiah the Recluse, a 6th-century Father of the Philokalia, teaches that Christians should "daily have death

---

* Bishop Ignatius, Vol. III, pp. 138–139; Life of St. Anthony, Eastern Orthodox Books, ed., p. 41.

** Homily on Patience and Gratitude, appointed to be read at Orthodox church services on the seventh Saturday of Pascha and at funeral services.

*** *Fifty Spiritual Homilies,* 16:13; A.J. Mason tr., Eastern Orthodox Books, Willits, Ca., 1974, p. 141.

before our eyes and take care how to accomplish the departure from the body and how to pass by the powers of darkness who are to meet us in the air" (Homily 5:22). "When the soul leaves the body, angels accompany it; the dark powers come out to meet it, desiring to detain it, and testing it to see if they might find something of their own in it" (Homily 17).

Again, St. Hesychius, Presbyter of Jerusalem (5th century), teaches: "The hour of death will find us, it will come, and it will be impossible to escape it. Oh, if only the prince of the world and the air who is then to meet us might find our iniquities as nothing and insignificant and might not be able to accuse us justly!" (Homily on Sobriety in the Philokalia.)

St. Gregory the Dialogist (†604), in his Homilies on the Gospel, writes: "One must reflect deeply on how frightful the hour of death will be for us, what terror the soul will then experience, what remembrance of all the evils, what forgetfulness of past happiness, what fear, and what apprehension of the Judge. Then the evil spirits will seek out in the departing soul its deeds; then they will present before its view the sins towards which they had disposed it, so as to draw their accomplice to torment. But why do we speak only of the sinful soul, when they come even to the chosen among the dying and seek out their own in them, if they have succeeded with them? Among men there was only One Who before His suffering fearlessly said: *Hereafter I talk not much with you: For the prince of this world cometh, and hath nothing in Me* (John 14:30)" (Homilies on the Gospels, 39, on Luke 19:42–47; Bishop Ignatius, III, p. 278).

St. Ephraim the Syrian (†373) thus describes the hour of death and the judgment at the toll-houses: "When the fearful hosts come, when the divine takers-away command the soul to be translated from the body, when they draw us away by force and lead us away to the unavoidable judgment place—then, seeing them, the poor man ... comes all into a shaking as if from an earthquake, is all in trembling.... The divine takers-away, taking the soul, ascend in the air where stand the chiefs, the authorities and world-rulers of the opposing powers. These are our accusers, the fearful publicans, registrars, tax-collectors; they meet it on the way, register, examine, and count out the sins and debts of this man—the sins of youth and old age, voluntary and involuntary, committed in deed, word, and thought. Great is the fear here, great the trembling of the poor soul, indescribable the want which it suffers then from the incalculable multitudes of its enemies surrounding it there in myriads, slandering it so as not to allow it to ascend to heaven, to dwell in the light of the living, to enter the land of life. But the holy angels, taking the soul, lead it away."*

The Divine services of the Orthodox Church also contain many references to the toll-houses. Thus, in the *Octoechos,* the work of St. John Damascene (8th century), we read: "O Virgin, in the hour of my death rescue me from the hands of the demons, and the judgment, and the accusation, and the frightful testing, and the bitter toll-houses, and the fierce prince, and the eternal condemnation, O Mother of God" (Tone 4, Friday, 8th Canticle of the Canon at Matins). Again: "When my soul shall be about to be released from the bond with the flesh, intercede for me, O Sovereign Lady ... that I may pass unhindered through the princes of darkness standing in the air" (Tone 2, Saturday, Aposticha Theotokion at Matins). Bishop Ignatius cites seventeen other such examples from the Divine service books, which of course are not a complete list.

---

* St. Ephraim the Syrian, *Collected Works* (in Russian), Moscow, 1882, vol. 3, pp. 383–385.

The most thorough discussion among the early Church Fathers of the doctrine of the aerial toll-houses is set forth in the Homily on the Departure of the Soul of St. Cyril of Alexandria (†444) which is always included in editions of the Slavonic Sequential Psalter (that is, the Psalter arranged for use in Divine services). Among much else in this Homily, St. Cyril says: "What fear and trembling await you, O soul, in the day of death! You will see frightful, wild, cruel, unmerciful and shameful demons, like dark Ethiopians, standing before you. The very sight of them is worse than any torment. The soul, seeing them, becomes agitated, is disturbed, troubled, seeks to hide, hastens to the angels of God. The holy angels hold the soul; passing with them through the air and rising, it encounters the toll-houses which guard the path from earth to heaven, detaining the soul and hindering it from ascending further. Each toll-house tests the sins corresponding to it; each sin, each passion has its tax collectors and testers."

Many other Holy Fathers, before and after St. Cyril, discuss or mention the toll-houses. After quoting many of them, the above-mentioned 19th-century historian of Church dogma concludes: "Such an uninterrupted, constant, and universal usage in the Church of the teaching of the toll-houses, especially among the teachers of the 4th century, indisputably testifies that it was handed down to them from the teachers of the preceding centuries and is founded on apostolic tradition."*

3. The Toll-Houses in Lives of Saints

The Orthodox Lives of Saints contain numerous accounts—some of them very vivid—of how the soul passes

---

* Metropolitan Macarius of Moscow, *Orthodox Dogmatic Theology*, vol. 2, p. 535.

through the toll-houses after death. The most detailed account is to be found in the Life of St. Basil the New (March 26), which describes the passage through the toll-houses of Blessed Theodora, as related by her in a vision to a fellow disciple of the Saint, Gregory. In this account twenty specific toll-houses are mentioned, with the kinds of sins tested in each set forth. Bishop Ignatius quotes this account at some length (vol. III, pp. 151–158). This account already exists in an English translation, however (*Eternal Mysteries Beyond the Grave,* pp. 69–87), and it contains nothing significant that is not to be found in other Orthodox sources on the toll-houses, so we shall omit it here in order to give some of these other sources. These other sources are less detailed, but follow the same basic outline of events.

In the account of the Soldier Taxiotes, for example (Lives of Saints, March 28), it is related that he returned to life after six hours in the grave and told of the following experience:

"When I was dying, I saw Ethiopians who appeared before me. Their appearance was very frightful; my soul beholding them was disturbed. Then I saw two splendid youths, and my soul leaped out into their arms. We began slowly to ascend in the air to the heights, as if flying, and we reached the toll-houses that guard the ascent and detain the soul of each man. Each toll-house tested a special form of sin: one lying, another envy, another pride; each sin has its own testers in the air. And I saw that the angels held all my good deeds in a little chest; taking them out, they would compare them with my evil deeds. Thus we passed by all the toll-houses. And when, nearing the gates of heaven, we came to the toll-house of fornication, those who guard the way there detained me and presented to me all my fleshly deeds of fornication, committed from my childhood up to now. The angels who were leading me said: 'All the bodily sins which you committed in the city, God has forgiven because you repented of them.' To this my adversaries said to me: 'But when you left the city, in the village you committed adultery with a farmer's wife.' The angels, hearing this and finding no good deed which could be measured out for my sin, left me and went away. Then the evil spirits seized me and, overwhelming me with blows, led me down to earth. The earth opened, and I was let down by narrow and foul-smelling descents into the underground prison of hell." (The rest of this Life in English may be read in *Eternal Mysteries Beyond the Grave*, pp. 169–171.)

Bishop Ignatius quotes also other experiences of the toll-houses in the Lives of St. Eustratius the Great Martyr (4th century, Dec. 13), St. Niphon of Constantia in Cyprus, who saw many souls ascending through the toll-houses (4th century, Dec. 23), St. Symeon the fool for Christ of Emesa (6th century, July 21), St. John the Merciful, Patriarch of Alexandria (7th century, *Prologue* for Dec. 19), St. Symeon of Wondrous Mountain (7th century, *Prologue* for March 13); and St. Macarius the Great (4th century, Jan. 19).

Bishop Ignatius was unacquainted with many early Orthodox sources in the West which were never translated into Greek or Russian; but these too abound in descriptions of the toll-houses. The *name* of "toll-houses," it would seem, is restricted to Eastern sources, but the *reality* described in Western sources is identical.

St. Columba, for example, the founder of the island monastery of Iona in Scotland (†597), many times in his life saw the battle of the demons in the air for the souls of the newly departed. St. Adamnan (†704) relates these in his Life of the Saint; here is one incident:

St. Columba called together his monks one day, telling them: "Now let us help by prayer the monks of the Abbot

Comgell, drowning at this hour in the Lough of the Calf; for behold, at this moment they are warring in the air against hostile powers who try to snatch away the soul of a stranger who is drowning along with them." Then, after prayer, he said: "Give thanks to Christ, for now the holy angels have met these holy souls, and have delivered that stranger and triumphantly rescued him from the warring demons."*

St. Boniface, the 8th-century Anglo-Saxon "Apostle to the Germans," relates in one of his letters the account given to him personally by a monk of the monastery at Wenlock who died and came back to life after some hours. "Angels of such pure splendor bore him up as he came forth from the body that he could not bear to gaze upon them.... 'They carried me up,' he said, 'high into the air ...' He reported further that in the space of time while he was out of the body, a greater multitude of souls left their bodies and gathered in the place where he was than he had thought to form the whole race of mankind on earth. He said also that there was a crowd of evil spirits and a glorious choir of the higher angels. And he said that the wretched spirits and the holy angels had a violent dispute concerning the souls that had come forth from their bodies, the demons bringing charges against them and aggravating the burden of their sins, the angels lightening the burden and making excuses for them.

"He heard all his own sins, which he had committed from his youth on and had failed to confess or had forgotten or had not recognized as sins, crying out against him, each in its own voice, and accusing him grievously.... Everything he had done in all the days of his life and had neglected to confess and many which he had not known to be sinful, all these were now

---

* St. Adamnan, *Life of St. Columba,* tr. by Wentworth Huyshe, George Routledge & Sons, Ltd., London, 1939, Part III, ch. 13, p. 207.

shouted at him in terrifying words. In the same way the evil spirits, chiming in with the vices, accusing and bearing witness, naming the very times and places, brought proofs of his evil deeds.... And so, with his sins all piled up and reckoned out, those ancient enemies declared him guilty and unquestionably subject to their jurisdiction.

" 'On the other hand,' he said, 'the poor little virtues which I had displayed unworthily and imperfectly spoke out in my defense.... And those angelic spirits in their boundless love defended and supported me, while the virtues, greatly magnified as they were, seemed to me far greater and more excellent than could ever have been practiced by my own strength.' "*

4. A Modern Experience of the Toll-Houses

The reaction of a typical "enlightened" man of modern times when he personally encountered the toll-houses after his "clinical death" (which lasted for 36 hours) may be seen in the book already mentioned above, "Unbelievable for Many but Actually a True Occurrence." "Having taken me by the arms, the angels carried me right through the wall of the ward into the street. It had already grown dark, snow was silently falling in large flakes. I saw this, but the cold and in general the difference in temperature between the room and outside I did not feel. Evidently these like phenomena lost their significance for my changed body. We began quickly to ascend. And the degree to which we had ascended, the increasingly greater became the expanse of space that was revealed before our eyes, and finally it took on such terrifyingly vast proportions that I was seized with

---

* *The Letters of Saint Boniface,* tr. by Ephraim Emerton, Octagon Books (Farrar, Strauss and Giroux), New York, 1973, pp. 25–27.

a fear from the realization of my insignificance in comparison to this desert of infinity....

"The conception of time was absent in my mental state at this time, and I do not know how long we were moving upwards, when suddenly there was heard at first an indistinct noise, and following this, having emerged from somewhere, with shrieks and rowdy laughter, a throng of some hideous beings began rapidly to approach us.

"Evil spirits!—I suddenly comprehended and appraised with unusual rapidity that resulted from the horror I experienced at that time, a horror of a special kind and until then never before experienced by me. Evil spirits! O, how much irony, how much of the most sincere kind of laughter this would have aroused in me but a few days ago. Even a few hours ago somebody's report, not even that he saw evil spirits with his own eyes, but only that he believed in their existence as in something fundamentally real, would have aroused a similar reaction! As was proper for an 'educated' man at the close of the 19th century, I understood this to mean foolish inclinations, passions in a human being, and that is why the very word itself had for me, not the significance of a name, but a term which defined a certain abstract conception. And suddenly this certain 'abstract conception' appeared before me as a living personification!...

"Having surrounded us on all sides, with shrieks and rowdy sounds the evil spirits demanded that I be given over to them; they tried somehow to seize and tear me away from the angels, but evidently did not dare to do this. In the midst of their rowdy howling, unimaginable and just as repugnant to one's hearing as their sight was for my eyes, I sometimes caught up words and whole phrases. 'He is ours: he has renounced God'—they suddenly cried out almost in unison, and here they lunged at us with such boldness that for a moment fear froze the flow of all thought in my mind. 'That is a lie! That is untrue!'—I wanted to shout, coming to myself; but an obliging memory bound my tongue. In some way unknown to me, I suddenly recalled such a slight, insignificant occurrence, which in addition was related to so remote a period of my youth that, it seems, I in no way could have been able to recall it to mind."

Here the author recalls an incident from his school years: Once, in a philosophical discussion such as students have, one of his comrades expressed the opinion: "Why must I believe? Is it also not possible that God does not exist?" To this the author replied: "Maybe not." Now, confronted with the demon-accusers of the toll-houses, the author recalls:

"This phrase was in the full sense of the word an 'idle statement': the unreasonable talk of my friend could not have aroused within me a doubt in the existence of God. I did not particularly listen to his talking—and now it turned out that this idle statement of mine did not disappear without leaving a trace in the air. I had to justify myself, to defend myself from the accusation that was directed against me, and in such a manner the New Testament statement was verified in practice: We really shall have to give an account for all our idle words, if not by the Will of God, Who sees the secrets of man's heart, then by the anger of the enemy of salvation.

"This accusation evidently was the strongest argument that the evil spirits had for my perdition, they seemed to derive new strength in this for the daring of their attacks on me, and now with furious bellowing they spun about us, preventing us from going any further.

"I recalled a prayer and began praying, appealing for help to those holy ones whose names I knew and whose names came to mind. But this did not frighten my enemies. A sad, ignorant Christian only in name, I now, it seems, almost for the first time in my life remembered Her Who is called the Intercessor for Christians.

"And evidently my appeal to Her was intense, evidently my soul was filled with terror, because hardly had I remembered and pronounced Her name, when about us there suddenly appeared a kind of white mist which soon began to enfold within itself the ugly throng of evil spirits. It concealed them from my eyes before they could withdraw from us. Their bellowing and cackling was still heard for a long while, but according to how it gradually weakened in intensity and became more dull, I was able to judge that the terrible pursuit was gradually being left behind."*

5. The Toll-Houses Experienced before Death

Thus, it may be seen from innumerable clear examples how important and vivid an experience for the soul is the encounter with the demons of the aerial toll-houses after death. This experience, however, is not necessarily limited to the time just after death. We have seen above that the experience of St. Anthony the Great with the toll-houses was during an "out-of-body" experience while standing at prayer. Similarly, St. John of the Ladder describes an experience which occurred to one monk *before* his death:

"On the day before his death, he went into an ecstasy of mind and with open eyes he looked to the right and left of his bed and, as if he were being called to account by someone, in the hearing of all the bystanders he said: 'Yes indeed, that is true; but that is why I fasted for so many years.' And then again: 'Yes,

---

* "Unbelievable for Many but Actually a True Occurrence," in *Orthodox Life*, July-August, 1976.

it is quite true; but I wept and served the brethren.' And again: 'No, you are slandering me.' And sometimes he would say: 'Yes, it is true. Yes, I do not know what to say to this. But in God there is mercy.' And it was truly an awful and horrible sight—this invisible and merciless inquisition. And what was most terrible, he was accused of what he had not done. How amazing! Of several of his sins the hesychast and hermit said: 'I do not know what to say to this,' although he had been a monk for nearly forty years and had the gift of tears.... And while thus being called to account he was parted from his body, leaving us in uncertainty as to his judgment, or end, or sentence, or how the trial ended."*

Indeed, the encounter with the toll-houses after death is only a specific and final form of the general battle in which each Christian soul is engaged during his whole lifetime. Bishop Ignatius writes: "Just as the resurrection of the Christian soul from the death of sin is accomplished during its earthly wandering, precisely so is mystically accomplished, here on earth, its testing by the aerial powers, its captivity by them or deliverance from them; at the journey through the air (after death) this freedom or captivity is only made manifest" (Vol. III, p. 159). Some saints, such as Macarius the Great—whose passage through the toll-houses was seen by several of his disciples—ascend through the demonic "tax-collectors" without opposition, because they have already fought them and won the battle in this life. Here is the incident from his Life:

"When the time came for the death of St. Macarius, the Cherubim who was his guardian angel, accompanied by a multitude of the heavenly host, came for his soul. With the

---

* *Ladder of Divine Ascent,* tr. by Archimandrite Lazarus Moore, Eastern Orthodox Books, 1977, pp. 120–121.

ranks of angels there also descended choirs of apostles, prophets, martyrs, hierarchs, monks and righteous ones. The demons disposed themselves in ranks and crowds in their toll-houses in order to behold the passage of the God-bearing soul. It began to ascend. Standing far from it, the dark spirits shouted from their toll-houses: 'O Macarius, what glory you have been vouchsafed!' The humble man answered them: 'No! I still fear, because I do not know whether I have done anything good.' Meanwhile he swiftly ascended to heaven. From other higher toll-houses the aerial powers again cried out: 'Just so! You have escaped us, Macarius.' 'No,' he replied, 'I still need to flee.' When he already had come to the gates of heaven, lamenting out of malice and envy, they cried out: 'Just so! You did escape us, Macarius!' He replied: 'Guarded by the power of my Christ, I have escaped your nets!' " (*Patericon of Scetis.*)

"The great saints of God pass through the aerial guards of the dark powers with such great freedom because during earthly life they enter into uncompromising battle with them and, gaining the victory over them, acquire in the depths of their heart complete freedom from sin, become the temple and sanctuary of the Holy Spirit, making their rational dwelling-place inaccessible for the fallen angels" (Bishop Ignatius, vol. III, pp. 158–159).

6. The Particular Judgment

In Orthodox dogmatic theology the passage through the aerial toll-houses is a part of the *particular judgment* by means of which the fate of the soul is determined until the Last Judgment. Both the particular judgment and the Last Judgment are accomplished by angels, who serve as the instruments of God's justice: *At the end of the world, the angels shall come forth, and sever the wicked from among the just, and shall cast them into the furnace of fire* (Matt. 13:49).

Orthodox Christians are fortunate to have the teaching of the aerial toll-houses and the particular judgment clearly set forth in numerous Patristic writings and Lives of Saints, but actually any person who carefully reflects on nothing more than the Holy Scripture will come to a very similar teaching. Thus, the Protestant Evangelist Billy Graham writes in his book on angels: "At the moment of death the spirit departs from the body and moves through the atmosphere. But the Scripture teaches us that the devil lurks there. He is 'the prince of the power of the air' (Eph. 2:2). If the eyes of our understanding were opened, one would probably see the air filled with demons, the enemies of Christ. If satan could hinder the angel of Daniel for three weeks on his mission to earth, we can imagine the opposition a Christian may encounter at death.... The moment of death is satan's final opportunity to attack the true believer; but God has sent His angels to guard us at that time."*

7. The Toll-Houses: A Touchstone of Authentic After-Death Experience

All that has been described in this chapter is quite clearly not the same as the "flashbacks" of one's life that are so often described today in "after-death" experiences. The latter experience—which often occurs before death also—has nothing of the Divine, nothing of judgment, about it; it seems to be rather a psychological experience, a recapitulation of one's own conscience. The lack of judgment and even the "sense of humor"

* Billy Graham, *Angels, God's Secret Messengers*, Doubleday, New York, 1975, pp. 150–151.

which many have described in the invisible being who attends the "flashbacks" is, first of all, a reflection of the terrible lack of seriousness which most people in the Western world now have with regard to life and death. And this is also why even the Hindus of "backward" India have more frightening experiences of death than do most Westerners: even without the true enlightenment of Christianity, they have still preserved a more serious attitude to life than have most people in the frivolous "post-Christian" West.

The passage through the toll-houses—which is a kind of touchstone of authentic after-death experience—is not described at all in today's experiences, and the reason for this is not far to seek. From many signs—the absence of the angels who come for the soul, the absence of judgment, the frivolousness of many of the accounts, even the very shortness of the time involved (usually some five to ten minutes, compared with the several hours to several days in the incidents from saints' Lives and other Orthodox sources)—it is clear that today's experiences, although sometimes very striking and not explainable by any natural laws known to medical science, are not very profound. If these are actual experiences of death, then they involve only the very beginning of the soul's after-death journey; they occur in the anteroom of death, as it were, before God's decree for the soul has become final (manifested by the coming of the angels for the soul), while there is still a possibility for the soul to return to the body by natural means.

It still remains for us, however, to give a satisfactory explanation of the experiences that are occurring today. What are these beautiful landscapes that are often seen? Where is this "heavenly" city that is beheld? What is this whole "out-of-the-body" realm which is undeniably being contacted today?

The answer to these questions may be found in an investigation of a rather different kind of literature from the Orthodox sources mentioned above—a literature which is also based on personal experience, and is much more thorough in its observations and conclusions than the "after-death" experience of today. This is the literature to which Dr. Moody and other investigators are also turning, and in which they are finding indeed remarkable parallels to the clinical cases that have inspired the contemporary interest in life after death.

8. The Teaching of Bishop Theophan the Recluse on the Aerial Toll-Houses

Bishop Ignatius Brianchaninov was the leading defender of the Orthodox teaching of the aerial toll-houses in 19th-century Russia, when unbelievers and modernists were already beginning to scoff at it; but Bishop Theophan the Recluse was no less a firm defender of this teaching, which he saw as an integral part of the whole Orthodox teaching on the unseen warfare or spiritual struggle against demons. Here we give one of his statements on the toll-houses, which is part of his commentary on the eightieth verse of Psalm 118: *Let my heart be blameless in Thy statutes, that I may not be put to shame.*

"The prophet does not mention how and where one 'may not be put to shame.' The nearest 'not being put to shame' occurs during the arising of inward battles....

"The second moment of not being put to shame is the time of death and the passage through the toll-houses. No matter how absurd the idea of the toll-houses may seem to our 'wise men,' they will not escape passing through them. What do these toll-gatherers seek in those who pass through? They seek whether people might have some of their goods. What kind of goods? Passions. Therefore, in the person whose heart is pure and a stranger to passions, they cannot find anything to wrangle over; on the contrary, the opposing quality will strike them like arrows of lightning. To this someone who has a little education expressed the following thought: The toll-houses are something frightful. But it is quite possible that the demons, instead of something frightful, might present something seductive. They might present something deceptive and seductive, according to all the kinds of passions, to the soul as it passes through one after the other. When, during the course of earthly life, the passions have been banished from the heart and the virtues opposed to them have been planted, then no matter what seductive thing you might present, the soul, having no kind of sympathy for it, passes it by, turning away from it with disgust. But when the heart has not been cleansed, the soul will rush to whatever passion the heart has most sympathy for; and the demons will take it like a friend, and then they know where to put it. Therefore, it is very doubtful that a soul, as long as there remain in it sympathies for the objects of any passion, will not be put to shame at the toll-houses. Being put to shame here means that the soul itself is thrown into hell.

"But the final being put to shame is at the Last Judgment, before the face of the All-seeing Judge...."*

---

* *The One-Hundred Eighteenth Psalm, Interpreted by Bishop Theophan,* Moscow, 1891, reprinted Jordanville, 1976, pp. 289–290; see the English summary printed by New Diveyevo Convent, Spring Valley, N.Y., 1978, p. 24.

CHAPTER SEVEN

"Out-of-Body" Experiences in Occult Literature

RESEARCHERS in today's "after-death" experiences almost invariably turn for elucidation of these experiences to that form of literature which claims to be based on experience of the "out-of-body" realm: the occult literature down the ages from the Egyptian and Tibetan *Books of the Dead* down to the occult teachers and experimenters of our own day. Hardly any of these researchers on the other hand, pay very serious attention to the Christian teaching on life after death, or to the Scriptural and Patristic sources upon which it is based. Why is this?

The reason is very simple: the Christian teaching comes from God's revelation to man of the fate of the soul after death, and it emphasizes chiefly the ultimate state of the soul in heaven or hell. While there is also an abundant Christian literature describing what happens to the soul after death, based on firsthand after-death or out-of-body experiences (as presented in the chapter above on the "toll-houses"), this literature definitely occupies a secondary place when compared to the primary Christian teaching of the soul's final state. The literature based on Christian experience is chiefly useful in elucidating and making more vivid the basic points of Christian doctrine.

In occult literature, however, exactly the opposite is the case: the chief emphasis is on the soul's experience in the "out-of-body" realm, while the ultimate state of the soul is usually left vague or open to personal opinions and guesses, supposedly based on these experiences. Today's researchers are much more easily attracted to the experiences of occult writers (which seem to be capable of at least some degree of "scientific" investigation) than to the teaching of Christianity, which requires a commitment of belief and trust and the leading of a spiritual life in accord with it.

In this chapter we will try to point out some of the pitfalls of this approach, which is by no means as "objective" as it seems to some people, and offer an evaluation of the occult "out-of-body" experiences from the point of view of Orthodox Christianity. In order to do this, we must look at some of the occult literature which today's researchers are using to elucidate "after-death" experiences.

1. The Tibetan Book of the Dead

The *Tibetan Book of the Dead** is an 8th-century Buddhist book which probably hands down pre-Buddhist traditions from a much earlier period. Its Tibetan title is "Liberation by Hearing on the After-Death Plane," and it is described by the English editor as "a mystic manual for guidance through the other world of many illusions and realms" (p. 2). It is read at the body of the newly-deceased for the benefit of the soul, because, as the text itself says, "during the moments of death various misleading illusions occur" (p. 151). These, as the editor notes, "are not visions of reality, but nothing more than ... (one's own) intellectual impulses which have assumed personified form (p. 31).

---

* Ed. by W. Y. Evans-Wentz, Oxford University Press, Paperback ed., 1960.

In the later stages of the 49 days of "after-death" experiences described in the book, there are visions of both "peaceful" and "wrathful" deities—all of which, in accordance with Buddhist doctrine, are regarded as illusionary. (We shall discuss below, in examining the nature of this realm, why these visions are indeed largely illusionary.) The end of this whole process is the final fall of the soul into a "reincarnation" (also discussed below), which Buddhist teaching regards as an evil to be avoided by Buddhist training. Dr. C. G. Jung, in his Psychological Commentary on the book, finds these visions very similar to descriptions of the after-death world in the spiritistic literature of the modern West—both "give one a sickening impression of the utter inanity and banality of communications from the 'spirit world.'" (p. 11).

In two respects there are striking similarities between the *Tibetan Book of the Dead* and today's experiences, and this accounts for the interest of Dr. Moody and other researchers in this book. First, the "out-of-body" experience described in the first moments of death is essentially the same as that described in today's experiences (as well as in Orthodox literature): the soul of the deceased appears as a "shining illusory body" which is visible to other beings of like nature but not to men in the flesh; at first it does not know whether it is alive or dead; it sees people around the body, hears the wailing of mourners, and has all sense faculties; it has unimpeded motion and can go through solid objects (pp. 98–100, 156–160). Second, there is a "primary clear light seen at the moment of death" (p. 89), which today's researchers identify with the "being of light" described by many people today.

There is no reason to doubt that what is described in the *Tibetan Book of the Dead* is based on some kind of "out-of-body" experience; but we shall see below that the actual after-death state is only one of these experiences, and we must beware of accepting just any "out-of-body" experience as a revelation of what actually happens to the soul after death. The experiences of Western mediums also can be genuine; but they certainly do not transmit actual messages from the dead, as they pretend to do.

There is some similarity between the *Tibetan Book of the Dead* and the much earlier Egyptian Book of the Dead.* The latter describes the soul after death as undergoing many trans-formations and encountering many "gods." There is no living tradition of interpretation of this book, however, and without this the modern reader can only guess at the meaning of some of its symbolism. According to this book the deceased takes in succession the form of a swallow, a hawk of gold, a serpent with human legs and feet, a crocodile, a heron, a lotus flower, etc., and meets strange "gods" and other-worldly beings (the "Four Holy Apes," the hippopotamus-goddess, various gods with heads of dogs, jackals, apes, birds, etc.).

The elaborate and confused experiences of the "after-death" realm as described in this book are in sharp contrast to the clarity and simplicity of Christian experiences. Although also based, it may well be, on some kind of actual "out-of-body" experiences, this book is as full of illusory visions as the *Tibetan Book of the Dead* and certainly cannot be taken as an actual description of the state of the soul after death.

2. The Writings of Emanuel Swedenborg

Another of the occult texts which contemporary research-ers are investigating holds more hope for being understood, for

---

* *The Book of the Dead*, tr. by E. A. Wallis Budge, Bell Publishing Co., N.Y., 1960.

it is from our own modern times, is thoroughly Western in mentality, and purports to be Christian. The writings of the Swedish visionary Emanuel Swedenborg (1688–1722) describe the visions of another world which began to appear to him in mid-life. Before the visions began, he was a typical intellectual of 18th-century Europe, fluent in many languages, a scholar and scientist and inventor, a man active in public life as an overseer of Sweden's mining industries and a member of the House of Nobles—in short, a "universal man" in the early age of science, when it was still possible for one man to master almost all the knowledge of his day. He wrote some 150 scientific works, some of which (such as his 4-volume anatomical treatise, *The Brain*) were far ahead of his time.

Then, in the 56th year of his life, he turned his attention to the invisible world and in the last 25 years of his life he produced an immense number of religious works describing heaven, hell, angels and spirits—all based on his own personal experience.

His descriptions of the invisible realms are disconcertingly earth-like: in general, however, they are in agreement with the descriptions of most occult literature. When a person dies, according to Swedenborg's account, he enters the "world of spirits," which is halfway between heaven and hell.* This world although it is spiritual and not material, is so much like material reality that a person does not know at first that he has died (461); he has the same kind of "body" and sense faculties as when in his earthly body. At the moment of death there is a vision of light—something bright and hazy (450)—and there

---

* Emanuel Swedenborg, *Heaven and Hell,* tr. By George F. Dole, Swendenborg Foundation, Inc., N.Y., 1976, section 421; sections in parentheses in the text above are all from this book.

is a "review" of one's life and its good and evil deeds. He meets his friends and acquaintances from this world (494), and for some time he continues an existence very similar to the one he had on earth, except that everything is much more "inward"; one is drawn to those things and persons for which one has love, and reality is determined by thought—as soon as one thinks of a loved one, that person becomes present as though called (494). Once one becomes used to being in this spirit world, he is taught by his friends concerning heaven and hell, and is taken to various cities, gardens and parks (495).

In this intermediate "world of spirits" one is "prepared" for heaven in a process of education that takes anywhere from a few days to a year (498). But "Heaven" itself, as described by Swedenborg, is not too different from the "world of spirits", and both are very similar to earth (171). There are courtyards and halls as on earth, parks and gardens, houses and bedrooms for "angels", with many changes of clothing for them. There are governments and laws and law-courts—all, of course, more "spiritual" than on earth. There are church buildings and church services, with clergymen who give sermons and who become confused if anyone in the congregation disagrees with them. There are marriages, schools, the raising and educating of children, public life—in short, almost everything to be found on earth that can become "spiritual." Swedenborg himself talked with many of the "angels" in heaven (all of whom, he believed, were only the souls of the dead), as well as with the strange inhabitants of Mercury, Jupiter, and other planets; he argued with Martin Luther in "heaven" and converted him to his own beliefs, but was unsuccessful in persuading Calvin out of his belief in predestination. "Hell" is described as a similarly earth-like place where the inhabitants are characterized by self-love and evil actions.

One can easily understand why Swedenborg was dismissed by most of his contemporaries as a madman, and why even until quite recently his visions have seldom been taken seriously. Still, there have always been some who recognized that, for all the strangeness of his visions, he was in actual contact with unseen reality: his younger contemporary, the German philosopher Immanuel Kant, one of the chief founders of modern philosophy, took him very seriously and believed the several examples of Swedenborg's "clairvoyance" that were known throughout Europe; and the American philosopher Emerson, in his long essay on him in *Representative Men,* called him "one of the mastodons of literature, not to be measured by whole colleges of ordinary scholars." Today, of course, the revival of interest in occultism has brought him to the fore as a "mystic" and "seer" not bound by doctrinal Christianity, and in particular the researchers in "after-death" experiences find remarkable parallels between their findings and his description of the first moments after death.

There can be little doubt that Swedenborg was in actual contact with invisible spirits and that he received his "revelations" from them. An examination of *how* he received these "revelations" will show us what is the actual realm these spirits inhabit.

The history of Swedenborg's contacts with invisible spirits—which he recorded in great detail in his voluminous *Journal of Dreams* and *Spiritual Journal* (2300 pages)—reveal precisely the characteristics of one entering into contact with the demons of the air, as described by Bishop Ignatius. From childhood Swedenborg practiced a form of meditation, involving relaxation and intense concentration; in time, he began to see a splendid flame during his meditation, which he accepted with trust and interpreted as a sign of "approval" of his ideas. This prepared him for the opening up of communication with the realm of spirits. Later he began to have dreams of Christ and of being received into a society of "immortals," and he gradually became aware of the presence of "spirits" around him. Finally, the spirits began to appear to him in a waking state. The first of these latter experiences occurred when he was travelling in London: One night, after overeating, he suddenly saw a blackness and crawling reptiles on the floor, and then a man sitting in the corner of the room, who said only "Eat not so much" and disappeared in blackness. Although he was frightened at this apparition, he trusted it as something "good" because it gave "moral" advice. Then, as he himself related, "during the same night the same man revealed himself to me again, but I was not frightened now. He then said that he was the Lord God, the Creator of the World, and the Redeemer, and that he had chosen me to explain to men the spiritual sense of the Scripture, and that he himself would explain to me what I should write on this subject; that same night were opened to me, so that I became thoroughly convinced of their reality, the worlds of spirits, heaven and hell.... Afterwards the Lord opened, daily very often, my bodily eyes, so that in the middle of the day I could see into the other world, and in a state of perfect wakefulness converse with angels and spirits."*

It is quite clear from this description that Swedenborg was opened up to contact with the *aerial realm of fallen spirits* and that all his later revelations came from this source. The "heaven" and the "hell" which he saw were also parts of this aerial realm, and the "revelations" which he recorded are a description of the

---

* R. L. Tafel, *Documents Concerning Swedenborg,* vol. 1, pp. 35–6. See Wilson Van Dusen, *The Presence of Other Worlds (The Psychological-Spiritual Findings of Emanuel Swedenborg),* Harper and Row, N.Y., 1973, pp. 19–63, for a description of the opening of Swedenborg's "spiritual eyes."

illusions of this realm which the fallen spirits often produce for the gullible, with their own aims in view. A look at some other occult literature will show us more of the characteristics of this realm.

3. The "Astral Plane" of Theosophy

19th and 20th century Theosophy, which is an amalgamation of the occult ideas of East and West, teaches in detail concerning this aerial realm, which it sees as composed of a number of "astral planes." ("Astral," meaning "of the stars," is a fanciful term to refer to the level of reality "above the earthly.") According to one résumé of the teaching, "the (astral) planes comprise the habitations of all supernatural entities, the locale of gods and demons, the void where the thoughtforms dwell, the region inhabited by spirits of the air and other elements, and the various heavens and hells with their angelic and demonic hosts.... With the help of ritual procedures, trained persons believe that they can 'rise on the planes,' and experience these regions in full awareness."*

According to this teaching, one enters the "astral plane" (or "planes," depending on whether this realm is viewed as a whole or in its separate "layers") at death, and, as in Swedenborg's teaching, there is no sudden change in one's state and no judgment; one continues to live as before, only outside the body, and begins to "pass through all the sub-planes of the astral plane, on his way to the heaven-world."** Each sub-plane is

---

* Benjamin Walker, *Beyond the Body: The Human Double and the Astral Planes,* Routledge and Kegan Paul, London, 1974, pp. 117–8.
** A. E. Powell, *The Astral Body,* The Theosophical Publishing House, Wheaton, Ill., 1972, p. 123.

increasingly refined and "inward," and the progression through them, far from involving fear and uncertainty as do the Christian "toll-houses," is a time of pleasure and joy: "The joy of life on the astral plane is so great that physical life in comparison with it seems no life at all.... Nine out of ten much dislike returning to the body" (Powell, p. 94).

Theosophy, the invention of the Russian medium Helena Blavatskaya, was founded in the late 19th century in an attempt to give a systematic explanation of the mediumistic contacts with the "dead" which had been multiplying in the Western world since the great outbreak of spiritistic phenomena in America in 1848. To this day its teaching on the "astral plane" (although often not called by that name) is the standard one used by mediums and other dabblers in the occult to explain their experiences in the world of spirits. Although Theosophical books on the "astral plane" are filled with the same "sickening inanity and banality" that Dr. Jung finds to characterize all spiritistic literature, still, behind this triviality there is a basic underlying philosophy of other-world reality that strikes a responsive chord in researchers today. Today's humanistic world-view is much more favorably disposed to an other-world that is pleasant rather than painful, that allows for gentle "growth" or "evolution" rather than the finality of judgment, that permits "another chance" to prepare oneself for a higher reality rather than determining one's eternal lot by one's behavior in earthly life. The teaching of Theosophy gives exactly these characteristics demanded by the "modern soul" and it claims to be based on experience.

In order to give an Orthodox Christian answer to this teaching we must look more closely at the specific experiences which are undergone on the "astral plane." But where shall we look? The communication of mediums are notoriously unreliable and hazy; and in any case the contact made with the "spirit world" through mediums is too shadowy and indirect to constitute convincing proof of the nature of that world. The "after-death" experiences of today, on the other hand, are too brief and inconclusive to be taken as evidence of the actual nature of the other world.

But there *is* a kind of experience on the "astral plane" that can be studied in more detail. In Theosophical language it is called "astral projection" or "the projection of the astral body." It is possible, through the cultivation of certain mediumistic techniques, not merely to enter into contact with discarnate spirits, as ordinary mediums do (when their seances are genuine), but actually to enter into their realm of being and "travel" in their midst. One may well be skeptical on hearing of such experiences in ancient times but it so happens that this experience has become relatively common—and not only among occultists—in our own times, and there is already an extensive literature of firsthand experience in this realm.

4. "Astral Projection"

It is well known to Orthodox Christians that man can in fact be raised above the limitations of his bodily nature and journey to invisible realms. The exact nature of this journey will not concern us here. The Apostle Paul himself did not know whether he was "in the body or out of the body" when he was caught up to the third heaven (II Cor. 12:2), and there is no need for us to speculate as to how the body can become refined enough to enter heaven (if his experience was actually "in the body"), or what kind of "subtle body" the soul may be clothed in during an "out- of-body" experience—if indeed such things can be known in this life. It is enough for us to know that the soul (in whatever kind of "body") can indeed be raised up by God's grace and behold paradise, as well as the aerial realm of spirits under heaven.

Often in Orthodox literature such experiences are described as being "out of the body," as was St. Anthony's experience of the "toll-houses" while standing at prayer, described above. Bishop Ignatius Brianchaninov mentions two ascetics in the 19th century whose souls likewise left their bodies while they were at prayer—Elder Basilisk of Siberia, whose disciple was the famous Zosima, and Schema-Elder Ignatius (Isaiah), a personal friend of Bishop Ignatius (Bishop Ignatius, *Collected Works,* vol. III, p. 75). The most striking "out-of-body" experience in the Orthodox Lives of Saints is probably that of St. Andrew the Fool for Christ of Constantinople (10th century), who, while his body evidently lay in the snow of the city streets, was raised up in spirit to behold paradise and the third heaven, a part of which he described to his disciple who recorded the experience (Lives of Saints, Oct. 2).

Such experiences occur only by the grace of God and quite apart from the will or desire of men. But "astral projection" is an "out-of-body" experience that can be sought and initiated by means of certain techniques. This experience is a special form of what Bishop Ignatius describes as the "opening of the senses," and it is clear that—since contact with spirits is forbidden to men except by God's direct action—the realm that can be reached by this means is not heaven, but only the aerial realm of the under-heaven, the realm inhabited by the fallen spirits.

Theosophical texts which describe this experience in detail are so full of occult opinions and interpretations as to be largely useless in giving one an idea of the actual *experiences* of this realm. In the 20th century, however, there has been another kind of literature dealing with this experience: parallel to the rise of research and experiments in the field of "parapsychology," some individuals have discovered, whether by accident or by experiment, that they are able to have the experience of "astral projection," and they have written books describing their experiences in non-occult language; and some researchers have compiled and studied accounts of "out-of-body" experiences and have written about them in scientific rather than occult language. Here we shall look at several of these books.

The "earthly" side of "out-of-body" experiences is well described in a book by the Director of the Institute of Psychophysical Research at Oxford, England.* In answer to an appeal made in September, 1966, in the British press and on the radio, the Institute received some 400 replies from persons who claimed to have had personal out-of-body experiences. Such a response indicates both that these experiences are by no means rare in our days, and that those who have had them are much more willing than in previous years to discuss them without fear of being thought "crazy." Dr. Moody and other researchers have discovered the same things with regard to "after-death" experiences. These 400 persons were given two questionnaires to fill out, and the book was the result of a comparison and analysis of the replies to these questionnaires.

The experiences described in this book were almost all involuntary ones which were triggered by various physical conditions: stress, fatigue, illness, an accident, anesthetization, sleep. Almost all of them occurred in the proximity of the body (not in any "spirit" realm), and the observations made are very similar to those made by people who have had "after-death"

---

* Celia Green, *Out-of-the-Body Experiences,* Ballantine Books, N.Y., 1975.

experiences: one views one's own body from "outside," possesses all sense faculties (even though in the body one might have been deaf or blind), is unable to touch or interact with one's environment, "floats" in the air with an extreme sense of pleasantness and well-being; one's mind is clearer than usual. Some persons described meetings with deceased relatives, or journeying to a landscape which seemed not part of ordinary reality.

One investigator of "out-of-body" experiences, the English geologist Robert Crookall, has gathered an enormous number of examples of them, both from occultists and mediums on the one hand and from ordinary people on the other. He summarizes the experience as follows: "A replica-body, or 'double' was 'born' from the physical body and took up a position above it. As the 'double' separated from the body, there was a 'blackout' in consciousness (much as the changing of gears in a car causes a momentary break in the transmission of power).... There was often a panoramic review of the past life, and the vacated physical body was commonly seen from the released 'double.'... Contrary to what one would expect, no one described pain or fear as having been caused by leaving the body—everything seemed perfectly natural.... Consciousness, as it operated through the separated 'double,' was more extensive than in ordinary life.... There were sometimes telepathy, clairvoyance, and foreknowledge. 'Dead' friends were often seen. Many of the deponents expressed great reluctance to re-enter the body and so return to earth-life.... This general pattern of events in out-of-body experiences, hitherto unrecognized, cannot be explained adequately on the hypothesis that all such experiences were dreams and that all the 'doubles' described were mere hallucinations. It can, on the other hand, be readily explained on the hypothesis that these were genuine experiences and that the 'doubles' seen were objective (though ultra-physical) bodies."*

This description is virtually identical, point-by-point, with Dr. Moody's "model" of after-death experiences (*Life After Life*, pp. 23–24). This identity is so precise that it can only be one and the same experience that is being described. If this is so, it is finally possible to define the experience that Dr. Moody and other investigators have been describing, and which has caused so much interest and discussion in the Western world for several years now. It is not precisely an "after-death" experience; it is rather the "out-of-body" experience which is only the antechamber to other much more extensive experiences, whether of death itself or of what is sometimes called "astral travelling" (on which see below). Although the "out-of-body" state might be called the "first moment" of death—if death actually follows—it is a gross mistake to conclude from it anything whatever about the "after-death" state, unless it be the bare facts of the survival and consciousness of the soul after death, which hardly anyone who actually believes in the soul's immortality denies in any case.** Further, because the "out-of-body" state is not necessarily bound up with death at all, we must be extremely discerning in sifting the evidence supplied by extensive experiences in this realm; in particular, we must ask whether the visions of "heaven" (or "hell") which some are undergoing today have anything to do with the true Christian understanding of heaven and hell, or whether they are only an

---

* Robert Crookall, *Out-of-the-Body Experiences,* The Citadel Press, Secaucus, N.J., 1970, pp. 11–13.
** Only a few sects far from historical Christianity teach that the soul "sleeps" or is "unconscious" after death: the Jehovah's Witnesses, Seventh-Day Adventists, etc.

interpretation of some merely natural (or demonic) experience in the "out-of-body" realm.

Dr. Crookall—who has been the most thorough investigator in this field up to now, applying to it the same caution and concern for detail that characterize his earlier books on the fossil plants of Great Britain—has gathered much material on "paradise" and "hades" experiences. He finds them both to be natural and virtually universal experiences in the "out-of-body" state, and he distinguishes them as follows: "Those who left their bodies naturally tended to glimpse bright and peaceful ('Paradise') conditions, a kind of glorious earth; while (those who were) forcibly ejected ... tended to be in the relatively dim, confused, and semi-dreamlike conditions that correspond to the 'Hades' of the ancients. The former met many helpers (including the 'dead' friends and relatives already mentioned); the latter sometimes encountered discarnate would-be hinderers" (pp. 14–15). Persons who have what Dr. Crookall calls a "mediumistic bodily constitution" invariably pass first of all through a dark, misty "Hades" region, and then into a region of bright light that seems like Paradise. This "Paradise" is variously described (by both mediums and non-mediums) as "the most beautiful scenery ever seen," "a scene of wondrous beauty—a vast parklike garden and the light there is a light that never was seen on sea or land," "lovely scenery" with "people dressed in white" (p. 117), "the light became intense," "the whole earth was aglow" (p. 137).

To explain these experiences, Dr. Crookall hypothesizes the existence of a "total earth" which comprises, on the lowest level, the physical earth which we know in everyday life, surrounded by an interpenetrating non-physical sphere with "Hades" and "Paradise" belts at its lower and upper boundaries (p. 87). This is, roughly, a description of what in Orthodox language is known as the aerial realm of fallen spirits of the under-heaven, or the "astral plane" of Theosophy; Orthodox descriptions of this realm, however, make no "geographical" distinctions between "upper" and "lower," and emphasize more the demonic deceptions which are an integral part of this realm. Dr. Crookall, being a secular researcher, knows nothing of this aspect of the aerial realm, but he does testify, from his "scientific" point of view, to an extremely important fact for the understanding of "after-death" and "out-of-body" experiences: *the "heaven" and "hell" seen by persons in these experiences are only parts (or appearances) of the aerial realm of spirits and have nothing to do with the true heaven and hell of Christian doctrine, which are the eternal dwelling-places of human souls (and their resurrected bodies) as well as of immaterial spirits.* Persons in the "out-of-body" state are not free to "wander" into the true heaven and hell, which are opened to souls only by the express will of God. If some "Christians" at "death" see almost immediately a "heavenly city" with "pearly gates" and "angels", it is only an indication that what is seen in the aerial realm depends to some extent on one's own past experiences and expectations, even as dying Hindus see their own Hindu temples and "gods." True Christian experiences of heaven and hell (as we shall see in the next chapter) are of a different dimension altogether.

5. "Astral Travelling"

Almost all of the recent "after-death" experiences have been extremely brief; if they had been longer, actual death would have resulted. But in the "out-of-body" state that is not bound up with near-death conditions, a longer experience is possible. If this experience is of sufficient duration, one can leave one's immediate environment behind and enter an entirely new landscape—not merely for a brief glimpse of a "garden" or a "bright place" or a "heavenly city," but for an extended "adventure" in the aerial realm. The "astral plane" is evidently quite close to every man, and certain critical experiences (or mediumistic techniques) can "project" one into contact with it. In one of his books, Dr. Carl Jung describes the experience of one of his patients, a woman who had an "out-of-body" experience while undergoing a difficult birth. She saw the doctors and nurses around her, but behind her she was aware of a glorious landscape which seemed to be the boundary of another dimension; she felt that if she turned toward it, she would leave this life—but she returned to her body instead.*

Dr. Moody has recorded a number of such experiences, which he calls the "border" or "limit" experience (*Life after Life*, pp. 54–57).

Those who deliberately induce the experience of "astral projection" are often able to enter into this "other dimension." Just in recent years one man's descriptions of his "journeys" in this dimension have achieved a certain fame, which has allowed him to establish an institute for experiments in the "out-of-body" state. One of the students of this institute has been Dr. Elizabeth Kubler-Ross, who agrees with Monroe's conclusions regarding the similarity of "out-of-body" experiences and the "after-death" state. Here we shall summarize the findings of this experimenter.**

Robert Monroe is a successful American business executive (president of the board of directors of a multi-million dollar

---

* C. G. Jung, *The Interpretation of Nature and the Psyche,* Routledge and Kegan Paul, London, 1955, p. 128.
** Robert A. Monroe, *Journeys Out of the Body,* Anchor Books (Doubleday), Garden City, New York, 1977 (first printing, 1971).

corporation) and an agnostic in religion. His "out-of-body" experiences began in 1958, before he had any interest in occult literature, when he was conducting his own experiments in data-learning techniques during sleep; this involved exercises in concentration and relaxation similar to some techniques of meditation. After starting these experiments, he had the un-usual experience of seeming to be struck with a beam of light, which caused temporary paralysis. After this sensation had been repeated several times, he began "floating" out of the body, and then began to experiment with inducing and developing this experience. In this beginning of his occult "journeys," he reveals the same basic characteristics—a passive meditation, an experi-ence of "light," a basic attitude of trust and openness to new and strange experiences, all in conjunction with a "practical" outlook on life and a lack of any profound awareness or experi-ence of Christianity—that opened Swedenborg to his adven-tures in the world of spirits.

At first Monroe's "journeys" were to recognizable places on earth—nearby places in the beginning, then places farther away—with some successful attempts to bring back actual evidence of the experiences. Then he began to contact "ghost-like" figures, the first contact being as part of a mediumistic experiment (the "Indian guide" sent by the medium actually came for him!—p. 52). Finally, he began to enter into contact with strange landscapes seemingly not of earth.

Taking detailed notes on his experiences (which he re-corded as soon as he returned to the body), he categorized them all as belonging to three "locales": "Locale I" is the "here-now," the normal this-worldly environment. "Locale II" is a "non-ma-terial" environment seemingly immense, with characteristics identical with those of the "astral plane." This locale is the "natural environment" of the "Second Body," as Monroe calls the entity that travels in this realm; it "interpenetrates" the physical world, and its laws are those of thought: "as you think, so you are," "like attracts like," in order to travel one need only *think* of one's destination. Monroe visited various "places" in this realm, where he saw such things as a group of people wearing long robes in a narrow valley (p. 81), and a number of uniformed people who called themselves a "target army" waiting for assignments (p. 82). "Locale III" is a seemingly earth-like reality that is, however, unlike anything known on this earth, with strangely anachronistic features; Theosophists would probably understand this as just another more "solid" part of the "astral plane."

After largely overcoming his initial feeling of fear when finding himself in these unknown realms, Monroe began to explore them and to describe the many intelligent beings he encountered there. On some "journeys" he encountered "dead" friends and conversed with them, but more often he found strange impersonal beings who sometimes "helped" him but just as often failed to respond when he called, who gave vague "mystical" messages that sound like the communications of mediums, who might shake his hand but were just as likely to dig a hook into his offered hand (p. 89). Some of these beings he recognized as "hinderers": beast-like creatures with rubbery bodies that easily change into the shapes of dogs, bats, or his own children (pp. 137–140), and others who tease and torment him and merely laugh when he calls (not in faith, it is true, but only as another "experiment") on the name of Jesus Christ (p. 119).

Having no faith of his own, Monroe opened himself to the "religious" suggestions of the beings of this realm. He was given "prophetic" visions of future events, which sometimes did, in fact, come to pass as he saw them (pp. 145ff). Once, when a white ray of light appeared to him on the boundary of the out-of-body state, he asked it for an answer to his questions about this realm. A voice from the ray answered: "Ask your father to tell you of the great secret." At the next opportunity Monroe accordingly prayed: "Father, guide me. Father, tell me the great secret" (pp. 131–2). It is obvious from all this that Monroe, although remaining "secular" and "agnostic" in his own religious outlook, gave himself over freely to be used by the beings of the occult realm (who, of course, are demons).

Just like Dr. Moody and other investigators in this realm, Monroe writes that "in twelve years of non-physical activities, I find no evidence to substantiate the biblical notions of God and afterlife in a place called heaven" (p. 116). However, just like Swedenborg, Theosophists, and investigators like Dr. Crookall, he finds in the "non-material" environment he explored "all of the aspects we attribute to heaven and hell, which are but part of Locale II" (p. 73). In the area seemingly "closest" to the material world he encountered a gray-black area populated by "nibbling and tormenting beings"; this, he thinks, may be the "border of hell" (pp. 120–121), rather like the "Hades" region Dr. Crookall has identified.

Most revealing, however, is Monroe's experience of "heaven." Three times he travelled to a place of "pure peace," floating in warm, soft clouds which were swept by constantly-changing colored rays of light; he vibrated in harmony with the music of wordless choirs; there were nameless beings around him in the same state, with whom he had no personal contact. He felt this place to be his ultimate "Home," and was lonely for it for some days after the experience ended (pp. 123–5). This "astral heaven," of course, is the ultimate source of the Theosophist teaching on the "pleasantness" of the other world; but how far it is from the true Christian teaching of the Kingdom of Heaven, far outside this aerial realm, which in its fullness of love and personality and the conscious presence of God has become utterly remote from the unbelievers of our times, who ask nothing more than a "nirvana" of soft clouds and colored lights! The fallen spirits can easily provide such an experience of "heaven"; but only Christian struggle and the grace of God can raise one into the true heaven of God.

On several occasions, Monroe has encountered the "God" of his heaven. This event, he says, can occur anywhere in "Locale II." "In the midst of normal activity, wherever it may be, there is a distant Signal, almost like heraldic trumpets. Everyone takes the Signal calmly, and with it, everyone stops speaking or whatever he may be doing. It is the Signal that He (or They) is coming through His Kingdom.

"There is no awestruck prostration or falling down on one's knees. Rather, the attitude is most matter-of-fact. It is an occurrence to which all are accustomed and to comply takes absolute precedence over everything. There are no exceptions.

"At the Signal, each living thing lies down ... with head turned to one side so that one does not see Him as He passes by. The purpose seems to be to form a living road over which He can travel.... There is no movement, not even thought, as He passes by....

"In the several times that I have experienced this, I lay down with the others. At the time, the thought of doing otherwise was inconceivable. As He passes, there is a roaring musical sound and a feeling of radiant, irresistible living force of ultimate power that peaks overhead and fades in the distance.... It is an action as casual as halting for a traffic light at a busy intersection, or waiting at the railroad crossing when the signal indicates that a train is coming; you are unconcerned and yet feel unspoken respect for the power represented in the passing train. The event is also impersonal.

"Is this God? Or God's son? Or His representative?" (pp. 122–3).

It would be difficult to find, in the occult literature of the world, a more vivid account of the worship of satan in his own realm by his impersonal slaves. In another place, Monroe describes his own relationship to the prince of the realm into which he has penetrated. One night, some two years after the start of his "out-of-body" journeys, he felt himself bathed in the same kind of light that accompanied the beginning of these experiences, and he felt the presence of a very strong, intelligent, personal force which rendered him powerless and with no will of his own. "I received the firm impression that I was inextricably bound by loyalty to this intelligent force, always had been, and that I had a job to perform here on earth" (pp. 260–261). In another similar experience with this unseen force or "entity" several weeks later, it (or they) seemed to enter and "search" his mind, and then, "they seemed to soar up into the sky, while I called after them, pleading.* Then I was sure that their mentality and intelligence were far beyond my understanding. It is an impersonal, cold intelligence, with none of the emotions of love or compassion which we respect so much.... I sat down and cried, great deep sobs as I have never cried before, because then I knew without any qualification or future hope of change that

---

* This latter experience is very similar to that undergone by many people today in close encounters with "Unidentified Flying Objects" (UFOs). The occult experience of encountering the fallen spirits of the air is always one and the same experience, even though it is expressed in different images and symbols in accordance with human expectations. (For a discussion of the occult side of UFO encounters, see *Orthodoxy and the Religion of the Future*, St. Herman Monastery Press, 2nd Edition, 1979, ch. VI.)

the God of my childhood, of the churches, of religion throughout the world was not as we worshiped him to be—that for the
rest of my life, I would 'suffer' the loss of this illusion" (p. 262).
One could scarcely imagine a better description of the encounter with the devil which so many of our unsuspecting contemporaries are now undergoing, being helpless to resist it because
of their estrangement from true Christianity.

The value of Monroe's testimony regarding the nature and
the beings of the "astral plane" is great. Although he himself
became deeply involved in it and actually gave his soul over in
submission to the fallen spirits, he described his experiences in
a straightforward, non-occult language and from a relatively
normal human point of view that make his book a persuasive
warning against "experiments" in this realm. Those who know
the Orthodox Christian teaching on the aerial world, as well as
on the true heaven and hell which are outside it, can only be the
more firmly convinced of the reality of the fallen spirits and
their realm, as well as of the great danger of contacting them
even through a seemingly "scientific" approach.* As Orthodox
Christian observers, we do not need to know how much of his
experience was "real" and how much was a result of spectacles
and illusions engineered for him by the fallen spirits; deception
is so much a part of the aerial realm that there is no point in
even trying to unravel its precise forms. But that he did encounter the realm of the fallen spirits cannot be doubted.

The "astral plane" can also be contacted (but not necessarily in an "out-of-body" state) through the use of certain drugs.
Recent experiments in administering LSD to dying persons has

---

* Monroe's observation, made also by many other experimenters in this area,
that "out-of-body" experiences are invariably accompanied by a high degree
of sexual excitement, only confirms the fact that these experiences attract the
lower side of man's nature and have nothing whatever spiritual about them.

produced very convincing "near-death" experiences, together
with a "condensed replay" of one's entire life, a vision of
blinding light, encounters with the "dead" and with non-
human "spiritual beings," and the communication of spiritual
messages concerning the truths of "cosmic religion," reincarnation, and the like. Dr. Kubler-Ross has also been involved in
these experiments.*

It is well known that the shamans of primitive tribes enter
into contact with the aerial world of fallen spirits in "out-of-
body" states, and once "initiated" into this experience are able
to visit the "world of spirits" and communicate with its beings.**

The same experience was common among the initiates of
the "mysteries" of the ancient pagan world. In the *Life* of St.
Cyprian and Justina (Oct. 2) we have the first-hand testimony
of a former sorcerer concerning his experiences in this realm:

"On Mt. Olympus Cyprian studied all manner of diabol-
ical arts: he mastered various demonic transformations, learned
how to change the nature of the air.... In this place he saw a
numberless legion of demons, with the prince of darkness at
their head; some stood before him, others served him, still
others cried out in praise of their prince, and some were sent
into the world in order to corrupt people. Here he likewise saw
in their false forms the pagan gods and goddesses, and also
diverse phantoms and specters, the invocation of which he
learned in a strict forty-day fast.... Thus he became a sorcerer,
magician, and destroyer of souls, a great friend and faithful slave
of the prince of hell, with whom he conversed face to face, being

---

* Stanislav Grof and Joan Halifax, *The Human Encounter with Death*, E.P.
Dutton, New York, 1977.
** See M. Eliade, *Shamanism*, Routledge and Kegan Paul, London, 1961.

vouchsafed to receive from him great honor, as he himself testified. 'Believe me,' he said, 'I have seen the prince of darkness himself.... I greeted him and his ancients.... He promised to make me a prince after my departure from the body, and for the course of earthly life to help me in everything.... The outward appearance of the prince of darkness was like a flower. His head was covered by a crown (not an actual, but a phantom one) made of gold and brilliant stones, as a result of which the whole space around him was illuminated; and his clothing was astonishing. When he would turn to one or the other side, that whole place would tremble, a multitude of evil spirits of various degrees stood obediently at this throne. I gave myself over entirely into his service at that time, obeying his every command" (*The Orthodox Word,* 1976, no. 70, pp. 136–138).

St. Cyprian does not state explicitly that he had these experiences out of the body; it would indeed seem that more advanced sorcerers and adepts do not need to leave the body in order to achieve full contact with the aerial realm. Swedenborg, even while describing his own "out-of-body" experiences, stated that most of his contact with spirits was, on the contrary, in the body, but with his "doors of perception" opened (*Heaven and Hell,* Sections 440–442). Still, the characteristics of this realm, and one's "adventures" in it, are the same whether one happens to be "in" or "out" of the body.

One of the famous pagan sorcerers of antiquity (2nd century), in describing his initiation into the mysteries of Isis, gives a classic example of the "out-of-body" experience, the contact with the aerial realm, that could be used to describe some of today's "out-of-body" and "after-death" experiences:

"I will record (of my initiation) as much as I may lawfully record for the uninitiated, but only on condition that you believe it. *I approached the very gates of death and set one foot on*

Proserpine's threshold, yet was permitted to return, rapt through all the elements. At midnight I saw the sun shining as if it were noon; I entered the presence of the gods of the underworld and the gods of the upper world, stood near and worshipped them. Well, now you have heard what happened, but I fear you are still none the wiser."*

Conclusions about the "Out-of-Body" Realm

All that has been said here about "out-of-body" experiences is sufficient to place today's "after-death" experiences in their proper perspective. Let us summarize what we have found:

1. These are, purely and simply, "out-of-body" experiences, something well known especially in occult literature, which have been happening with increasing frequency in recent years to ordinary people who are not at all involved in occultism. These experiences, however, in actual fact tell us almost nothing of what happens to the soul after death, except that it does survive and is conscious.

2. The realm into which the soul immediately enters when it leaves the body and begins to lose contact with what we know as "material reality" (whether after death or in a simple "out-of-body" experience) is neither heaven nor hell, but an invisible realm close to earth which is variously called the "After-death" or "Bardo plane" (*Tibetan Book of the Dead*), the "world of spirits" (Swedenborg and spiritism), the "astral plane" (Theosophy and most of occultism), "Locale II" (Monroe)—or, in Orthodox language, the aerial world of the under-heaven where fallen spirits dwell and are active in deceiving men for their

---

* Apuleius, *The Golden Ass*, tr. by Robert Graves, Farrar, Straus and Young, New York, 1951, p. 280. Proserpine (or Persephone) was the Queen of Hades in Greek and Roman mythology.

damnation. This is not the "other world" that awaits man after death, but only the invisible part of *this* world that man must pass through to reach the truly "other" world of heaven or hell. For those who have truly died, and are being conducted by angels out of earthly life, this is the realm where the Particular Judgment begins at the aerial "toll-houses," where the spirits of the air reveal their real nature and their hostility towards mankind; for all others, it is a realm of demonic deception at the hands of these same spirits.

3. *The beings contacted in this realm are always (or almost always) demons,* whether they are invoked by mediumism or other occult practices, or encountered in "out-of-body" experiences. They are not angels, for these dwell in heaven and only pass through this realm as messengers of God. They are not the souls of the dead, for they dwell in heaven or hell and only pass through this realm immediately after death on their way to judgment for their actions in this life. Even those most adept in "out-of-body" experiences cannot remain in this realm for long without danger of permanent separation from the body (death), and even in occult literature such adepts are rarely described as meeting each other.

4. *Experiences in this realm are not to be trusted, and certainly are not to be taken at their "face-value."* Even those with a firm grounding in Orthodox Christian teaching can be easily deceived by the fallen spirits of the air with regard to any "vision" they may see; but those who enter this realm with no knowledge of it and accept its "revelations" with trust are nothing more than pitiful victims of the fallen spirits.

It may be asked: What of the feelings of "peace" and "pleasantness" which seem to be almost universal in the "out-of-body" state. What of the vision of "light" which so many see? Are these only deceptions also?

In a sense, it may be, these experiences are "natural" to the soul when separated from the body. Our physical bodies in this fallen world are bodies of pain, corruption, and death. When separated from this body, the soul is immediately in a state more "natural" to it, closer to the state God intends for it; for the resurrected "spiritual body" in which man will dwell in the Kingdom of Heaven has more in common with the soul than with the body we know on earth. Even the body with which Adam was created in the beginning had a nature different from the body after Adam's fall, being more refined and not subject to pain or travail.

In this sense, the "peace" and "pleasantness" of the out-of-body experience may be considered real and not a deception. Deception enters in, however, the instant one begins to interpret these "natural" feelings as something "spiritual"—as though this peace were the true peace of reconciliation with God, and the "pleasantness" were the true spiritual pleasure of heaven. This is, in fact, how may people interpret their "out-of-body" and "after-death" experiences, because of their lack of true spiritual experience and awareness. That this is a mistake may be seen from the fact that even the crudest unbelievers have the same experience of pleasantness when they "die." We have already seen this in an earlier chapter in the case of Hindus, an atheist, and a suicide. Another striking example is that of the agnostic British novelist, Somerset Maugham, who, when he had a brief "death" experience just before his actual death at the age of 80, experienced first an ever-increasing light and "then the most exquisite sense of release," as he described it in his own words (see Allen Spreggett, *The Case for Immortality*, New American Library, New York, 1974, p. 73). This experience was not in the least spiritual; it was but one more "natural" experience in a life that ended in unbelief.

As a sensuous or "natural" experience, therefore, it would seem that death is indeed pleasant. This pleasantness may be experienced equally by one whose conscience is clean before God, and by one who does not deeply believe in God or eternal life at all, and therefore has no awareness of how he may have displeased God during his lifetime. A "bad death" is experienced, as one writer has well said, only by "those who know that God exists, and yet have lived their lives as though He did not"*—i.e., those whose consciences torment them and counteract by their pain the natural "pleasure" of physical death. The distinction between believers and unbelievers occurs, then, not at the moment of death itself, but later, at the Particular Judgment. The "pleasantness" of death may be real enough, but it has no necessary connection whatever with the eternal fate of the soul, which may well be one of torment.

All the more is this true of the vision of "light." This *may* be something merely natural also—a reflection of the true state of light for which man was created. If so, it is still a serious mistake to give it the "spiritual" meaning which the spiritually inexperienced invariably give it. Orthodox ascetic literature is filled with warnings against trusting any kind of "light" that might appear to one; and when one begins to interpret such a light as an "angel" or even "Christ," it is clear that one has already fallen into deception, weaving a "reality" out of one's own imagination even before the fallen spirits have begun their own work of deception.

It is also "natural" for the soul apart from the body to have a heightened awareness of reality and to exercise what is now called "extra-sensory perception" (ESP). It is an obvious

---

* David Winter, *Hereafter: What Happens after Death?* Harold Shaw Publishers, Wheaton, Ill., 1977, p. 90.

fact, noted both in Orthodox literature and in modern scientific investigations, that the soul just after "death" (and often just before death) sees things that bystanders do not see, knows when someone is dying at a distance, etc. A reflection of this may be seen in the experience Dr. Moody calls "the vision of knowledge," when the soul seems to have an "enlightenment" and to see "all knowledge" in front of it (*Reflections on Life after Life,* pp. 9–14). St. Boniface describes the immediate experience after death of the "monk of Wenlock" thus: "He felt like a man seeing and wide-awake, whose eyes had been veiled by a dense covering and then suddenly the veil was lifted and everything made clear which had previously been invisible, veiled and unknown. So with him, when the veil of the flesh was cast aside the whole universe seemed to be brought together before his eyes so that he saw in one view all parts of the earth and all seas and peoples" (Emerton, *Letters of St. Boniface,* p. 25).

Some souls seem to be naturally sensitive to similar experiences, even while still in the body. St. Gregory the Great notes that "sometimes it is through a subtle power of their own that souls can foresee the future," as opposed to those who foresee the future by God's revelation (*Dialogues,* IV, 27, p. 219). But such "psychics" invariably fall into deception when they begin interpreting or developing this talent, which can be properly used only by persons of great sanctity and (of course) Orthodoxy of belief. The American "psychic" Edgar Cayce is a good example of the pitfalls of such "ESP": once he discovered that he had a talent for accurate medical diagnosis in a trance-state, he began to trust *all* the messages received in this state and ended by giving himself off as a prophet of the future (sometimes with spectacular wrongness, as with the West-coast cataclysm which failed to occur in 1969), offering astrological readings, and tracing out the "past lives" of men in "Atlantis," ancient Egypt, and elsewhere.

The "natural" experiences of the soul when it is especially sensitive or is separated from the body—whether these be experiences of "peace" and pleasantness, light, or "ESP"—are therefore only the "raw material" of the soul's heightened awareness, but give (we must say again) very little positive information about the state of the soul after death, and all too often lead one to unwarranted interpretations of the "other world" as well as into direct contact with the fallen spirits whose realm this is. Such experiences are all of the "astral" world and have in themselves nothing spiritual or heavenly; even when the experience itself is real, the interpretations given to it are not to be trusted.

5. By the very nature of things, *a true knowledge of the aerial realm of spirits and its manifestations cannot be acquired by experience alone.* The boast of all branches of occultism that their knowledge is sure because it is based on "experience" is precisely the fatal flaw of all occult "knowledge." Rather, the experiences of this realm, because they occur in the aerial realm and are often produced by demons with the ultimate intent of deceiving and destroying men's souls, *are by their very nature bound up with deception,* quite apart from the fact that man, not being at home in this realm, can never fully orient himself in it and be sure of its reality as he can of the material realm. Buddhist doctrine (as expressed in the *Tibetan Book of the Dead)* is certainly correct when it speaks of the illusionary nature of the appearances of the "Bardo plane"; but it is wrong when it concludes from this, on the basis of experience alone, that there is no objective reality whatever behind these appearances. The reality of this invisible realm cannot be known for what it actually is unless this be revealed by a source outside and above it.

The contemporary approach to this realm by means of personal and/or "scientific" experimentation is, for the same reason, bound to result in misleading and deceptive conclusions. Almost all contemporary researchers accept or at least are highly sympathetic to the occult teaching regarding this realm, for the single reason that it is based on experience, which is also the basis of science. But "experience" in the material world is something quite different from "experience" in the aerial realm. The raw material being experienced and studied in the one case is morally "neutral," and it can be studied objectively and verified by others; but in the other case the "raw material" is hidden, extremely difficult to grasp, and, in many cases, *has a will of its own*—a will to deceive the observer. For this reason, serious investigations such as those of Dr. Moody, Dr. Crookall, Drs. Osis and Haraldsson, and Dr. Kubler-Ross almost inevitably end by being used for the spread of occult ideas, which are the "natural" ideas to be drawn from a study of the occult aerial realm. Only with the idea (which has become rare today) that there is a revealed *truth* that is above all experience, can this occult realm be enlightened, its true nature recognized and a discernment made between this lower realm and the higher realm of heaven.

It has been necessary to devote this long chapter to "out-of-body" experiences in order to define as precisely as possible the nature of the experiences now being undergone by a large number of ordinary people, not merely mediums and occultists. (In the conclusion of this book we shall try to explain why such experiences have become so common today.) It is quite clear that these experiences are real, and cannot be dismissed as "hallucinations." But it is equally clear that these experiences are not spiritual, and the attempts of those who have undergone them to interpret them as "spiritual experiences" which reveal the true nature of life after death and the ultimate state of the soul—only serve to increase the spiritual confusion of contemporary mankind and reveal how far its awareness is from true spiritual knowledge and experience.

In order to see this the better, we shall now turn to an examination of several cases of *true* experiences of the other world—the eternal world of heaven which is opened to man only by the will of God, and which is quite distinct from the aerial realm we have been examining here, which is still part of *this* world which will have an end.

A NOTE ON "REINCARNATION"

Among the occult ideas which are now being widely discussed and sometimes accepted by those who have "out-of-body" and "after-death" experiences, and even by some scientists, is the idea of reincarnation: that the soul after death does not undergo the Particular Judgment and then dwell in heaven or hell awaiting the resurrection of the body and the Last Judgment, but (evidently after a longer or shorter stay on the "astral plane") comes back to earth and occupies a new body, whether of a beast or of another man.

This idea was widespread in pagan antiquity in the West, before it was replaced by Christian ideas; but its spread today is largely owing to the influence of Hinduism and Buddhism, where it is commonly accepted. Today the idea is usually "humanized," in that people assume their "previous lives" were as men, whereas the more common idea both among Hindus and Buddhists and among ancient Greeks and Romans is that it is rather rare to achieve "incarnation" as a man, and that most of today's "incarnations" are as beasts, insects, and even plants.

Those who believe in this idea say that it accounts for all of the many "injustices" of earthly life, as well as for seemingly unexplainable phobias: if one is born blind, or in conditions of poverty, it is as a just reward for one's actions in a "previous life" (or, as Hindus and Buddhists say, because of one's "bad karma"); if one is afraid of water, it is because one drowned in a "previous existence."

Believers in reincarnation do not have any very thorough philosophy of the origin and destination of the soul, nor any convincing proofs to support their theory; its main attractions are the superficial ones of seeming to provide "justice" on earth, of explaining some psychic mysteries, and of providing some semblance of "immortality" for those who do not accept this on Christian grounds.

On deeper reflection, however, the theory of reincarnation offers no real explanation of injustices at all: if one suffers in this life for sins and mistakes in another lifetime which one cannot remember, and for which (if one was "previously" a beast) one cannot even be held responsible, and if (according to Buddhist teaching) there is even no "self" that survives from one "incarnation" to the next, and one's past mistakes were literally someone else's—then there is no recognizable justice at all, but only a blind suffering of evils whose origin is not to be traced out. The Christian teaching of the fall of Adam, which is the origin of all the world's evils, offers a much better explanation of injustices in the world; and the Christian revelation of God's perfect justice in His judgment of men for eternal life in heaven or hell renders unnecessary and trivial the idea of attaining "justice" through successive "incarnations" in this world.

In recent decades the idea of reincarnation has achieved a remarkable popularity in the Western world, and there have been numerous cases suggesting the "remembrance" of "past lives"; many people also return from "out-of-body" experiences believing that these experiences suggest or instill the idea of reincarnation. What are we to think of these cases?

Very few of these cases, it should be noted, offer "proof" that is any more than vaguely circumstantial, and could easily be the product of simple imagination: a child is born with a mark on his neck, and subsequently "remembers" that he was hanged as a horse thief in a "previous life"; a person fears heights, and then "remembers" that he died by falling in his "past life"; and the like. The natural human tendency of fantasy renders such cases useless as "proof" of reincarnation.

In many cases, however, such "previous lives" have been discovered by a hypnotic technique known as "regressive hypnosis," which has in many cases given striking results in the recall of events long forgotten by the conscious mind, even as far back as infancy. The hypnotist brings a person "back" to infancy, and then asks: "What about *before that?*" Often, in such cases, a person will "remember" his "death" or even a whole different lifetime; what are we to think of such memories?

Well-trained hypnotists themselves will admit the pitfalls of "regressive hypnosis." Dr. Arthur C. Hastings, a California specialist in the psychology of communication, notes that "the most obvious thing that happens under hypnosis is that the person is extremely open to any subtle, unconscious, nonverbal, as well as verbal suggestions of the hypnotist and they are extremely compliant. If you ask them to go to a past life, and they don't *have* a past life, they will invent one for you! If you suggest that they saw a UFO, they would have seen a UFO."* A Chicago-based hypnotist, Dr. Larry Garrett, who has done some 500 hypnotic regressions himself, notes that these regressions are often inaccurate even when it is only a matter of remembering a past event in *this* life: "A lot of times people fabricate things, from either wishful thinking, fantasies, dreams, things such as this.... Anyone who is into hypnosis and does any type of regression would find out that many times people have such a vivid imagination that they will sit there and make up all kinds of things just to please the hypnotist" (*The Edge of Reality*, pp. 91–92).

Another researcher on this question writes: "This method is fraught with hazards, chief of which is the unconscious mind's tendency toward dramatic fantasy. What comes out in hypnosis may be, in effect, a dream of the kind of previous existence the subject would like to have lived or believes, correctly or incorrectly, that he did live.... One psychologist instructed a number of hypnotized subjects to remember a previous existence, and they did, without exception. Some of these accounts were replete with colorful details and seemed convincing.... However, when the psychologist rehypnotized them they were able, in trance, to trace every element in the accounts of previous existence to some normal source—a person they had known in childhood, scenes from novels they had read or movies they had seen years before, and so on."**

But what of those cases, publicized widely of late, when there is "objective proof" of one's "previous life"—when a person "remembers" details of time and places he could not

---

* J. Allen Hynek and Jacques Vallee, *The Edge of Reality*, Henry Regnery Co., Chicago, 1975, p. 107.
** Allen Spraggett, *The Case for Immortality*, New American Library, New York, 1974, pp. 137–8.

possibly have known by himself, and which can be checked by historical documents?

Such cases seem very convincing to those already inclined to believe in reincarnation; but this kind of "proof" is not different from the standard information provided by the "spirits" at seances (which can also be of a very striking kind), and there is no reason to suppose that the source is different. If the "spirits" at seances are quite clearly demons, then the information on one's "previous lives" can also be supplied by demons. The aim in both cases is the same: to confuse men with a dazzling display of seemingly "supernatural" knowledge, and thus to deceive them concerning the true nature of life after death and leave them spiritually unprepared for it.

Even occultists who are favorable in general to the idea of reincarnation admit that the "proof" for reincarnation can be interpreted in various ways. One American popularizer of occult ideas believes that "most reported instances giving evidence of reincarnation could possibly be cases of possession."* "Possession," according to such occultists, occurs when a "dead" person takes possession of a living body and the latter's personality and very identity seem to change, thus causing the impression that one is being dominated by the characteristics of one's "previous life." Those beings that "possess" men, of course, are demons, no matter how much they may masquerade as the souls of the dead. The recent famous *Twenty Cases Suggestive of Reincarnation* by Dr. Ian Stevenson seems, indeed, to be a collection of cases of such "possession."

The early Christian Church fought the idea of reincarnation, which entered the Christian world through Eastern teachings such as those of the Manicheans. Origen's false teaching of

---

* Suzy Smith, *Life is Forever,* G.P. Putnam's Sons, New York, 1974, p. 171.

the "pre-existence of souls" was closely related to these teachings, and at the Fifth Ecumenical council in Constantinople in 553 it was strongly condemned and its followers anathematized. Many individual Fathers of the Church wrote against it, notably St. Ambrose of Milan in the West (*On Belief in the Resurrection,* Book II), St. Gregory of Nyssa in the East (*On the Soul and the Resurrection*), and others.

For the present-day Orthodox Christian who is tempted by this idea, or who wonders about the supposed "proof" of it, it is perhaps sufficient to reflect on three basic Christian dogmas which conclusively refute the very possibility of reincarnation:

1. *The resurrection of the body.* Christ rose from the dead in the very body which had died the death of all men, and became the first-fruits of all men, whose bodies will also be resurrected on the last day and rejoined to their souls in order to live eternally in heaven or hell, according to God's just judgment of their life on earth. This resurrected body, like that of Christ Himself, will be different from our earthly bodies in that it will be more refined and more like the angelic nature, without which it could not dwell in the Heavenly Kingdom, where there is no death or corruption; but it will still be the *same body,* miraculously restored and made fit by God for eternal life, as Ezekiel saw in his vision of the "dry bones" (Ezek. 37:1–14). In heaven the redeemed will recognize each other. The body is thus an inalienable part of the whole person who will live forever, and the idea of many bodies belonging to the same person denies the very nature of the Heavenly Kingdom which God has prepared for those who love Him.

2. *Our redemption by Jesus Christ.* God took flesh and through His life, suffering, and death on the Cross redeemed us from the dominion of sin and death. Through His Church, we are saved and made fit for the Heavenly Kingdom, with no

"penalty" to pay for our past transgressions. But according to the idea of reincarnation, if one is "saved" at all it is only after many lifetimes of working out the consequences of one's sins. This is the cold and dreary legalism of the pagan religions which was totally abolished by Christ's sacrifice on the Cross; the thief on His right hand received salvation in an instant through his faith in the Son of God, the "bad karma" of his evil deeds being obliterated by the grace of God.

3. *The Judgment. It is appointed unto men once to die, but after this the judgment* (Heb. 9:27). Human life is a single, definite period of trial, after which there is no "second chance," but only God's judgment (which is both just and merciful) of a man according to the state of his soul when his life is finished.

In these three doctrines the Christian revelation is quite precise and definite, in contrast to the pagan religions which do not believe either in the resurrection or in redemption, and are vague about judgment and the future life. The one answer to all supposed experiences or remembrances of "previous lives" is precisely the clear-cut teaching of Christianity about the nature of human life and God's dealings with men.

CHAPTER EIGHT

True Christian Experiences of Heaven

1. The "Location" of Heaven and Hell

WE have now seen, through numerous accounts of Holy Fathers and in Lives of Saints, that the soul after death enters immediately into the aerial realm of the under-heaven, whose characteristics we have examined in detail. We have also seen that the progress of the soul through this aerial realm, once the body has actually died and the soul is finished with earthly things, is described as an ascent through the toll-houses, where the Particular Judgment begins in order to determine the fitness of the soul to dwell in heaven. Those souls that are convicted of unrepented sins are cast down by the fallen spirits into hell; those that pass successfully through the trials of the toll-houses ascend freely, guided by angels, to heaven.

What is this heaven? Where is it? Is heaven a place? Is it "up"?

As with all matters concerning life after death, we should not ask such questions out of mere curiosity, but solely in order to understand better the teaching on this subject which the Church has handed down to us, and to escape the confusions which modern ideas and some psychic experiences can cause even in Orthodox Christians.

It so happens that the question of the "location" of heaven (and hell) is one that has been very widely misunderstood in modern times. It was only a few years ago that the Soviet dictator Krushchev was laughing at religious people who still believed in heaven—he had sent "cosmonauts" into space and they had not seen it!

No thinking Christian, of course, believes in the atheist caricature of a heaven "in the sky," although there are some naive Protestants who would place heaven in a distant galaxy or constellation; the whole visible creation is fallen and corrupt, and there is no place in it anywhere for the invisible heaven of God, which is a spiritual and not a material reality. But many Christians, in order to escape the mockery of unbelievers and avoid even the slightest taint of any materialistic conception, have gone to an opposite extreme and declare that heaven is "nowhere." Among Roman Catholics and Protestants there are sophisticated apologies which proclaim that heaven is "a state, not a place," that "up" is only a metaphor, the Ascension of Christ (Luke 24:50–51, Acts 1:9–11) was not really an "ascension," but only a change of state. The result of such apologies is that heaven and hell become very vague and indefinite conceptions, and the sense of their reality begins to disappear—with disastrous results for Christian life, because these are the very realities toward which our whole earthly life is directed.

All such apologies, according to the teaching of Bishop Ignatius Brianchaninov, are based on the false idea of the modern philosopher Descartes that everything that is not material is "pure spirit" and is not limited by time and space. This is not the teaching of the Orthodox Church. Bishop Ignatius writes: "The fantasy of Descartes concerning the independence of spirits on space and time is a decisive absurdity. Everything that is limited is necessarily dependent on space" (vol. III, p.

312). "The numerous quotations cited above from the Divine service books and the works of the Fathers of the Orthodox Church decide with complete satisfaction the question as to where paradise and hell are located.... With what clarity the teaching of the Orthodox Eastern Church indicates that *the location of paradise is in the heaven* and *the location of hell is in the bowels of the earth"* (vol. III, pp. 308–9; the emphasis is his). Here we shall only indicate just how this teaching is to be interpreted.

It is certainly true, as Bishop Ignatius' numerous citations indicate, that all Orthodox sources—the Holy Scripture, Divine services, Lives of Saints, writings of Holy Fathers—speak of paradise and heaven as "up" and hell as "down," under the earth. And it is also true that since angels and souls are limited in space (as we have seen in the chapter above on "The Orthodox Doctrine of Angels"), they must always be in one definite *place*—whether heaven, hell, or earth. We have already quoted the teaching of St. John Damascene that "when the angels are in heaven they are not on earth, and when they are sent to earth by God they do not remain in heaven" (*Exact Exposition of the Orthodox Faith*, II. 3, p. 206), which is only the same doctrine taught earlier by St.Basil the Great (*On the Holy Spirit*, ch. 23), St.Gregory the Dialogist (*Morals on the Book of Job*, Book II, 3), and indeed all the Orthodox Fathers.

Heaven, therefore, is certainly a place, and it is certainly *up* from any point on the earth, and hell is certainly *down*, in the bowels of the earth; but these places and their inhabitants cannot be seen by men until their spiritual eyes are opened, as we have seen earlier with regard to the aerial realm. Further, these places are not within the "coordinates" of our space-time system: an airliner does not pass "invisibly" through paradise, nor an earth satellite through the third heaven, nor can the souls waiting in hell for the Last Judgment be reached by drilling for them in the earth. They are not *there,* but in a different *kind* of space that begins right here but extends, as it were, in a different direction.

There are indications, or at least hints, of this other kind of reality even in everyday, this-worldly experience. For example, the existence of volcanos and of great heat in the center of the earth is taken by many Saints and Fathers as a direct indication of the existence of hell in the bowels of the earth.* Of course, hell is not "material" in the sense that the lava that flows up from under the crust of the earth is material; but there does seem to be a kind of "overlapping" of the two kinds of reality—an "overlapping" that can be seen first of all in the nature of man himself, who is capable, under certain circumstance or by God's will, of perceiving both kinds of reality even in this life. Modern scientists themselves have come to admit that they are no longer sure of the ultimate nature and boundaries of matter, nor where it leaves off and "psychic" reality begins.

Numerous incidents in the Lives of Saints show how this other kind of space "breaks into" the "normal" space of this world. Often, for example, the soul of a newly deceased man is seen rising to heaven, as when St. Benedict saw the soul of St. Germanus of Capua carried to heaven by angels in a ball of fire (St. Gregory's *Dialogues,* II, 35), or the residents of Afognak saw St. Herman's soul ascending in a pillar of fire, or the Elder Philaret of Glinsk saw the soul of St. Seraphim of Sarov ascending. The Prophet Elisha beheld the Prophet Elijah taken up in a fiery chariot into heaven (III Kings 2:11). Often, also, souls

---

* See the Life of St. Patricius of Prussa, May 19; St. Gregory's *Dialogues,* IV, 36 and 44; Bishop Ignatius Brianchaninov, vol. III, p. 98.

are beheld going through the toll-houses; such cases are especially numerous in the Life of St. Niphon of Constantia (Dec. 23) and St. Columba of Iona—some of the latter were quoted above in the chapter on the toll-houses. In the Life of Blessed Theophilus of Kiev, the one witness of the righteous one's death saw how at this time "something flashed before his gaze and a current of cool air struck his face. Dimitry looked upwards in amazement and became petrified. In the cell, the ceiling began to rise and the blue sky, as if extending its arms, was preparing to receive the holy soul of the dying righteous one."*

Beyond the general knowledge that heaven and hell are indeed "places," but not places in this world, in our space-time system—we need not be curious. These "places" are so different from our earthly notions of "place" that we shall become hopelessly confused if we attempt to piece together a "geography" of them. Some Lives of Saints indicate clearly that "heaven" is above "paradise"; others indicate that there are at least "three heavens"—but it is not for us to define the "boundaries" of these places or to try to distinguish their characteristics. Such descriptions are given to us, in God's Providence, in order to inspire us to struggle to reach them by a Christian life and death—but not in order to apply to them worldly categories of logic and knowledge which do not fit them. St. John Chrysostom rightly recalls us to our proper concern in studying about heaven and hell: "You ask where hell is; but why should you know it? You must know that hell exists, not where it is hidden.... In my opinion, it is somewhere outside this whole world.... Let us attempt to find out not where it is, but how to escape it" (Homilies on Romans, 31:3–4).

---

* See the Life of Blessed Theophilus (Feofil), Holy Trinity Monastery, Jordanville, N.Y., 1970, p. 125.

It is not given us to understand very much of the other-worldly reality in this life, although we do know enough to answer the rationalists who say that heaven and hell are "nowhere" and therefore non-existent because they cannot see them. These places are indeed "somewhere," and some living on earth have been there and returned to tell of them; but these places are seen by us in the flesh more by faith than by knowledge: *Now we see through a glass darkly, but then face to face. Now I know in part, but then I shall know even as I am known* (I Cor. 13:12).

2. Christian Experiences of Heaven

True Christian experiences of heaven always bear one and the same stamp of other-worldly experience. Those who have beheld heaven have not merely travelled to a different *place;* they have also entered into a whole different *spiritual state.* We who have not experienced this personally must be satisfied with the description of certain outward features which, taken together, distinguish these experiences rather clearly from all of the experiences of the aerial realm which we have examined above.

Numerous Lives of Saints contain descriptions of souls entering heaven, as seen from the earth. In the Life of St. Anthony the Great we read: "Another time, Anthony was sitting in the mountain, and looking up he saw one carried on high, and a joyful band meeting him. Filled with wonder, he pronounced them a band of the blessed, and prayed to learn what this might be. And straightway came a voice to him, saying 'This is the soul of Ammon, the monk of Nitria, who led an ascetic life down to his old age'" (*Life of St. Anthony,* Eastern Orthodox Books edition, p. 38).

Abba Serapion thus described the death of St. Mark of Thrace: "Looking up, I beheld the soul of the Saint already being delivered from the bonds of the body. It was covered by angelic hands with a bright white garment and raised up by them to heaven. I beheld the aerial path to heaven and the opened heavens. Then I saw the hordes of demons standing on this path and heard an angelic voice addressed to the demons: 'Sons of darkness! Flee and hide yourselves from the face of the light of righteousness!' The holy soul of Mark was detained in the air for about one hour. Then a voice was heard from heaven, saying to the angels: 'Take and bring here him who put the demons to shame.' When the soul of the saint had passed without any harm to itself through the hordes of demons and had already drawn near to the opened heaven, I saw as it were the likeness of a hand stretched out from heaven receiving the immaculate soul. Then this vision was hidden from my eyes, and I saw nothing more" (Lives of Saints, April 5).

From these accounts we may already see three characteristics of the true Christian experience of heaven: It is an ascent; the soul is conducted by angels; it is greeted by and joins the company of the inhabitants of heaven.

Experiences of heaven are of various kinds. Sometimes a soul is conducted to heaven before death to be shown its wonders or the place prepared there for the soul. Thus, St. Maura, after resisting the two false visions of the fallen spirits during her martyrdom (described above as an example of the temptations that can occur at the hour of death), described the God-given experience that followed: "I also beheld a third man, very comely of appearance; his face shone like the sun. He took me by the hand, led me up to heaven and showed me a throne covered with white garments, and a crown, most beautiful in appearance. Amazed at such beauty, I asked the man that had led me up to heaven: 'Whose is this, my lord?' He told me: 'This is the reward for your struggle.… But now return to your body. In the morning, at the sixth hour, the angels of God will come to take your soul up to heaven."*

There is also the experience of beholding heaven in vision from afar, as when the First Martyr St. Stephen beheld *the heavens opened, and the Son of Man standing on the right hand of God* (Acts 7:56). Here, however, we shall study only the specific experience that is most comparable to today's "after-death" experiences: the ascent to heaven, either at death or in a Divinely-granted experience, whether "in" or "out" of the body.

St. Salvius of Albi, a 6th-century hierarch of Gaul, after being dead for the better part of a day, returned to life and gave this account to his friend, St. Gregory of Tours: "When my cell shook four days ago, and you saw me lying dead, I was raised up by two angels and carried to the highest peak of heaven, until I seemed to have beneath my feet not only this miserable earth, but also the sun and moon, the clouds and stars. Then I was conducted through a gate that shone more brightly than the light of the sun and entered a building where the whole floor shone with gold and silver. The light was impossible to describe. The place was filled with a multitude of people, neither male nor female, stretching so far in all directions that one could not see where it ended. The angels made a way for me through the crowd of people in front of me, and we came to the place towards which our gaze had been directed even when we had been far away. Over this place hung a cloud more brilliant than any light, and yet no sun or moon or star could be seen; indeed,

---

* Lives of Saints, May 3, English translation in *Orthodox Life*, May-June, 1978, pp. 9–17.

the cloud shone more brightly than any of these with its own brilliance. A voice came out of the cloud, as the voice of many waters. Sinner that I am, I was greeted with great respect by a number of beings, some dressed in priestly vestments and others in ordinary dress; my guides told me that these were the martyrs and other holy men whom we honor here on earth and to whom we pray with great devotion. As I stood here there was wafted over me a fragrance of such sweetness that, nourished by it, I have felt no need of food or drink until this very moment. Then I heard a voice which said: 'Let this man go back into the world, for our churches have need of him.' I heard the voice, but I could not see who was speaking. Then I prostrated myself on the ground and wept. 'Alas, alas, O Lord!' I said. 'Why hast Thou shown me these things only to take them away from me again?...' The voice which had spoken to me said: 'Go in peace. I will watch over you until I bring you back once more to this place.' Then my guides left me and I turned back through the gate by which I had entered, weeping as I went."*

Several more important characteristics are added in this experience: the brightness of the light of heaven; the invisible presence of the Lord, Whose voice is heard; the Saint's awe and fear before the Lord; and a tangible sensing of Divine grace, in the form of an indescribable fragrance. Further, it is specified that the multitudes of "people" encountered in heaven are (in addition to the angels who conduct souls) the souls of martyrs and holy men.

The monk of Wenlock, after being raised up by angels and passing through the toll-houses, "saw also a place of wondrous beauty, wherein a multitude of very handsome men were enjoy-

---

* St. Gregory of Tours, *The History of the Franks,* Book VII, 1; *Vita Patrum,* St. Herman Monastery Press, 1988, pp. 296–7.

ing extraordinary happiness, and they invited him to come and share in their happiness if it were permitted to him. And a fragrance of wonderful sweetness came to him from the breath of the blessed souls rejoicing together. The holy angels told him that this was the famed Paradise of God." Further on, "he beheld shining walls of gleaming splendor of amazing length and enormous height. And the holy angels said: 'This is that sacred and famous city, the heavenly Jerusalem, where holy souls live in joy forever.' He said that those souls and the walls of that glorious city ... were of such dazzling brilliance that his eyes were utterly unable to look upon them"(*The Letters of St. Boniface,* pp. 28–29).

Perhaps the fullest and most striking experience of heaven recorded in Christian literature is that of St. Andrew, the Fool for Christ of Constantinople (9th century). This experience was written down in the Saint's own words by his friend Nicephorus; we give only some excerpts from it here:

Once, during a terrible winter when St. Andrew lay in a city street frozen and near death, he suddenly felt a warmth within him and beheld a splendid youth with a face shining like the sun, who conducted him to paradise and the third heaven. "By God's will I remained for two weeks in a sweet vision.... I saw myself in a splendid and marvelous paradise.... In mind and heart I was astonished at the unutterable beauty of the paradise of God, and I took sweet delight walking in it. There were a multitude of gardens there, filled with tall trees which, swaying in their tips, rejoiced my eyes, and from their branches there came forth a great fragrance.... One cannot compare these trees in their beauty to any earthly tree.... In these gardens there were innumerable birds with wings golden, snow-white, and of various colors. They sat on the branches of the trees of paradise and sang so wondrously that from the sweetness of their singing I was beside myself.... After this a kind of fear fell upon me, and it seemed to me that I was standing at the peak of the firmament of heaven. Before me a youth was walking with a face as bright as the sun, clothed in purple.... When I followed in his steps I saw a great and splendid Cross, in form like a rainbow, and around it stood fiery singers like flames and sang sweet hymns, glorifying the Lord Who had once been crucified on the Cross. The youth who was going before me, coming up to the Cross, kissed it and gave me a sign that I should also kiss the Cross.... In kissing it I was filled with unutterable spiritual sweetness, and I smelled a fragrance more powerful than that of paradise. Going past the Cross, I looked down and saw under me as it were the abyss of the sea.... My guide, turning to me, said, 'Fear not, for we must ascend yet higher.'

"And he gave me his hand. When I seized it we were already above the second firmament. There I saw wondrous men, their repose, and the joy of their feasting which cannot be communicated by the human tongue.... And behold, after this we ascended above the third heaven, where I saw and heard a multitude of heavenly powers hymning and glorifying God. We went up to a curtain which shone like lightning, before which great and frightful youths were standing, in appearance like fiery flames.... And the youth who was leading me said to me: 'When the curtain opens, you shall see the Master Christ. Bow down to the throne of His glory.' Hearing this, I rejoiced and trembled, for I was overcome by terror and unutterable joy.... And behold, a flaming hand opened the curtain, and like the Prophet Isaiah I beheld my Lord, *sitting upon a throne, high and lifted up, and above it stood the Seraphim* (Isaiah 6:1). He was clothed in a purple garment; His face was most bright, and His eyes looked on me with love.

Seeing this, I fell down before Him, bowing down to the most bright and fearful throne of His glory. The joy that overcame me on beholding His face cannot be expressed in words. Even now, remembering this vision, I am filled with unutterable joy. In trembling I lay there before my Master…. After this all the heavenly host sang a most wondrous and unutterable hymn, and then—I myself do not understand how—again I found myself walking in paradise."*

When St. Andrew reflected that he had not seen the Mother of God in heaven, an angel told him: "Did you wish to see here the Queen Who is more brighter than the heavenly powers? She is not here; She has gone away to the world which lies in great misfortune, to help people and to comfort the sorrowing. I would have shown you Her holy place, but now there is no time, for you must again return." Here once more the fact is affirmed that angels and saints can be in only one place at a time.

Even in the 19th century, a similar true vision of heaven was beheld by a disciple of Elder Paisius Velichkovsky, Schema-monk Theodore of Svir. Towards the end of his life he experienced God's grace very strongly. Shortly after one such experience he fell into a sickness and for three days was in a sort of coma. "When a state of ecstasy began in him and he came out of himself, there appeared to him a certain invisible youth, who was sensed and beheld by the feeling of the heart alone; and this youth led him by a narrow path towards the left. Father Theodore himself, as he later related, had the feeling that he had already died, and he said to himself: 'I have died. I do not know whether I shall be saved or perish.'

---

* Lives of Saints, October 2; English translation in *The Orthodox Word*, 1979, no. 86, pp. 125–7.

"'You are saved!' an invisible voice said to him in answer to this thought. And suddenly a power like a violent whirlwind carried him off and transported him to the right side.

"'Taste the sweetness of the betrothals of paradise which I give to those who love Me,' an invisible voice declared. With these words, it seemed to Father Theodore that the Saviour Himself placed His right hand on his heart, and he was transported into an unutterably pleasant dwelling, as it were, but one that was completely invisible and indescribable in the words of earthly language. From this feeling he went over to another even more exalted one, and then to a third one; but all these feelings, as he said himself, he could remember only with his heart, but could not understand with his mind.

"Then he saw something like a temple, and in it, near the altar, something like a tent, in which there were five or six men. A mental voice said: 'For the sake of these men your death is set aside. For them you will live.' Then the spiritual stature of some of his disciples was revealed to him, and the Lord declared to him the trials which were to disturb the evening of his days.... But the Divine voice assured him that the ship of his soul would not suffer from these fierce waves, for its invisible guide was Christ."*

Other experiences of heaven from the Lives of Saints and ascetics could be given, but they do no more than repeat the characteristics already described here. It will be instructive, however—especially for purposes of a comparison with contemporary "after-death" experiences—to present the experience of a modern *sinner* in heaven. Thus, the author of "Unbelievable for Many" (whose testimony has already been quoted several

---

* From the *Life of Optina Elder Leonid,* St. Herman Brotherhood, 1976, pp. 275–6 (in Russian). [English ed., *St. Leonid of Optina,* 1990, pp. 223–4.]

times above), after escaping the demons of the toll-houses by the intercession of the Mother of God, described how, still being conducted by his angel-guides, "we were continuing to move upward…when I saw a bright light above me; it resembled, as it seemed to me, our sunlight, but was much more intense. There evidently is some kind of kingdom of light. Yes, precisely a kingdom, full of the power of light—because there was no shade with this light. 'But how can there be light without shade?' immediately my perplexed conceptions made their appearance.

"And suddenly we were quickly carried into the field of this light, and it literally blinded me. I shut my eyes, brought my hands up to my face, but this did not help since my hands did not give shade. And what did such protection mean here anyway?

" 'My God, what is this, what kind of light is this? Why for me it is like regular darkness! I cannot look, and as in darkness, can see nothing….'

"This incapacity to see, to look, increased in me the fear before the unknown, natural in this state of being found in a world unknown to me, and with alarm I thought: 'What will come next? Shall we soon pass this sphere of light, and is there a limit, an end?'

"But something different happened. Majestically, without wrath, but authoritatively and firmly, the words resounded from above: *Not ready!* And after that … an immediate stop came to our rapid flight upward—we quickly began to descend" (pp. 26–27).

In this experience the quality of the light of heaven is made clearer: it is of a kind that cannot be borne by one who is not prepared for it by the Christian life of struggle such as Sts. Salvius and Andrew endured.

3. Characteristics of the True Experience of Heaven

Let us now summarize the main characteristics of these true experiences of heaven and see how they differ from the experiences of the aerial world as described in previous chapters.

(1) The true experience of heaven invariably occurs at the end of a process of *ascent,* usually through the toll-houses (if the soul has any "tolls" to pay there). In today's "out-of-body" and "after-death" experiences, on the other hand, the toll-houses and their demons are *never* encountered, and only occasionally is a process of ascent described.

(2) The soul is *always* conducted to heaven by an angel or angels, and never "wanders" into it or goes of its own will or motive power. This is surely one of the most striking differences between genuine experiences of heaven and the contemporary experiences of Pentecostals and others who describe "after-death" experiences of "paradise" and "heaven": the latter are virtually identical with secular and even atheist experiences of "paradise," as we have already seen, except in incidental points of interpretation, which can easily be supplied by the human imagination in the "astral plane"; but virtually never in such experiences is the soul conducted by angels. Of this St. John Chrysostom, in interpreting Luke 16:19–31, writes: "Lazarus then was conducted away by angels, but the soul of the other (the rich man) was taken by certain frightful powers who, it may be, were sent for this. *For the soul by itself cannot depart to that life,* because this is impossible. If we, in going from city to city, have need of a guide, how much more will the soul be in need of guides

when it is torn away from the body and presented for the future life?"*

This point, indeed, may be taken as one of the touchstones of the authentic experience of heaven. In the contemporary experiences the soul is most frequently offered a choice to remain in "paradise" or go back to earth; while the genuine experience of heaven occurs not by the choice of man but only at the command of God, fulfilled by His angels. The common "out-of-body" experience of "paradise" in our days has no need of a guide because it takes place *right here*, in the air above us, still *in this world;* while the presence of the guiding angels is necessary if the experience takes place *outside* this world, in a different kind of reality, where the soul cannot go by itself. (This is not to say that demons cannot masquerade as "guiding angels" also, but they seldom seem to do so in today's experiences.)

(3) The experience occurs in bright light, and is accompanied by manifest signs of Divine grace, in particular a wonderful fragrance. Such signs, it is true, sometimes are present in today's "after-death" experiences also, but there is a fundamental difference between them that can scarcely be over-emphasized. Today's experiences are superficial, even sensuous; there is nothing to distinguish them from the similar experiences of unbelievers save the Christian imagery which the observer sees in (or adds to) the experience; these are no more than the *natural* experience of pleasure in the "out-of-body" state with a thin "Christian" covering. (Perhaps, also, in some of them the fallen spirits are already adding their deceptions to entice the observer further into pride and confirm his superficial idea of Christian-

---

* Homily "To the People of Antioch," III, "On Lazarus," II, as cited in Metr. Macarius, *Orthodox Dogmatic Theology,* II, p. 536.

ity; but here there is no need to determine this.) In the true Christian experiences, on the other hand, the depth of the experience is confirmed by truly miraculous occurrences: St. Salvius was so "nourished" by the fragrance that he needed no food or drink for over three days, and the fragrance vanished and his tongue became sore and swollen only the moment that he revealed his experience; St. Andrew was gone for two weeks; K. Uekskuell was "clinically dead" for 36 hours. In today's experiences, to be sure, there are sometimes "miraculous recoveries" from near or seeming death, but never anything as extraordinary as the above occurrences, and never anything to indicate that those who have experienced them have actually seen *heaven* as opposed to a pleasing appearance in the "out-of-body" realm (the "astral plane"). The difference between today's experiences and the true experience of heaven is exactly the same as the difference between today's superficial "Christianity" and true Orthodox Christianity. The "peace," for example, that can be experienced by a person who has "accepted Jesus as his personal Saviour" or who has had the very common experience of contemporary "speaking in tongues," or has had a vision of "Christ" (something by no means rare today), but who knows nothing of the life of conscious Christian struggle and repentance and has never partaken of the true Body and Blood of Christ in the Holy Mysteries instituted by Christ Himself— simply cannot be compared in any way with the peace that is revealed in the lives of the great Orthodox Saints. The contemporary experiences are literally "counterfeits" of the real experience of heaven.

(4) The true experience of heaven is accompanied by a feeling of such awe and fear before the greatness of God, and a feeling of such unworthiness to be beholding it, as are seldom found even among Orthodox Christians today, let alone those

outside the Church of Christ. St. Salvius' heartfelt expressions of his unworthiness, St. Andrew's trembling prostration before Christ, even K. Uekskuell's blindness in the light he was unworthy to behold—are unheard of in today's experiences. Those who are seeing "paradise" in the aerial realm today are "pleased," "happy," "satisfied"—seldom anything more; if they behold "Christ" in some form, it is only to indulge in the familiar "dialogues" with him that characterize experiences in the "charismatic" movement. The element of the Divine and of man's awe before it, the fear of God, are absent in such experiences.

Other characteristics of the true experience of heaven, as recorded especially in the Orthodox Lives of Saints, could be set forth; but those discussed above are sufficient to distinguish them emphatically from today's experiences. Let us only remember, whenever we dare to talk of such exalted and otherworldly experiences, that they are far above our low level of feeling and understanding, and that they are given to us more as *hints* than as complete descriptions of what cannot properly be described in human language at all. *Eye hath not seen, nor ear heard, neither have entered into the heart of man, the things which God hath prepared for them that love Him* (I Cor. 2:9).

A NOTE ON VISIONS OF HELL

For Orthodox believers the reality of hell is as certain as that of heaven. Our Lord Himself on many occasions spoke of those men whom, because they did not obey His commandments, He will send *into the everlasting fire prepared for the devil and his angels* (Matt. 25:41). In one of His parables, He gives the vivid example of the rich man who, condemned to hell because of his unrighteous deeds in this life, looks up to paradise which he has lost and begs the Patriarch Abraham there to allow Lazarus, the beggar whom he disdained while alive, to come and *dip the tip of his finger in water and cool my tongue; for I am tormented in this flame.* But Abraham replies that *between us and you there is a great gulf fixed,* and there is no contact between the saved and the damned (Luke 16:24, 26).

In Orthodox literature visions of hell are as common as visions of heaven and paradise. Such visions and experiences, unlike visions of heaven, occur more commonly to ordinary sinners than to saints, and their purpose is always clear. St. Gregory in his *Dialogues* states: "In His unbounded mercy, the good God allows some souls to return to their bodies shortly after death, so that the sight of hell might at last teach them to fear the eternal punishments in which words alone could not make them believe" (*Dialogues* IV, 37, p. 237). St. Gregory then describes several experiences of hell and tells of the impression they produced on the beholders. Thus, a certain Spanish hermit Peter died and saw "hell with all its torments and countless pools of fire." On returning to life, Peter described what he had seen, "but even had he kept silent, his penitential fasts and night watches would have been eloquent witnesses to his terrifying visit to hell and his deep fear of its dreadful torments. God had shown Himself most merciful by not allowing him to die in this experience with death" (p. 238).

The 8th-century English chronicler, Venerable Bede, relates how a man from the province of Northumbria returned after being "dead" one whole night and related his experience of both paradise and hell. In hell, he found himself in dense darkness; "frequent masses of dusky flame suddenly appeared before us, rising as though from a great pit and falling back into it again…. As the tongues of flame rose, they were filled with the souls of men which, like sparks flying up with the smoke, were sometimes flung high in the air, and at others dropped back into the depths as the vapors of the fire died down. Furthermore, an indescribable stench welled up with these vapors, and filled the whole of this gloomy place…. I suddenly heard behind me the sound of a most hideous and desperate lamentation, accompanied by harsh laughter…. I saw a throng of wicked spirits dragging with them five human souls howling and lamenting into the depths of the darkness while the devils laughed and exulted…. Meanwhile, some of the dark spirits emerged from the fiery depths and rushed to surround me, harassing me with their glowing eyes and foul flames issuing from their mouths and nostrils…."*

In the Life of Taxiotes the Soldier it is related that after Taxiotes was stopped by the demonic "tax-collectors" at the toll-houses, "the evil spirits took me and began to beat me. They led me down into the earth, which had parted to receive us. I was conducted through narrow entrances and confining, evil-smelling cracks. When I reached the very depths of hell, I saw there the souls of sinners, confined in eternal darkness. Existence there cannot be called life, for it consists of nothing but suffering, tears that find no comfort, and a gnashing teeth that can find no description. That place is forever full of the desperate cry: 'Woe, woe! Alas, alas!' It is impossible to describe all the suffering which hell contains, all its torments and pains. The departed groan from the depths of their heart, but no one pities them; they weep, but no one comforts them; they beg, but no one listens to them and delivers them. I too was confined in

---

* Bede, *A History of the English Church and People,* tr. by Leo Sherley-Price, Penguin Books, 1975, Book V, 12, pp. 290–291.

those dark regions, full of terrible sorrows, and wept and bitterly sobbed for six hours."*

The monk of Wenlock beheld a similar scene in the "lowest depths" of the earth, where "he heard a horrible, tremendous, and unspeakable groaning and weeping of souls in distress. And the angel said to him: 'The murmuring and crying which you hear down there comes from those souls to which the loving kindness of the Lord shall never come, but an undying flame shall torture them forever'" (*The Letters of St. Boniface,* p. 28).

Of course, we should not be overly fascinated by the literal details of such experiences, and even less than in the case of paradise and heaven should we try to piece together a "geography" of hell based on such accounts. The Western notions of "purgatory" and "limbo" are attempts to make such a "geography"; but Orthodox tradition knows only the one reality of hell in the underworld. Furthermore, as St. Mark of Ephesus teaches (see his Second Homily on Purgatorial Fire in Appendix I), what is seen in experiences of hell is often an image of future torments rather than a literal depiction of the present state of those awaiting the Last Judgment in hell. But whether it is an actual beholding of present realities or a vision of the future, the experience of hell as recorded in Orthodox sources is a powerful means of awakening one to a life of Christian struggle, which is the only means of escaping eternal torment; this is why God grants such experiences.

Are there any comparable experiences of hell in today's "after-death" literature?

Dr. Moody and most other investigators today have found almost no such experiences, as we have already seen. Earlier we

---

* Lives of Saints, March 28; *Eternal Mysteries Beyond the Grave,* p. 170.

explained this fact as due to the "comfortable" spiritual life of men today, who often have no fear of hell or knowledge of demons, and thus do not expect to see such things after death. However, a recent book on life after death has suggested another explanation which seems to be of equal value, while at the same time denying that the experience of hell is really as rare as it seems. Here we shall briefly examine the findings of this book.

Dr. Maurice Rawlings, a Tennessee physician who specializes in internal medicine and cardiovascular diseases, has himself resuscitated many persons who have been "clinically dead." His own interviews of these persons have taught him that, "contrary to most published life-after-death cases, not all death experiences are good. Hell also exists! After my own realization of this fact I started collecting accounts of unpleasant cases that other investigators apparently had missed. This has happened, I think, because the investigators, normally psychiatrists, have never *resuscitated* a patient. They have not had the opportunity to be on the scene. The unpleasant experiences in my study have turned out to be at least as frequent as the pleasant ones."* "I have found that most of the bad experiences are soon suppressed deeply into the patient's subliminal or subconscious mind. These bad experiences seem to be so painful and disturbing that they are removed from conscious recall so that only the pleasant experiences—or no experiences at all—are recollected" (p. 65).

Dr. Rawlings describes his "model" of these experiences of hell: "As with those who have had good experiences, those reporting bad experiences may have trouble realizing they are dead as they watch people work on their dead bodies. They may also enter a dark passage after leaving the room, but instead of

---

* Maurice Rawlings, *Beyond Death's Door,* Thomas Nelson, Inc., Nashville, 1978, pp. 24–25.

emerging into bright surroundings they enter a dark, dim environment where they encounter grotesque people who may be lurking in the shadows or along a burning lake of fire. The horrors defy description and are difficult to recall" (pp. 63–64). Various descriptions are given—including some by "regular church members" who are surprised to find themselves in such a state—of manifestations of imps and grotesque giants, of a descent into blackness and a fiery heat, of a pit and an ocean of fire (pp. 103–110).

In general, these experiences—both in their shortness and in the absence of any angelic or demonic guides—lack the complete characteristics of genuine other-worldly experiences, and some of them are quite reminiscent of Robert Monroe's adventures in the "astral plane." But they do supply an important corrective to the widely reported experience of "pleasantness" and "paradise" after death: the "out-of-body" realm is by no means all pleasantness and light, and those who have experienced its "hellish" side are closer to the truth of things than those who experience only "pleasure" in this state. The demons of the aerial realm expose something of their true nature to such ones, even giving them a hint of the torments to come for those who have not known Christ and been obedient to His commandments.

CHAPTER NINE

The Meaning of Today's "After-Death" Experiences

If they hear not Moses and the Prophets,
neither will they be persuaded, though
one rose from the dead. —Luke 16:31

1. What do Today's Experiences "Prove"?

THUS we have seen that the "after-death" and "out-of-body" experiences which are so much under discussion today are quite distinct from the genuine experiences of the other world which have been manifested over the centuries in the lives of God-pleasing men and women. Further, the contemporary experiences have been so emphasized and have become so "fashionable" in recent years not because they are actually "new" (there were whole collections of similar experiences in 19th-century England and America), nor necessarily because they have been occurring with more frequency in these years, but chiefly because the public mind in the Western world, and especially in America, was "ready" for them. The public interest seems to be part of a widespread reaction against 20th-century materialism and unbelief, a sign of a more widespread interest in religion. Here we shall ask what the significance of this new "religious" interest might be.

But first, let us state once more what these experiences "prove" about the truth of religion. Most investigators seem to agree with Dr. Moody that the experiences do *not* corroborate the "conventional" Christian view of heaven (*Life after Life*, pp. 70, 98); even the experiences of those who *think* they saw heaven do not hold up when compared with authentic visions of heaven in the past; even the experiences of hell are more "hints" than any kind of proof of the actual existence of hell.

One must therefore qualify as exaggerated the statement of Dr. Kubler-Ross that contemporary "after-death" research "will confirm what we have been taught for two thousand years—that there is life after death," and that it will help us "to know, rather than to believe" this (Foreword to *Life after Life*, pp. 7–8). Actually, these experiences may be said to "prove" no more than a minimum doctrine of the bare *survival* of the human soul outside the body, and of the bare *existence* of a non-material reality, while giving decisively *no* information on the further state or even existence of the soul after the first few minutes of "death," nor of the ultimate nature of the non-material realm. From this point of view the contemporary experiences are much less satisfactory than the accounts given over the centuries in Lives of Saints and other Christian sources; we know much more from these latter sources—provided, of course, that we trust those who have given this information to the same degree that the contemporary researchers trust those whom they have interviewed. But even so, our basic attitude towards the other world still remains one of *belief rather than knowledge;* we may know with reasonable certainty that there is "something" after death—but exactly what it is, we believe rather than know.

Further, that which Dr. Kubler-Ross and others of like mind think they know about life after death, based on "after-death" experiences, is in open contradiction to what Orthodox Christians believe about it, based on revealed Christian teaching and also on "after-death" experiences in Orthodox literature. The Christian after-death experiences all affirm the existence of heaven, hell, and judgment, of the need for repentance, struggle, and fear of losing one's soul eternally; while the contemporary experiences, like those of shamans, pagan initiates, and mediums, seem to point to a "summerland" of pleasant experiences in the "other world," where there is no judgment but only "growth," and death is not to be feared but only welcomed as a "friend" that introduces one to the pleasures of "life after death."

We have already discussed in earlier chapters the reason for the difference in these two experiences: the Christian experience is of the genuinely other world of heaven and hell, while the spiritistic experience is only of the aerial part of *this* world, the "astral plane" of the fallen spirits. Today's experiences clearly belong to the latter category—but we could not know this unless we accepted (on faith) the Christian revelation of the nature of the other world. Similarly, If Dr. Kubler-Ross and other researchers accept (or are sympathetic to) a non-Christian interpretation of these experiences, it is not because today's experiences *prove* this interpretation, but because these researchers themselves *already have faith in a non-Christian interpretation of them.*

The significance of today's experiences, therefore, lies in the fact that they are becoming widely known at just the right time to serve as a "confirmation" of a non-Christian view of life after death; they are being used as part of a non-Christian religious movement. Let us look now more closely at the nature of this religious movement.

2. The Connection with Occultism

Over and over again, in the investigators of "after-death" experiences, one may see a more or less evident connection with occult ideas and practices. Here we may define "occult" (which literally refers to what is "hidden") as pertaining to any contacts of men with unseen spirits and powers in a way forbidden by God's revelation (see Leviticus 19:31, 20:6, etc.). This contact may be sought by men (as in spiritistic seances) or instigated by the fallen spirits (when they appear spontaneously to men). The opposite of "occult" is "spiritual" or "religious," which terms refer to that contact with God and His angels and saints which is permitted by God: prayer on man's part, and true, grace-giving manifestations of God, angels, and saints on the other.

As an example of this occult connection, Dr. Hans Holzer (*Beyond This Life,* Pinnacle Books, Los Angeles, 1977) finds the significance of "after-death" experiences to lie in their opening men up to communication with the dead, and he finds them to give the same kind of messages as those provided by the "dead" at spiritistic seances. Dr. Moody, and indeed very many of today's researchers, as we have seen, look to occult texts such as the writings of Swedenborg and the *Tibetan Book of the Dead* to explain today's experiences. Robert Crookall, perhaps the most scientific investigator in this field, uses the communications of mediums as one of his primary sources of information on the "other world." Robert Monroe and others involved in "out-of-body" experiences are open practitioners of occult experimentation, even to the extent of receiving guidance and advice from the "discarnate entities" they encounter.

Most symptomatic of all these investigators, perhaps, is the woman who has become the leading spokesman for the new attitude towards death which is emerging from today's "after-death" experiences: Dr. Elizabeth Kubler-Ross.

No Christian, surely, can fail to sympathize with the cause which Dr. Kubler-Ross has chosen to champion: a humane and helpful attitude towards the dying, in contrast with the cold, helpless, and often fearful attitude which has often prevailed not only among doctors and nurses in hospitals, but even among clergymen who are supposed to have the "answer" to the questions raised by the fact of death. Since the publication of her book *On Death and Dying* (Macmillan Publishing Co., New York) in 1969, the whole subject of death has become much less a "taboo" one among medical professionals, helping also to create an intellectual atmosphere favorable to the discussion of what happens *after* death—a discussion which was set off in turn by the publication of Dr. Moody's first book in 1975. It is no accident that so many of the present books on life after death are accompanied by prefaces or at least brief comments by Dr. Kubler-Ross.

To be sure, anyone who accepts the traditional Christian view of life as a testing-ground for eternity, and death as the entrance into eternal blessedness or eternal misery, according to one's faith and life on earth—will find her book discouraging. To have a humane attitude toward a dying person, to help him "prepare" for death, without placing faith in Christ and hope of salvation in the first place—is, when all is said and done, to remain in the same dreary realm of "humanism" to which mankind has been reduced by modern unbelief. The experience of dying can be made more pleasant than it usually is in today's hospitals; but if there is no knowledge of what comes after death, or that there *is* anything after death, the work of people like Kubler-Ross is reduced to the level of giving harmless colored pills to the incurably ill to make them at least *feel* that "something is being done."

In the course of her research, however (although she did not mention it in her first book), Dr. Kubler-Ross has indeed come across evidence that there is something after death. Although she has not yet published her own book of "after-death" experiences, she has made clear in her frequent lectures and interviews that she has seen enough to know *for certain* that there is life after death.

The chief source of her "knowledge" of this is, however, not the "after-death" experiences of others, but her own rather startling experiences with "spirits." Her first such experience occurred in her office at the University of Chicago in 1967, when she was discouraged and thinking of giving up her newly begun research in death and dying. A woman came to her office and introduced herself as a patient who had died ten months before; Kubler-Ross was skeptical, but relates how she was finally persuaded by the "ghost": "She said she knew I was considering giving up my work with dying patients and that she came to tell me not to give it up.... I reached out to touch her. I was reality-testing. I was a scientist, a psychiatrist, and I didn't believe in such things." She finally persuaded the "ghost" to write a note, and a later handwriting analysis confirmed that it was the handwriting of the deceased patient. Dr. Kubler-Ross states that this incident "came at a cross-roads where I would have made the wrong decision if I hadn't listened to her."* The dead never appear thus so matter-of-factly among the living; this "other-worldly" visitation, if genuine, could only have been

---

* Interview by James Pearre of the Chicago Tribune, printed in the San Francisco *Sunday Examiner and Chronicle,* Nov. 14, 1976, Section B, p. 7.

that of a fallen spirit out to deceive his victim. For such a spirit, the perfect imitation of human handwriting is an easy thing.

Later, Dr. Kubler-Ross' contacts with the "spirit-world" became much more intimate. In 1978, before an enthralled audience of 2200 in Ashland, Oregon, she related how she was first brought into contact with her "spirit guides." A spiritistic-type assembly was rather mysteriously arranged for her, evidently in southern California, with 75 people singing together in order to "raise the necessary energy to create this event. I was moved and touched that they would do that for me. Not more than two minutes later, I saw huge feet in front of me. There was an immense man standing in front of me." This "man" told her that she was to be a teacher and needed this firsthand experience to give her strength and courage for her work. "About a half-minute later, another person literally materialized about 1/2 inch from my feet.... I understood that he was my guardian angel.... He called me Isabelle, and he asked me if I remembered how, 2000 years ago, we both had worked with the Christ." Later a third "angel" appeared in order to teach her more about "joy." "My experience of these guides has been one of the greatest kind, of totally unconditional love. And I just want to tell you that we are never alone. Each of us has a guardian angel who is never more than two feet away from us at any time. And we can call on these beings. They will help us."*

At a holistic health conference in San Francisco in September, 1976, Dr. Kubler-Ross shared with an audience of 2300 physicians, nurses, and other medical professionals a "profound mystical experience" that had occurred to her only the night before. (This experience is apparently the same one she de-

---

* As reported by Gaea Laughingbird in *Berkeley Monthly,* June, 1978, p. 39.

scribed in Ashland.) "Last night, I was visited by Salem, my spirit guide, and two of his companions, Anka and Willie. They were with us until three o'clock in the morning. We talked, laughed and sang together. They spoke and touched me with the most incredible love and tenderness imaginable. This was the highlight of my life." In the audience, "as she concluded, there was a momentary silence and then the mass of people rose as one in tribute. Most of the audience, largely physicians and other health care professionals, was seemingly moved to tears."*

It is well known in occult circles that "spirit guides" (who, of course, are the fallen spirits of the aerial realm) do not manifest themselves so readily unless a person is rather advanced in mediumistic receptivity. But perhaps even more striking than Dr. Kubler-Ross' involvement with "familiar spirits" is the enthusiastic response her accounts of this involvement produce on audiences composed, not of occultists and mediums, but of ordinary middle-class and professional people. Surely this is one of the religious "signs of the times": men have become receptive to contacts with the "spirit world" and are ready to accept the occult explanation of these contacts which contradict Christian truth.

Quite recently, extensive publicity has been given to scandals at Dr. Kubler-Ross' newly established retreat in southern California, "Shanti Nilaya." According to these accounts, many of the "workshops" at Shanti Nilaya are centered on old-fashioned mediumistic seances, and a number of former participants have declared that the seances are fraudulent.** It may be that there is more wishful thinking than reality in Dr. Kubler-

---

* Reported by Lennie Kronisch in *Yoga Journal,* September-October, 1976, pp.18–20.
** See *The San Diego Union,* Sept. 2, 1979, pp. A-1, 3, 6, 14.

Ross' "spirit contacts"; but this does not affect the teaching which she and others are giving about life after death.

3. The Occult Teaching of Today's Investigators

The teaching on life after death of Dr. Kubler-Ross and other investigators of "after-death" experiences today may be summarized in a few points. Dr. Kubler-Ross, it should be noted, expresses these points with the certainty of someone who thinks she has had immediate experience of the "other world"; but scientists like Dr. Moody, while much more cautious and tentative in tone, cannot help but promote the same teaching. This is the teaching on life after death that has entered the air of the late 20th century and seems unaccountably "natural" to all students of it who do not have a firm grasp on any other teaching.

(1) *Death is not to be feared.* Dr. Moody writes: "In some form or other, almost every person has expressed to me the thought that he is no longer afraid of death" (*Life after Life,* p. 68). Dr. Kubler-Ross relates: "Recorded histories reveal that dying is painful but death itself ... is a totally peaceful experience, free of pain and fear. Everyone, without exception, describes a feeling of equanimity and wholeness."* One may see here the basic trust in one's psychic experiences that characterizes all who are deceived by the fallen spirits. There is nothing whatever in today's "after-death" experiences to indicate that death itself will be merely a repetition of them, and that not for a few minutes only, but *permanently;* this trust of pleasant psychic experiences is part of the religious spirit that is now in

---

* As reported by Elizabeth Kemf in *East-West Journal,* March, 1978, p. 52.

the air, and it produces a false sense of well-being that is fatal to spiritual life.

(2) *There is no judgment to come, and no hell.* Dr. Moody reports, on the basis of his interviews, that "in most cases, the reward-punishment model of the afterlife is abandoned and disavowed, even by many who had been accustomed to thinking in those terms. They found, much to their amazement, that even when their most apparently awful and sinful deeds were made manifest before the being of light, the being responded not with anger and rage, but rather only with understanding, and even with humor" (*Life after Life,* p. 70). Dr. Kubler-Ross observes of her interviewees, in a more doctrinaire tone: "All have a sense of 'wholeness.' God is not judgmental; man is" (Kemf, p. 52). It does not seem even to occur to such investigators that this absence of judgment in "after-death" experiences might be a misleading first impression, or that the first few minutes of death are not the place for judgment; they are merely interpreting the experiences in accordance with the religious spirit of the times, which does not wish to believe in judgment and hell.

(3) *Death is not as unique and final an experience as Christian doctrine has described it, but is rather only a harmless transition to a "higher state of consciousness."* Dr. Kubler-Ross thus defines it: "Death is simply a shedding of the physical body, like the butterfly coming out of a cocoon. It is a transition into a higher state of consciousness, where you continue to perceive, to understand, to laugh, to be able to grow, and the only thing you lose is something that you don't need anymore, and that is your physical body. It's like putting away your winter coat when spring comes ... and that's what death is about" (Kemf, p. 50). We shall state below how this contrasts with the true Christian teaching.

(4) *The purpose of life on earth, and of life after death, is not the eternal salvation of one's soul, but an unlimited process of "growth" in "love" and "understanding" and "self-realization."* Dr. Moody finds that "many seemed to have returned with a new model and a new understanding of the world beyond—a vision which features not unilateral judgement, but rather co-operative development towards the ultimate end of self-realization. According to these new views, development of the soul, especially in the spiritual faculties of love and knowledge, does not stop upon death. Rather it continues on the other side, perhaps eternally...." *(Life after Life,* p. 70). Such an occult view of life and death does not come from the fragmentary experiences being publicized today; rather, it comes from the occult *philosophy* that is in the air today.

(5) *"After-death" and "out-of-body" experiences are themselves a preparation for life after death.* The traditional Christian preparation for eternal life (faith, repentance, participating in the Sacraments, spiritual struggle) is of little importance compared with the increased "love" and "understanding" which are inspired by "after-death" experiences; and specifically (as in the recent program worked out by Kubler-Ross and Robert Monroe) one can train terminally-ill persons in "out-of-body" experiences "so that the persons will quickly gain a perception of what awaits them on the Other Side when they die" (Wheeler, *Journey to the Other Side,* p. 92). One of Dr. Moody's interviewees states categorically: "The reason why I'm not afraid to die is that I know where I'm going when I leave here, because I've been there before" *(Life after Life,* p. 69). What a tragic and ill-founded optimism!

Every one of these five points is part of the teaching of 19th-century Spiritualism as revealed at that time by the "spirits" themselves through mediums. It is a teaching literally devised by demons with the single clear intention of overthrowing the traditional Christian teaching on life after death and changing mankind's whole outlook on religion. The occult philosophy that almost invariably accompanies and colors today's "after-death" experiences is simply a filtering down to the popular level of the esoteric Spiritism of the Victorian age; it is a symptom of the evaporation of genuine Christian views from the minds of the masses of the Western world. The "after-death" experience itself, one may say, is incidental to the occult philosophy that is being spread through it; the experience promotes the philosophy not because its content as such is occult, but because the basic Christian safeguards and teaching that once protected men from such a foreign philosophy have now largely been removed, and virtually *any* experience of the "other world" will now be used for promoting occultism. In the 19th century only a few freethinkers and unchurched people believed in this occult philosophy; but now it is so much in the air that anyone who does not have a conscious philosophy of his own is drawn to accept it quite "naturally."

4. The "Message" of Today's "After-Death" Experiences

But why, finally, are "after-death" experiences so much "in the air" today, and what is their meaning as part of the "spirit of the times"? The most obvious reason for the increased discussion of these experiences today is the invention in recent years of new techniques for resuscitating the "clinically dead," which have made such experiences more commonly reported than ever before. This explanation, to be sure, does help to account for the quantitative increase of "after-death" reports, but it is too superficial to account for the spiritual impact of these experiences on mankind and the changing view of life after death which they are helping to cause.

A deeper explanation is to be found in the increasing openness and sensitivity of men to "spiritual" and "psychic" experiences in general, under the greatly increased influence of occult ideas on the one hand, and on the other hand the waning both of humanistic materialism and of Christian faith. Mankind is coming once more to an acceptance of the possibility of contact with "another world."

Further, this "other world" itself seems to be *opening itself up more to a mankind that is eager to experience it.* The "occult explosion" of recent years has been produced by—and in turn has helped to produce—a spectacular increase in actual "para-normal" experiences of all kinds. "After-death" experiences are at one end of the spectrum of these experiences, involving little or no conscious will to contact the "other world"; the activities of contemporary witchcraft and satanism are at the other end of the spectrum, involving a conscious attempt to contact and even serve the powers of the "other world"; and the myriad varieties of today's psychic experiences, from the "spoon-bending" of Uri Geller and parapsychological experi-ments in "out-of-body" travel and the like, to contact with and abductions by "UFO" beings—fall somewhere in be-tween these extremes. Significantly, a large number of these "paranormal" experiences have been occurring to "Chris-tians," and one kind of these experiences ("charismatic" ones) is widely accepted as a genuinely Christian phenomenon.* In actuality, however, the "Christian" involvement in all such

---

* An examination of the "charismatic" movement as a mediumistic phenomenon may be read in *Orthodoxy and the Religion of the Future,* St. Herman Monastery Press, 1979, ch. VII.

experiences is only a striking indication of the extent to which the Christian awareness of occult experience has been lost in our times.

One of the foremost authentic mediums of the 20th century, the late Arthur Ford—whose increase in respectability among "Christians" and unbelieving humanists alike is itself one of the "signs of the times"—has given a revealing hint as to what the increasing acceptance of and susceptibility to occult experiences means: "The day of the professional medium is about over. We've been useful as guinea pigs. Through us, scientists have learned something about the conditions necessary for it (contact with the 'spirit world') to happen."* That is: the occult experience hitherto restricted to a few "initiates" has now become accessible to thousands of ordinary people. Of course, it is not chiefly science that has brought this about, but mankind's increasing estrangement from Christianity and its thirst for new "religious experiences." Fifty or seventy-five years ago, only mediums and cultists on the fringes of society had contact with "spirit guides," cultivated "out-of-body" experiences, or "spoke in tongues"; today these experiences have become relatively common and are accepted as ordinary on all levels of society.

This marked increase in "other worldly" experiences today is doubtless one of the signs of the approaching end of this world. St. Gregory the Great, after describing various visions and experiences of life after death in his *Dialogues,* remarks that "the spiritual world is moving closer to us, manifesting itself through visions and revelations.... As the present world approaches its end, the world of eternity looms nearer.... The end

---

* *Psychics,* by the Editors of *Psychic Magazine,* Harper & Row, N.Y., 1972, p. 23.

of the world merges with the beginning of eternal life" (*Dialogues* IV, 43, p. 251).

St. Gregory adds, however, that through these visions and revelations (which are much more common in our time than they were in his) we still see the truths of the future life imperfectly, because the light is still "dim and pale, like the light of the sun in the early hours of the day just before dawn." How true this is of today's "after-death" experiences! Never before has mankind been given such striking and clear proofs—or at least "hints"—that there is another world, that life does not end with the death of the body, that there is a soul that survives death and is indeed more conscious and alive *after* death. For a person with a clear grasp of Christian doctrine, today's "after-death" experiences can only be a striking confirmation of the Christian teaching on the state of the soul immediately after death; and even today's occult experiences can only confirm for him the existence and nature of the aerial realm of fallen spirits.

But for the rest of mankind, including most of that part that still calls itself Christian, today's experiences, far from confirming the truths of Christianity are proving to be a subtle pointer to deception and false teaching, a preparation for the coming reign of Antichrist. Truly, even those who return from the "dead" today cannot persuade mankind to repent: *If they hear not Moses and the Prophets, neither will they be persuaded, though one rose from the dead* (Luke 16:31). In the end, it is only those who are faithful to "Moses and the Prophets"—that is, to the fullness of revealed truth—who are able to understand the true meaning of today's experiences. What the rest of mankind learns from these experiences is not repentance and the closeness of God's judgment—but a strange, enticing new gospel of pleasant "other-worldly" experience and the abolition of something which God has set up for the awakening of man to the reality of the true other world of heaven and hell: *the fear of death.*

Arthur Ford makes quite clear that the whole mission of mediums like himself has been "to use whatever special talents given me to remove for all time the fear of the death passage from earth minds."* This is the message of Dr. Kubler-Ross also, and it is the "scientific" conclusion of researchers like Dr. Moody: the "other world" is pleasant, one need not fear to enter it. Two centuries ago Emanuel Swedenborg summed up the "spirituality" of those who believe like this: "I have been permitted to enjoy not only the pleasures of the body and the senses, like those who live in the world, but I have also been permitted to enjoy such delights and felicities of life as, I believe, no persons in the whole world ever before enjoyed, which were greater and more exquisite than any person could imagine and believe.... Believe me, if I knew that the Lord would call me to Himself tomorrow, I would summon the musicians today, in order to be once more really gay in this world." When he foretold the date of his death to his landlady, he was as pleased "as if he was going to have a holiday, to go to some merry-making."**

We shall contrast this attitude now with the true Christian attitude towards death over the centuries. Here we shall see how perilous it is for a soul to have no discernment with regard to "spiritual experiences," to cast aside the safeguards of Christian teaching!

---

* Arthur Ford, *The Life Beyond Death,* G. P. Putnam's Sons, New York, 1971, p. 153.
** Quoted in George Trobridge, *Swedenborg: Life and Teaching,* Swedenborg Foundation, New York, 1968, pp. 175, 276.

5. The Christian Attitude Towards Death

The occult teaching on life after death, although it ends so far from the truth of things, does begin with an undoubted Christian truth: the death of the body is not the end of human life, but only the beginning of a new condition for the human personality, which continues its existence apart from the body. Death, which was not made by God but was brought into the creation by Adam's sin in Paradise, is the most striking form in which man faces the fallenness of his nature. A person's fate for eternity depends largely on how he regards his own death and how he prepares for it.

The true Christian attitude towards death has in it elements both of fear and uncertainty, just those emotions which occultism wishes to abolish. However, in the Christian attitude there is nothing of the abject fear which can be present in those who die with no hope of eternal life, and a Christian with his conscience at peace approaches death calmly and, according to God's grace, even with a certain sense of assurance. Let us look at the Christian death of several of the great monastic Saints of 5th-century Egypt.

"When the time came for the repose of St. Agatho, he spent three days in profound heedfulness to himself, conversing with no one. The brethren asked him: 'Abba Agatho, where are you?' 'I am standing before the judgment of Christ,' he answered. The brethren said: 'Are even you afraid, Father?' He replied: 'I have striven according to my strength to keep God's commandments, but I am a man, and how do I know that my deeds have been pleasing to God?' The brethren asked: 'Do you really have no hope in your way of life, which was in accordance with the will of God?' 'I cannot have such hope,' he replied, 'because one thing is the judgment of man, and another is the judgment of God.' They wished to ask him yet more, but he told them: 'Show love to me, and do not speak with me now, for I am not free.' And he died with joy. 'We saw him rejoicing,' his disciples related, 'as if he were meeting and greeting dear friends.'"*

Even great saints who die in the midst of obvious signs of God's grace retain a sobering humility about their own salvation. "When the time came for the great Sisoes to die, his face became illuminated and he said to the Fathers who were sitting with him: 'Here Abba Anthony has come.' After being silent for a little, he said: 'Here the choir of the prophets has come.' Then he became yet brighter and said: 'Here the choir of apostles has come.' And again, his face became twice as shining; he began to speak with someone. The Elders asked him to say with whom he was speaking. He replied: 'The angels have come to take me, but I am imploring them to leave me a short time for repentance.' The Elders said to him: 'Father, you have no need for repentance.' He replied to them: 'In truth, I do not know whether I have even placed a beginning of repentance.' But everyone knew that he was perfect. Thus spoke and felt a true Christian, despite the fact that during his lifetime he had raised the dead at his mere word and was filled with the gifts of the Holy Spirit. And again his face shone yet more: it shone like the sun. All were afraid. He said to them: 'Behold, the Lord has come and uttered: "Bring me the chosen vessel from the desert."' With these words he sent forth his spirit. Lightning was seen, and the room was filled with fragrance" (*Patericon of Scetis*, Bishop Ignatius, vol. III, p. 110).

---

* *Patericon of Scetis*, quoted in Bishop Ignatius, vol. III, pp. 107–8.

How different this profound and sober Christian attitude is when compared with the superficial attitude of some non-Orthodox Christians today who think they are already "saved" and will not even undergo the judgment of all men, and therefore have nothing to fear in death. Such an attitude, very widespread among present-day Protestants, is actually not too far from the occult idea that death is not to be feared because there is no damnation; certainly, even though inadvertently, it has helped give rise to the latter attitude. Blessed Theophylactus of Bulgaria, in his 11th-century commentary on the Gospels, wrote of such ones: "Many deceive themselves with a vain hope; they think that they will receive the Kingdom of Heaven and will unite themselves to the choir of those reposing in the height of virtues, having exalted fancies of themselves in their hearts.... Many are called, because God calls many, indeed everyone; but few are chosen, few are saved, few are worthy of God's choosing" (Commentary on Matt. 22:14).

The similarity between occult philosophy and the common Protestant view is perhaps the chief reason why the attempts of some Evangelical Protestants (see Bibliography) to criticize today's "after-death" experiences from the point of view of "Biblical Christianity" has been so unsuccessful. These critics themselves have lost so much of the traditional Christian teaching on life after death, the aerial realm, and the activities and deceptions of demons, that their criticisms are often vague and arbitrary; and their discernment in this realm is often no better than that of the secular researchers and causes them also to be taken in by deceptive "Christian" or "Biblical" experiences in the aerial realm.

The true Christian attitude towards death is based upon an awareness of the critical differences between this life and the next. Metropolitan Macarius of Moscow has summed up the

Scriptural and Patristic teaching on this point in these words: "Death is the boundary at which the time of struggles ends for man and the time of recompense begins, so that after death neither repentance nor correction of life is possible for us. Christ the Saviour expressed this truth in His parable of the rich man and Lazarus, from which it is clear that both the one and the other immediately after death received their recompense, and the rich man, no matter how much he was tormented in hell, could not be delivered from his sufferings through repentance (Luke 16:26)."*

Death, therefore, is precisely the reality that awakens one to the difference between this world and the next and inspires one to undertake the life of repentance and cleansing while this precious time is given to us. When St. Abba Dorotheus was asked by a certain brother why he spent his time carelessly in his cell, he replied: "Because you have not understood either the awaited repose or the future torment. If you knew them as you should, you would endure and not grow weak even though your cell should be filled with worms and you would be standing among them up to your neck."**

Similarly, St. Seraphim of Sarov, in our own modern times, taught: "Oh, if only you could know what joy, what sweetness await the souls of the righteous in heaven, then you would be determined in this temporal life to endure any sorrow, persecution, and calumny with gratitude. If this very cell of ours were full of worms, and if these worms were to eat our flesh throughout our whole temporal life, then with utmost desire we should consent to it, only not to be deprived of that

---

* Metr. Macarius, *Orthodox Dogmatic Theology*, vol. II, p. 524.
** Abba Dorotheus, *Soul-Profiting Instructions,* Holy Trinity Lavra, 1900. Instruction 12: "On the Fear of Future Torment," p. 137.

heavenly joy which God has prepared for those who love Him."*

The fearlessness of occultists and Protestants alike before death is the direct result of their lack of awareness of what awaits them in the future life and of what can be done now to prepare for it. For this reason, true experiences or visions of life after death generally have the effect of shaking one to the depths of one's being and (if one has not been leading a zealous Christian life) of changing his whole life to make preparation for the life to come. When St. Athanasius of the Kiev Caves died and came back to life after two days, his fellow monks "were terrified seeing him come back to life; then they began to ask how he had come back to life, and what he had seen and heard while he had been apart from the body. To all questions he answered only with the words: 'Save yourselves!' And when the brethren insistently asked him to tell them something profitable, he gave as his testament to them obedience and ceaseless repentance. Right after this Athanasius closed himself up in a cave, remained in it without leaving for twelve years, spending day and night in unceasing tears, eating a little bread and water every other day, and conversing with no one during all this time. When the hour of his death came, he repeated to the assembled brethren his instruction on obedience and repentance, and died with peace in the Lord."**

Similarly, in the West, Venerable Bede relates how the man of Northumbria, after being dead one whole night, came back

* *The Spiritual Instructions of St. Seraphim of Sarov,* St. Herman Monastery Press, 1978, p. 69.
** As related by Bishop Ignatius, vol. III, p. 129; see his Life in the *Kiev-Caves Patericon,* Holy Trinity Monastery, Jordanville, N.Y., 1967, pp. 153–5. St. Athanasius, called "the Resurrected," is commemorated on December 2.

to life and said: "I have truly risen from the grasp of death, and I am allowed to live among men again. But henceforth I must not live as I used to, and must adopt a very different way of life." He gave away all his possessions and retired to a monastery. Later he related that he had seen both heaven and hell, but "this man of God would not discuss these and other things that he had seen with any apathetic or careless-living people, but only with those who were haunted by fear of punishment or gladdened by the hope of eternal joys, and were willing to take his words to heart and grow in holiness."*

Even in our own modern times, the author of "Unbelievable for Many" was so shaken by his true experience of the other world that he entirely changed his life, became a monk, and wrote his account of his experiences in order to awaken others like himself who were living in the false security of unbelief about the next life.

Such experiences are numerous in Lives of Saints and other Orthodox sources, and they stand in sharp contrast to the experiences of people today who have seen "heaven" and the "other world" and yet remain in the false security that they are already "prepared" for life after death and that death itself is nothing to be feared.

The place of the remembrance of death in Christian life may be seen in the manual of Christian struggle, *The Ladder* of St. John (whose Sixth Step is devoted specifically to this): "As of all foods bread is the most essential, so the thought of death is the most necessary of all works…. It is impossible to spend the present day devoutly unless we regard it as the last of our whole life" (Step 6:4, 24). The Scripture well states: *In all you do, remember the end of your life, and then you will never sin*

---

* Bede, *A History of the English Church and People,* Book V, 12, pp. 289, 293.

(Sirach 7:36). The great St. Barsanuphius of Gaza gave as his advice to a brother: "Let your thoughts be strengthened with the remembrance of death, the hour of which is not known to any man. Let us strive to do good before we depart from this life—for we do not know on what day we shall be called—lest we turn out to be unprepared and remain outside the bridal chamber with the five foolish virgins" (St. Barsanuphius, Answer 799).

The great Abba Pimen, when he heard of the death of St. Arsenius the Great of Egypt, said: "Blessed is Arsenius! You wept over yourself for the course of earthly life! If we do not weep over ourselves here, we shall weep eternally. It is not possible to escape weeping: either here, voluntarily, or there, in torments, involuntarily" (*Patericon of Scetis,* in Bishop Ignatius, vol. III, p. 108).

Only a person with this sober Christian outlook on life can dare to say, with the Apostle Paul, that he has *a desire to depart, and to be with Christ* (Phil. 1:23). Only he who has lived the Christian life of struggle, repentance, and weeping over one's sins, can say with St. Ambrose of Milan: "The foolish are afraid of death as the greatest of evils, but wise men seek it as a rest after their toils and as the end of evils."*

Bishop Ignatius Brianchaninov concludes his celebrated "Homily on Death" with words that can stand for us also, a hundred years later, as a call to return to the one and only true Christian attitude towards death, putting away all rosy illusions of our present spiritual state as well as all false hopes for the future life:

---

* St. Ambrose, "Death as a Good," 8:32, in *Seven Exegetical Works,* tr. by Michael P. McHugh, Catholic University of America Press, 1972, Fathers of the Church, vol. 65, p. 94.

"Let us arouse in ourselves the remembrance of death by visiting cemeteries, visiting the sick, being present at the death and burial of our close ones, by frequently examining and renewing in our memories various contemporary deaths which we have heard of or seen…. Having understood the shortness of our earthly life and the vanity of all earthly acquisitions and advantages; having understood the frightful future that awaits those who have disdained the Redeemer and redemption and have offered themselves entirely as a sacrifice to sin and corruption—let us turn our mental eyes away from their steady gazing at the deceptive and enchanting beauty of the world which easily catches the weak human heart and forces it to love and serve it; let us turn them to the fearful but saving spectacle of the death that awaits us. Let us weep over ourselves while there is time; let us wash, let us cleanse with tears and confession our sins which are written in the books of the Sovereign of the world. Let us acquire the grace of the Holy Spirit—this seal, this sign of election and salvation; it is indispensable for a free passage through the spaces of the air and for entrance into the heavenly gates and mansions…. O ye who have been banished from Paradise! It is not for enjoyments, not for festivity, not for playing that we find ourselves on earth—but in order that by faith, repentance, and the Cross we might kill the death which has killed us and restore to ourselves the lost Paradise! May the merciful Lord grant the readers of this Homily, and him who has composed it, to remember death during this earthly life, and by the remembrance of it, by the mortification of oneself to everything vain, and by a life lived for eternity, to banish from oneself the fierceness of death when its hour shall come, and through it to enter into the blessed, eternal, true life. Amen" (Vol. III, pp. 181–183).

CHAPTER TEN

Summary of the Orthodox Teaching on the Fate of the Soul After Death

I N the first nine chapters of this book we have tried to set forth some of the basic aspects of the Orthodox Christian view of life after death, contrasting them with the widespread contemporary view as well as with older Western views which in a number of respects have departed from the ancient Christian teaching. In the West the authentic Orthodox doctrines of angels, of the aerial realm of fallen spirits, of the nature of human contacts with spirits, of heaven and hell, have been lost or distorted, with the result that an entirely misleading interpretation is being given to "after-death" experiences that are now occurring. The only adequate answer to this false interpretation is the Orthodox Christian doctrine.

This book has been too limited in compass to present the entire Orthodox teaching on the other world and life after death; our attempt has been the more limited one of presenting enough of this teaching to answer the questions raised by today's "after-death" experiences, and of pointing readers to the Orthodox texts which contain this teaching. Here, in conclusion, we present a final summary of the Orthodox teaching specifically on the fate of the soul after death. This summary consists of an article written a year before his death by one of the last great Russian Orthodox theologians of our times, Archbishop John Maximovitch. His words are printed here in italics, and explanatory titles, comments, and comparisons, together with quotes from various Holy Fathers, have been inserted between the paragraphs in regular Roman type.

LIFE AFTER DEATH
By Archbishop John Maximovitch

> I look for the resurrection of the dead,
> and the life of the age to come.
> —Nicene Creed

Limitless and without consolation would have been our sorrow for close ones who are dying, if the Lord had not given us eternal life. Our life would be pointless if it ended with death. What benefit would there then be from virtue and good deeds? Then they would be correct who say: "Let us eat and drink, for tomorrow we die!" But man was created for immortality, and by His resurrection Christ opened the gates of the Heavenly Kingdom, of eternal blessedness for those who have believed in Him and have lived righteously. Our earthly life is a preparation for the future life, and this preparation ends with our death. "It is appointed unto man once to die, but after this the judgment" (Heb. 9:27). Then a man leaves all his earthly cares; the body disintegrates, in order to rise anew at the General Resurrection.

But his soul continues to live, and not for an instant does it cease its existence. By many manifestations of the dead it has been given us to know in part what occurs to the soul when it leaves the body. When the vision of its bodily eyes ceases, its spiritual vision begins.

Bishop Theophan the Recluse, in a message to a dying woman, writes: "You will not die. Your body will die, but you will go over into a different world, being alive, remembering yourself and recognizing the whole world that surrounds you."*

After death the soul is more, not less, alive and aware than before death. St. Ambrose of Milan teaches: "Since the life of the soul remains after death, there remains a good which is not lost by death but is increased. The soul is not held back by any obstacle placed by death, but is more active, because it is active in its own sphere without any association with the body, which is more of a burden than a benefit to it."**

St. Abba Dorotheus, the 6th-century monastic Father of Gaza, summarizes the teaching of the early Fathers on this subject: "For as the Fathers tell us, the souls of the dead remember everything that happened here—thoughts, words, desires—and nothing can be forgotten. But, as it says in the Psalm, *In that day all their thoughts shall perish* (Ps. 145:4). The thoughts he speaks of are those of this world, about houses and possessions, parents and children, and business transactions. All these things are destroyed immediately when the soul passes out of the body.... But what he did against virtue or against his evil passions, he remembers, and nothing of this is lost.... In fact, the soul loses nothing that it did in this world but remembers

---

* From the Russian periodical, *Soul-Profiting Reading,* August 1894.
** St. Ambrose, "Death as a Good" (*De bono mortis*), in *Seven Exegetical Works,* tr. by Michael P. McHugh, Catholic University of America Press, 1972 (Fathers of the Church Series, vol. 65), ch. 4:15, p. 80.

everything at its exit from this body more clearly and distinctly once freed from the earthliness of the body."*

The great 5th-century monastic Father, St. John Cassian, sets forth quite clearly the active state of the soul after the death of the body, in answer to the early heretics who believed the soul was unconscious after death:

"Souls after the separation from this body are not idle, do not remain without consciousness; this is proved by the Gospel parable of the rich man and Lazarus (Luke 16:22–28).... The souls of the dead not only do not lose their consciousness, they do not even lose their dispositions—that is, hope and fear, joy and grief, and something of that which they expect for themselves at the Universal Judgment they begin already to foretaste.... They become yet more alive and more zealously cling to the glorification of God. And truly, if we were to reason on the basis of the testimony of Sacred Scripture concerning the nature of the soul, in the measure of our understanding, would it not be, I will not say extreme stupidity, but at least folly, to suspect even in the least that the most precious part of man (that is, the soul), in which, according to the blessed Apostle, the image and likeness of God is contained (I Cor. 11:7, Col. 3:10), after putting off this fleshly coarseness in which it finds itself in the present life, should become unconscious—that part which, containing in itself the whole power of reason, makes sensitive by its presence even the dumb and unconscious matter of the flesh? Therefore it follows, and the nature of reason itself demands, that the spirit after casting off this fleshy coarseness by which now it is weakened, should bring its mental powers into a better condi-

---

* Abba Dorotheus, *Discourses,* tr. by E. P. Wheeler, Kalamazoo, 1977, pp. 185–6.

tion, should restore them as purer and more refined, but should not be deprived of them."*

Today's "after-death" experiences have made men shockingly aware of the consciousness of the soul outside the body, of the keener and quicker state of its mental faculties. But this awareness by itself is not enough to protect one in that state from being deceived by appearances in the "out-of-body" realm; one must be in possession of the *full* Christian doctrine on this subject.

THE BEGINNING OF SPIRITUAL VISION

Often (this spiritual vision) begins in the dying even before death, and while still seeing those around them and even speaking with them, they see what others do not see.

This experience of the dying has been noticed throughout the ages, and its occurrence among the dying today is nothing new. What was stated above, however (Chapter One, part 2), should be repeated here: only in the grace-given visitations to the righteous, when saints and angels appear, can we be certain that it is actually beings from the other world who come. In the ordinary cases when the dying person begins to see departed relatives and friends, the experience is perhaps only a kind of "natural" introduction to the unseen world which he is about to enter; the actual nature of the images of the departed which then appear is perhaps known to God alone—there is no need for us to pry into it.

Apparently God grants this experience as the most evident way to inform the dying person that the other world is not, after

---

* First Conference, ch. 14, in the *Works of St. John Cassian the Roman,* Russian tr. by Bishop Peter, Moscow, 1892, pp. 178–9.

all, a totally strange place, that life in the other world is also characterized by the love that one has for one's close ones. Bishop Theophan expresses this touchingly in his words to the dying woman: "There your father and mother, brothers and sisters will meet you. Bow down to them, and give them our greetings, and ask their prayers for us. Your children will surround you, with their joyous greetings. It will be better for you there than here."

ENCOUNTERS WITH SPIRITS

But when it leaves the body, the soul finds itself among other spirits, good and evil. Usually it inclines toward those which are more akin to it in spirit, and if while in the body it was under the influence of certain ones, it will remain in dependence upon them when it leaves the body, however unpleasant they may turn out to be upon encountering them.

Here we are solemnly reminded that the other world, even though it will not be totally strange to us, will not be simply a pleasant meeting with loved ones in a "summerland" of happiness, but a spiritual encounter which will test the disposition of our soul in this life—whether it has become more inclined towards the angels and saints through a life of virtue and obedience to God's commandments, or whether by its negligence or unbelief it has made itself more fit for the company of fallen spirits. Bishop Theophan the Recluse has well said (see above, page 86–7) that even the trial at the aerial toll-houses may well turn out to be less one of accusations than of temptations.

While the fact of judgment in the next life is quite beyond doubt—both the Particular Judgment immediately after death, and the Last Judgment at the end of the world—the outward sentence of God will only answer to the *inward* disposition which the soul had developed in itself towards God and the spiritual beings.

THE FIRST TWO DAYS AFTER DEATH

For the course of two days the soul enjoys relative freedom and can visit places on earth which were dear to it, but on the third day it moves into other spheres.

Here Archbishop John simply repeats the teaching known to the Church since the 4th century, when the angel who accompanied St. Macarius of Alexandria in the desert told him, in explaining the Church's commemoration of the dead on the third day after death: "When an offering is made in church on the third day, the soul of the departed receives from its guardian angel relief from the sorrow it feels as a result of the separation from the body.... In the course of the two days the soul is permitted to roam the earth, wherever it wills, in the company of the angels that are with it. Therefore the soul, loving the body, sometimes wanders about the house in which its body had been laid out, and thus spends two days like a bird seeking its nest. But the virtuous soul goes about those places in which it was wont to do good deeds. On the third day, He Who Himself rose from the dead on the third day commands the Christian soul, in imitation of His resurrection, to ascend to the Heavens to worship the God of all."*

St. John Damascene, in the Orthodox funeral service, vividly describes the state of the soul, parted from the body but

---

* Quoted in "The Church's Prayer for the Dead," *Orthodox Life,* 1978, no. 1, p. 16.

still on earth, helpless to contact the loved ones whom it can see: "Woe is me! What manner of ordeal doth the soul endure when it is parted from the body! Alas! How many then are its tears, and there is none to show compassion! It raiseth its eyes to the angels; all unavailing is its prayer. It stretcheth out its hands to men, and findeth none to succour. Wherefore, my beloved brethren, meditating on the brevity of our life, let us beseech of Christ rest for him who hath departed hence, and for our souls great mercy."*

Bishop Theophan the Recluse, in a letter to the brother of the dying woman mentioned above, writes: "Your sister will not die: the body dies, but the personality of the dying one remains. It only goes over to another order of life.... It is not she whom they will put in the grave. She is in another place. She will be just as alive as she is now. In the first hours and days she will be around you. Only she will not say anything, and you won't be able to see her; but she will be right here. Have this in mind. We who remain weep over the departed, but for them it is immediately easier; that condition is a happier one. Those who have died and then have been brought back into the body have found it to be a very uncomfortable dwelling. Your sister will feel this also. She is better off there; and we are in agony, as if some kind of tragedy has happened to her! She will look and surely be astonished at this" (*Soul-Profiting Reading,* August, 1894).

It should be kept in mind that this description of the first two days of death constitutes a *general rule* which by no means covers all cases. In fact, most of the examples quoted from Orthodox literature in the course of this book do not fit this

---

* Orthodox Funeral Service for laymen, sticheron, tone 2; *Service Book,* tr. by Isabel Florence Hapgood, Houghton Mifflin, Boston, 1906, p. 385.

rule, and for an obvious reason: the saints, being not at all attached to the things of this world and living in constant expectation of their passage to the other world, are not attracted even to the places of their good deeds, but immediately begin their ascent to heaven. Others, like K. Uekskuell, begin their ascent before the end of the two days because of some special reason in God's Providence. On the other hand, the contemporary "after-death" experiences, fragmentary as they are, all do fit into this rule: the "out-of-body" state is but the beginning of the soul's initial period of bodiless "wandering" to the places of its earthly attachments; but none of these people has been dead long enough even to meet the angels who are to accompany them.

Some critics of the Orthodox teaching on life after death find such variations from the general rule of after-death experience to be proof of "contradictions" in the Orthodox teaching; but such critics are simply too literal-minded. The description of the first two days (and of the succeeding days as well) is by no means any kind of dogma; it is merely a "model" which indeed sets forth the most common order of the soul's experiences after death. The many cases, both in Orthodox literature and in accounts of modern experiences, where the dead have momentarily appeared to the living within the first day or two after death (sometimes in dreams) are examples of the truth that the soul does indeed usually remain close to earth for some short period.* By the third day (and often sooner), this period comes to an end.

---

* For some examples, see *Eternal Mysteries Beyond the Grave,* pp. 189–196. Genuine appearances of the dead after this first short period of the soul's "freedom" are much rarer and are always for some specific purpose allowed by God, and not according to one's own will (see below, Appendix II).

THE TOLL-HOUSES

At this time (the third day), it passes through legions of evil spirits which obstruct its path and accuse it of various sins, to which they themselves had tempted it. According to various revelations there are twenty such obstacles, the so-called "toll-houses," at each of which one or another form of sin is tested; after passing through one the soul comes upon the next one, and only after successfully passing through all of them can the soul continue its path without being immediately cast into gehenna. How terrible these demons and their toll-houses are may be seen in the fact that the Mother of God Herself, when informed by the Archangel Gabriel of Her approaching death, begged Her Son to deliver Her soul from these demons and, answering Her prayer, the Lord Jesus Christ Himself appeared from heaven to receive the soul of His Most Pure Mother and conduct it to heaven.* Terrible indeed is the third day for the soul of the departed, and for this reason it especially needs prayers then for itself.

Chapter Six above has set forth a number of the Patristic and hagiographical texts on the toll-houses, and there is no need to add to them here. Here again, however, we may note that descriptions of the toll-houses constitute a "model" of the soul's experiences after death, and individual experiences of them may vary considerably. Minor details such as the number of the toll-houses are, of course, quite secondary compared to the primary fact that the soul does indeed experience a judgment (the Particular Judgment) soon after death as a final summary of the "unseen warfare" it has conducted (or failed to conduct) on earth against the fallen spirits.

---

* This is visually depicted in the traditional Orthodox icon of the Dormition.

Bishop Theophan the Recluse writes, continuing the letter to the brother of the woman who was about to die:

"In the departed there soon begins the struggle of going through the toll-houses. Here she needs help! Stand then in this thought, and you will hear her cry to you: 'Help!' This is where you should direct all your attention and all your love for her. I think that it will be the truest testimony of love if, from the minute of the soul's departure, leaving concern for the body to others, you will go off and, being by yourself wherever you can, you will immerse yourself in prayer for her in her new condition and her new, unexpected needs. Having begun thus, remain in unceasing crying out to God to help her, for the course of six weeks, and indeed for longer than that. In the account of Theodora, the bag from which the angels took in order to be separated from the tax-collectors was the prayers of her elder. Your prayers will be the same; do not forget to do this. This is love!"

The "bag of gold" with which the angels "paid the debts" of Blessed Theodora at the toll-houses has often been misunderstood by critics of the Orthodox teaching; it is sometimes mistakenly compared to the Latin notion of the "excess merits" of saints. Again, such critics are too literal-minded in their reading of Orthodox texts. Nothing else is referred to here than the prayers of the Church for the reposed, in particular the prayers of a holy man and spiritual father. The form in which this is described—it should hardly be necessary to say—is metaphorical.

The Orthodox Church regards the teaching of the toll-houses as of such importance that it has included references to it in many of its Divine services (see a few of these above in the chapter on the toll-houses). In particular, the Church makes a special point of presenting this teaching to each one of its children who are dying; in the "Canon on the Departure of the Soul," read by the priest at the deathbed of each of the faithful, there are the following troparia:

"As I depart from earth, vouchsafe me to pass unhindered by the prince of the air, the persecutor, the tormenter, he who stands on the frightful paths and is their unjust interrogator" (Canticle 4).

"Translate me, O Sovereign Lady, into the sacred and precious hands of the holy angels, that being covered by their wings, I may not see the shameless and foul and dark form of the demons" (Canticle 6).

"O Thou Who gavest birth to the Lord Almighty, remove far from me the chief of the bitter toll-houses, the ruler of the world, when I am about to die, that I may glorify Thee forever, O Holy Theotokos" (Canticle 8).

Thus, the Orthodox Christian in dying is prepared by the Church's words for the trials in front of him.

THE FORTY DAYS

Then, having successfully passed through the toll-houses and bowed down before God, the soul for the course of 37 more days visits the heavenly habitations and the abysses of hell, not knowing yet where it will remain, and only on the fortieth day is its place appointed until the resurrection of the dead.

It is certainly not strange that the soul, having passed through the toll-houses and finished for good with earthly things, should then be introduced to the truly *other* world, in one part of which it will spend eternity. According to the revelation of the angel to St. Macarius of Alexandria, the

Church's special commemoration of the departed on the ninth day after death (apart from the general symbolism of the nine ranks of angels) occurs because up to then the soul is shown the beauties of Paradise, and only after this, for the remainder of the forty days, is it shown the torments and horrors of hell, before being assigned on the fortieth day to the place where it will await the resurrection of the dead and the Last Judgment. These numbers, once again, constitute a general rule, or "model" of after-death reality, and undoubtedly not all the departed complete their course precisely according to the "rule." We do know that Theodora, in fact, completed her "tour of hell" just on the fortieth day—as time is measured on earth (*Eternal Mysteries,* pp. 83–84).

THE STATE OF SOULS UNTIL THE LAST JUDGEMENT

Some souls find themselves (after the forty days) in a condition of foretasting eternal joy and blessedness, and others in fear of the eternal tortures which will come in full after the Last Judgment. Until then changes are still possible in the condition of souls, especially through offering for them the Bloodless Sacrifice (commemoration at the Liturgy), and likewise by other prayers.

The Church's teaching on the state of souls in heaven and hell before the Last Judgment is set forth below in more detail in the words of St. Mark of Ephesus (Appendix I).

The benefits of prayer, both public and private, for the souls in hell have been described in many Lives of Saints and ascetics and in Patristic writings. In the Life of the third-century Martyr Perpetua, for example, the fate of her brother Dimocrates was revealed to her in the image of a cistern filled with water which was too high for him to reach in the filthy, intensely hot place where he was confined. Through her intense prayer for a whole day and night the cistern was made accessible to him and she saw him in a bright place. By this she understood that he had been released from punishment.*

In the Life of an ascetic who died in our own 20th century there is a similar account. The Life of the Nun Athanasia (Anastasia Logacheva), a spiritual daughter of St. Seraphim of Sarov, relates:

"Now she undertook a labor of prayer for her own brother by blood, Paul, who had hanged himself while drunk. She went at first to Pelagia Ivanovna,** the blessed one who lived in the Diveyevo Convent, to take counsel from her as to what she could do to make easier the lot beyond the grave of her brother, who had unfortunately and dishonorably ended his earthly life. After counsel, the following was decided: Anastasia would lock herself up in her cell to fast and pray for him, every day reading 150 times the prayer, 'Virgin Mother of God, rejoice ...' At the end of forty days she saw a great abyss; at the bottom of it was a bloody stone, and upon it there lay two men with iron chains on their necks; one of them was her brother. When she informed the blessed Pelagia about this vision the latter advised her to repeat this labor. At the end of the second forty days she saw the same abyss, the same stone on which were the same two people with chains around their necks, but her brother was now standing and was going around the stone, but then fell again on

* Lives of Saints, February 1; English translation of this passage in *Orthodox Life,* 1978, no.1, pp. 23–24.
** Her complete Life in Russian is contained in Archimandrite Seraphim Chichagov, *The Diveyevo Chronicle,* St. Herman Brotherhood, 1978, pp. 530ff.

the stone; the chain was still around his neck. After she informed Pelagia Ivanovna about this dream, the latter advised her to perform the same labor for a third time. After forty more days Anastasia saw the same abyss and the same stone, but now there was only one man, unknown to her, and her brother had gone away from the stone and was hidden from sight. The one who remained on this rock said, 'It is good for you; you have powerful intercessors on the earth.' After this, blessed Pelagia said, 'Your brother has been delivered from tortures, but he has not received blessedness.' "*

There are many similar incidents in the Lives of Orthodox Saints and ascetics. If anyone is inclined to be too literal-minded about such visions, it should perhaps be said that of course the forms which such visions take (usually in dreams) are not necessarily "photographic" views of the way the soul appears in the other world, but rather are images which convey the spiritual truth of the soul's betterment in the other world through the prayers of those who remain on earth.

PRAYER FOR THE DEAD

How important commemoration at the Liturgy is may be seen in the following occurrence: Before the uncovering of the relics of St. Theodosius of Chernigov (1896), the priest-monk (the renowned Starets Alexis of Goloseyevsky Hermitage, of the Kiev-Caves Lavra, who died in 1916) who was conducting the re-vesting of the relics, becoming weary while sitting by the relics, dozed off and saw before him the Saint, who told him: "I thank you for laboring for me. I beg you also, when you will serve the Liturgy, to commemorate my

---

* *Soul-Profiting Reading,* June, 1902, p. 281.

parents"—and he gave their names (Priest Nikita and Maria). "How can you, O Saint, ask my prayers, when you yourself stand at the heavenly Throne and grant to people God's mercy?" the priest-monk asked. "Yes, that is true," replied St. Theodosius, "but the offering at the Liturgy is more powerful than my prayer."*

Therefore, panikhidas and prayer at home for the dead are beneficial for them, as are good deeds done in their memory, such as alms or contributions to the church. But especially beneficial for them is commemoration at the Divine Liturgy. There have been many appearances of the dead and other occurrences which confirm how beneficial is the commemoration of the dead. Many who died in repentance, but who were unable to manifest this while they were alive, have been freed from tortures and have obtained repose. In the Church prayers are ever offered for the repose of the dead, and on the day of the Descent of the Holy Spirit, in the kneeling prayers at vespers, there is even a special petition "for those in hell."

St. Gregory the Great, in answering in his *Dialogues* the question, "Is there anything at all that can possibly benefit souls after death?" teaches: "The Holy Sacrifice of Christ, our saving Victim, brings great benefits to souls even after death, provided their sins (are such as) can be pardoned in the life to come. For this reason the souls of the dead sometimes beg to have Liturgies offered for them.... The safer course, naturally, is to do for ourselves during life what we hope others will do for us after death. It is better to make one's exit a free man than to seek

---

* These names had been unknown before this vision. Several years after the canonization, St. Theodosius' own Book of Commemoration was found in the monastery where he had once been abbot, which confirmed these names and corroborated the vision. See the Life of Elder Alexis in *Pravoslavny Blagovestnik,* San Francisco, 1967, no. 1 (in Russian).

liberty after one is in chains. We should, therefore, despise this world with all our hearts as though its glory were already spent, and offer our sacrifice of tears to God each day as we immolate His sacred Flesh and Blood. This Sacrifice alone has the power of saving the soul from eternal death, for it presents to us mystically the death of the Only-begotten Son" (*Dialogues* IV: 57, 60, pp. 266, 272–3).

St. Gregory gives several examples of the dead appearing to the living and asking for or thanking them for the celebration of the Liturgy for their repose; once, also, a captive whom his wife believed dead and for whom she had the Liturgy celebrated on certain days, returned from captivity and told her how he had been released from his chains on some days—the very days when the Liturgy had been offered for him. (*Dialogues* IV: 57, 59, pp. 267, 270).

Protestants generally find the Church's prayer for the dead to be somehow incompatible with the necessity of finding salvation first of all in this life: "If you can be saved by the Church after death, then why bother to struggle or find faith in this life? Let us eat, drink, and be merry ..." Of course, no one holding such a philosophy has ever attained salvation by the Church's prayer, and it is evident that such an argument is quite artificial and even hypocritical. The Church's prayer cannot save anyone who does not wish salvation, or who never offered any struggle for it himself during his lifetime. In a sense, one might say that the prayer of the Church or of individual Christians for a dead person is but another result of that person's life: he would not be prayed for unless he had done something during his lifetime to inspire such prayer after his death.

St. Mark of Ephesus also discusses this question of the Church's prayer for the dead and the improvement it brings in their state, citing the example of the prayer of St. Gregory the

Dialogist for the Roman Emperor Trajan—a prayer inspired by a good deed of this pagan Emperor. (See below, Appendix I.)

WHAT WE CAN DO FOR THE DEAD

Every one of us who desires to manifest his love for the dead and give them real help, can do this best of all through prayer for them, and in particular by commemorating them at the Liturgy, when the particles which are cut out for the living and the dead are let fall into the Blood of the Lord with the words: "Wash away, O Lord, the sins of those here commemorated by Thy Precious Blood, by the prayers of Thy saints." We can do nothing better or greater for the dead than to pray for them, offering commemoration for them at the Liturgy. Of this they are always in need, and especially during those forty days when the soul of the deceased is proceeding on its path to the eternal habitations. The body feels nothing then: it does not see its close ones who have assembled, does not smell the fragrance of the flowers, does not hear the funeral orations. But the soul senses the prayers offered for it and is grateful to those who make them and is spiritually close to them.

O relatives and close ones of the dead! Do for them what is needful for them and what is within your power. Use your money not for outward adornment of the coffin and grave, but in order to help those in need, in memory of your close ones who have died, for churches, where prayers for them are offered. Show mercy to the dead, take care for their souls. Before us all stands that same path, and how we shall then wish that we would be remembered in prayer! Let us therefore be ourselves merciful to the dead.

As soon as someone has reposed, immediately call or inform a priest, so he can read the "Prayers on the Departure of the Soul," which are appointed to be read over all Orthodox Christians after death. Try, if it be possible, to have the funeral in church and to have the Psalter read over the deceased until the funeral. The funeral need not be performed elaborately, but most definitely it should be complete, without abbreviations; think at this time not of yourself and your convenience, but of the deceased, with whom you are parting forever. If there are several of the deceased in church at the same time, don't refuse if it be proposed to serve the funeral for all together. It is better for a funeral to be served for two or more of the deceased at the same time, when the prayer of the close ones who have gathered will be all the more fervent, than for several funerals to be served in succession and the services, owing to lack of time and energy, abbreviated; because each word of prayer for the reposed is like a drop of water to a thirsty man. Most definitely arrange at once for the serving of the forty-day memorial, that is, daily commemoration at the Liturgy for the course of forty days. Usually, in churches where there are daily services, the deceased whose funerals have been served there are commemorated for forty days and longer. But if the funeral is in a church where there are no daily services, the relatives themselves should take care to order the forty-day memorial wherever there are daily services. It is likewise good to send contributions for commemoration to monasteries, as well as to Jerusalem, where there is constant prayer at the holy places. But the forty-day memorial must be begun immediately after death, when the soul is especially in need of help in prayer, and therefore one should begin commemoration in the nearest place where there are daily services.

Let us take care for those who have departed into the other world before us, in order to do for them all that we can, remembering that "Blessed are the merciful, for they shall obtain mercy."

THE RESURRECTION OF THE BODY

One day this whole corruptible world will come to an end, and the everlasting Kingdom of Heaven will dawn, where the souls of the redeemed, joined to their resurrected bodies, will dwell forever with Christ, immortal and incorruptible. Then the partial joy and glory which souls know even now in heaven will be replaced by the fullness of joy of the new creation for which man was made; but those who did not accept the salvation which Christ came to earth to offer mankind will be tormented forever—together with their resurrected bodies—in hell. St. John Damascene, in the final chapter of his *Exact Exposition of the Orthodox Faith*, well describes this final state of the soul after death:

"We also believe in the resurrection of the dead, for there really will be one, there will be a resurrection of the dead. Now, when we say resurrection, we mean a resurrection of bodies. For resurrection is a raising up again of one who has fallen. But, since souls are immortal, how shall they rise again? Well, if death is defined as a separation of soul from body, the resurrection is the perfect rejoining of soul and body, and the raising up again of the dissolved and fallen living being. Therefore, the very body which is corrupted and dissolved will itself rise up incorruptible. For He Who formed it in the beginning from the dust of the earth is not incapable of raising it up again after it has again been dissolved and returned to the earth whence it was taken by the decision of its Creator....

"Now, if the soul had engaged alone in the contest for virtue, then it would also be crowned alone; and if it alone had indulged in pleasures, then it alone could be justly punished.

However, since the soul followed neither virtue nor vice without the body, it will be just for them to receive their recompense together....

"And so, with our souls again united to our bodies, which will have become incorrupt and put off corruption, we shall rise again and stand before the terrible judgment seat of Christ. And the devil and his demons, and his man, which is to say, the Antichrist, and the impious and sinners will be given over to everlasting fire, which will not be a material fire such as we are accustomed to, but a fire such as God might know. And those who have done good will shine like the sun together with the angels unto eternal life with our Lord Jesus Christ, ever seeing Him and being seen, enjoying the unending bliss which is from Him, and praising Him together with the Father and the Holy Spirit unto the endless ages of ages. Amen."*

---

* *Exact Exposition,* Book Four, ch. 27, in The Fathers of the Church, vol. 37, 1958, pp. 401, 402, 406.

APPENDIX I

THE ORTHODOX TEACHING OF

St. Mark of Ephesus

ON THE STATE OF SOULS
AFTER DEATH

THE ORTHODOX TEACHING on the state of souls after death is one that is often not fully understood, even by Orthodox Christians themselves; and the comparatively late Latin teaching of "purgatory" has caused further confusion in people's minds. The Orthodox doctrine itself, however, is not at all ambiguous or imprecise. Perhaps the most concise Orthodox exposition of it is to be found in the writings of St. Mark of Ephesus at the Council of Florence in 1439, composed precisely in order to answer the Latin teaching on "purgatory." These writings are especially valuable to us in that coming as they do from the last of the Byzantine Fathers, before the modern era with all its theological confusions, they both point us to the sources of the Orthodox doctrine and instruct us how to approach and understand these sources. These sources are: Scripture, Patristic homilies, church services, Lives of Saints, and certain revelations and visions of life after death, such as those contained in Book IV of the *Dialogues* of St. Gregory the Great.

Today's academic theologians tend to mistrust the latter two or three kinds of sources, which is why they are often uneasy when speaking on this subject and sometimes prefer to keep an "agnostic reticence" with regard to it (Timothy Ware, *The Orthodox Church,* p. 259). St. Mark's writings, on the other hand, show us how much "at home" with these sources genuine Orthodox theologians are; those who are "uncomfortable" with them perhaps reveal thereby an unsuspected infection with modern unbelief.

Of St. Mark's four replies on purgatory composed at the Council of Florence, the First Homily contains the most concise account of the Orthodox doctrine as against the Latin errors, and it is chiefly from it that this translation has been compiled. The other replies contain mostly illustrative material for the points discussed here, as well as answers to more specific Latin arguments.

The "Latin Chapter" to which St. Mark replies are those written by Julian Cardinal Cesarini (Russian translation in Pogodin, pp. 50–57), giving the Latin teaching, defined at the earlier "Union" Council of Lyons (1270), on the state of souls after death. This teaching strikes the Orthodox reader (as indeed it struck St. Mark) as one of an entirely too "literalistic" and "legalistic" character. The Latins by this time had come to regard heaven and hell as somehow "finished" and "absolute," and those in them as already possessing the fullness of the state they will have after the Last Judgment; thus, there is no need to pray for those in heaven (whose lot is already perfect) or those in hell (for they can never be delivered or cleansed from sin). But since many of the faithful die in a "middle" state — not perfect enough for heaven, but not evil enough for hell — the logic of the Latin arguments required a third place of cleansing ("purgatory"), where even those whose sins had already been forgiven had to be punished or give "satisfaction" for their sins before being sufficiently cleansed to enter heaven. These legalistic arguments of a purely human "justice" (which actually deny God's supreme goodness and love of mankind) the Latins proceeded to support by literalistic interpretations of certain Patristic texts and various visions; almost all of these interpretations are quite contrived and arbitrary, because not even the ancient Latin Fathers spoke of such a place as "purgatory," but only of the "cleansing" from sins after death, which some of them referred to (probably allegorically) as by "fire."

In the Orthodox doctrine, on the other hand, which St. Mark teaches, the faithful who have died with small sins unconfessed, or who have not brought forth fruits of repentance for sins they have confessed, are cleansed of these sins either in the trial of death itself with its fear, or after death, when they are confined (but not permanently) in hell, by the prayers and Liturgies of the Church and good deeds performed for them by the faithful. Even sinners destined for eternal torment can be given a certain relief from their torment in hell by these means also. There is no fire tormenting sinners now, however, either in hell (for the eternal fire will begin to torment them only after the Last Judgment), or much less in any third place like "purgatory"; all visions of fire which are seen by men are as it were images or prophecies of what will be in the future age. All forgiveness of sins after death comes solely from the goodness of God, which extends even to those in hell, with the cooperation of the prayers of men, and no "payment" or "satisfaction" is due for sins which have been forgiven.

It should be noted that St. Mark's writings concern primarily the specific point of the *state* of souls after death, and barely touch on the history of the events that occur to the soul immediately after death. On the latter point there is an abundant Orthodox literature, but this point was not under discussion at Florence.

All notes have been added by the translators.

FIRST HOMILY

REFUTATION OF THE LATIN CHAPTERS CONCERNING PURGATORIAL FIRE*

INASMUCH AS WE are required, preserving our Orthodoxy and the church dogmas handed down by the Fathers, to answer with love to what you have said, as our general rule we shall first quote each argument and testimony which you have brought forward in writing, in order that the reply and resolution to each of them might then follow briefly and clearly.

1. And so, at the beginning of your report you speak thus: "If those who truly repent have departed this life in love (towards God) before they were able to give satisfaction by means of worthy fruits for their transgressions or offenses, their souls are cleansed after death by means of purgatorial sufferings; but for the easing (or 'deliverance') of them from these sufferings, they are aided by the help which is shown them on the part of the faithful who are alive, as for example: prayers, Liturgies, almsgiving, and other works of piety."

To this we answer the following: Of the fact that those reposed in faith are without doubt helped by the Liturgies and prayers and almsgiving performed for them, and that this

---

* Translated from the Russian translation of Archimandrite Amvrossy Pogodin, in *St. Mark of Ephesus and the Union of Florence,* Jordanville, N.Y., 1963, pp. 58–73.

custom has been in force from antiquity, there is the testimony of many and various utterances of the Teachers, both Latin and Greek, spoken and written at various times and in various places. But that souls are delivered thanks to a certain purgatorial suffering and temporal fire which possesses such (a purgatorial) power and has the character of a help — this we do not find either in the Scriptures or in the prayers and hymns for the dead, or in the words of Teachers. But we have received that even the souls which are held in hell and are already given over to eternal torments, whether in actual fact and experience or in hopeless expectation of such, can be aided and given a certain small help, although not in the sense of completely loosing them from torment or giving hope for a final deliverance. And this is shown from the words of the great Macarius the Egyptian ascetic who, finding a skull in the desert, was instructed by it concerning this by the action of Divine Power.* And Basil the Great, in the prayers read at Pentecost, writes literally the following: "Who also, on this all-perfect and saving feast, are graciously pleased to accept propitiatory prayers for those who are imprisoned in hell, granting us a great hope of improvement for those who are imprisoned from the defilements which have

---

* In the "Alphabetical Collection" of sayings of the Desert Fathers, under "Macarius the Great," we read: "Abba Macarius said, Walking in the desert one day, I found the skull of a dead man, lying on the ground. As I was moving it with my stick, the skull spoke to me. I said to it, 'Who are you?' The skull replied, 'I was high priest of the idols and of the pagans who dwelt in this place; but you are Macarius, the Spirit-bearer. Whenever you take pity on those who are in torments, and pray for them, they feel a little respite.'" The skull further instructed St. Macarius concerning the torments of hell, concluding: "We have received a little mercy since we did not know God, but those who knew God and denied Him are down below us." (*The Sayings of the Desert Fathers*, tr. by Benedicta Ward, London, A. R. Mowbray & Co., 1975, pp. 115–6.)

imprisoned them, and that Thou wilt send down Thy consolation" (Third Kneeling Prayer at Vespers).

But if souls have departed this life in faith and love, while nevertheless carrying away with themselves certain faults, whether small ones over which they have not repented at all, or great ones for which—even though they have repented over them—they did not undertake to show fruits of repentance: such souls, we believe, must be cleansed from this kind of sins, but not by means of some purgatorial fire or a definite punishment in some place (for this, as we have said, has not at all been handed down to us). But some must be cleansed in the very departure from the body, thanks only to fear, as St. Gregory the Dialogist literally shows;* while others must be cleansed after the departure from the body, either while remaining in the same earthly place, before they come to worship God and are honored with the lot of the blessed, or—if their sins were more serious and bind them for a longer duration—they are kept in hell, but not in order to remain forever in fire and torment, but as it were in prison and confinement under guard.

All such ones, we affirm, are helped by the prayers and Liturgies performed for them, with the cooperation of the Divine goodness and love for mankind. This Divine cooperation immediately disdains and remits some sins, those committed out of human weakness, as Dionysius the Great (the Areopagite) says in the "Reflections on the Mystery of Those Reposed in Faith" (in *The Ecclesiastical Hierarchy*, VII, 7); while other sins, after a certain time, by righteous judgments it either likewise releases and forgives—and that completely—or lightens the responsibility for them until that final Judgment. And therefore we see no necessity whatever for any other punish-

---

* In Book IV of the *Dialogues*.

ment or for a cleansing fire; for some are cleansed by fear, while others are devoured by the gnawings of conscience with more torment than any fire, and still others are cleansed only by the very terror before the Divine Glory and the uncertainty as to what the future will be. And that this is much more tormenting and punishing than anything else, experience itself shows, and St. John Chrysostom testifies to us in almost all or at least most of his moral homilies, which affirm this, as likewise does the divine ascetic Dorotheus in his homily "On the Conscience ..."

2. And so, we entreat God and believe to deliver the departed from (eternal torment), and not from any other torment or fire apart from those torments and that fire which have been proclaimed to be forever. And that, moreover, the souls of the departed are delivered by prayer from confinement in hell, as if from a certain prison, is testified, among many others, by Theophanes the Confessor, called the Branded (for the words of his testimony for the Icon of Christ, words written on his forehead, he sealed by blood). In one of the canons for the reposed he thus prays for them: "Deliver, O Saviour, Thy slaves who are in the hell of tears and sighing" (Octoechos, Saturday canon for the reposed, Tone 8, Canticle 6, Glory).

Do you hear? He said "tears" and "sighing," and not any kind of punishment or purgatorial fire. And if there is to be encountered in these hymns and prayers any mention of fire, it is not a temporal one that has a purgatorial power, but rather that eternal fire and unceasing punishment. The saints, being moved by love for mankind and compassion for their fellow countrymen, desiring and daring what is almost impossible, pray for the deliverance of those departed in faith. For thus does St. Theodore the Studite, the confessor and witness of the truth himself, say, at the very beginning of his canon for the departed: "Let us all entreat Christ, performing a memorial today for those dead from the ages, that He might deliver from eternal fire those departed in faith and in hope of eternal life" (*Lenten Triodion*, Meat-Fare Saturday, Canon, Canticle 1). And then, in another troparion, in Canticle 5 of the Canon, he says: "Deliver, O our Saviour, all who have died in faith from the ever-scorching fire, and unillumined darkness, the gnashing of teeth, and the eternally-tormenting worm, and all torment."

Where is the "purgatorial fire" here? And if it in fact existed, where would it be more appropriate for the Saint to speak of it, if not here? Whether the saints are heard by God when they pray for this is not for us to search out. But they themselves knew, as did the Spirit dwelling in them by Whom they were moved, and they spoke and wrote in this knowledge; and likewise the Master Christ knew this, Who gave the commandment that we should pray for our enemies, and Who prayed for those who were crucifying Him, and inspired the First Martyr Stephen, when he was being stoned to death, to do the same. And although someone might say that when we pray for such people we are not heard by God, still we shall do everything that depends on us. And behold, some of the saints who prayed not only for the faithful, but even for the impious, were heard and by their prayers rescued them from eternal torment, as for example the First Woman-martyr Thecla rescued Falconila, and the divine Gregory the Dialogist, as it is related, rescued the Emperor Trajan.*

---

* The latter incident is related in some of the early Lives of St. Gregory, as for example in an 8th-century English Life: "Some of our people also tell a story related by the Romans of how the soul of the Emperor Trajan was refreshed and even baptized by St. Gregory's tears, a story marvelous to tell and marvelous to hear. Let no one be surprised that we say he was baptized, for without baptism none will ever see God; and a third kind of baptism is by tears. One day as he was crossing the Forum, a magnificent piece of work for which Trajan is said to have been responsible, he found on examining it

(Chapter 3 demonstrates that the Church prays also for those already enjoying blessedness with God—who, of course, have no need to go through "purgatorial fire.")

4. After this, a little further on, you desired to prove the above-mentioned dogma of purgatorial fire, at first quoting what is said in the book of Maccabees: *It is holy and pious ... to pray for the dead ... that they might be delivered from their sin* (II Maccabees 12:44–45). Then, taking from the Gospel according to Matthew the place in which the Saviour declares that *whosoever shall speak against the Holy Spirit, it shall not be forgiven him, neither in this world, nor in that which is to come* (Matt. 12:32), you say that from this one may see that there is a remission of sins in the future life.

---

carefully that Trajan, though a pagan, had done a deed so charitable that it seemed more likely to have been the deed of a Christian than of a pagan. For it is related that, as he was leading his army in great haste against the enemy, he was moved to pity by the words of a widow, and the emperor of the whole world came to a halt. She said, 'Lord Trajan, here are the men who killed my son and are unwilling to pay me recompense.' He answered: 'Tell me about it when I return and I will make them recompense you.' But she replied, 'Lord, if you never return, there will be no one to help me.' Then, armed as he was, he made the defendants pay forthwith the compensation they owed her, in his presence. When Gregory discovered this story, he recognized that this was just what we read about in the Scriptures, *Judge the fatherless, plead for the widow. Come now and let us reason together, saith the Lord.* Since Gregory did not know what to do to comfort the soul of this man who brought the words of Christ to his mind, he went to St. Peter's Church and wept floods of tears, as was his custom, until he gained at last by divine revelation the assurance that his prayers were answered, seeing that he had never presumed to ask this for any other pagan." (*The Earliest Life of Gregory the Great,* by an Anonymous Monk of Whitby, tr. by Bertram Colgrave, The University of Kansas Press, Lawrence, Kansas, 1968, ch. 29, pp. 127–9.) Since the Church does not offer public prayer for departed non-believers, it is evident that this deliverance from hell was the fruit of St. Gregory's own personal prayer. Although this is a rare occurrence, it gives hope to those who have dear ones who have died outside the faith.

But that from this there in no way follows the idea of purgatorial fire is clearer than the sun; for what is there in common between remission on the one hand, and cleansing by fire and punishment on the other? For if the remission of sins is accomplished for the sake of prayers, or merely by the Divine love of mankind itself, there is no need for punishment and cleansing (by fire). But if punishment, and also cleansing, are established (by God) ... then, it would seem, prayers (for the reposed) are performed in vain, and vainly do we hymn the Divine love of mankind. And so, these citations are less a proof of the existence of purgatorial fire than a refutation of it: for the remission of sins of those who have transgressed is presented in them as the result of a certain royal authority and love of mankind, and not as a deliverance from punishment or a cleansing.

5. Thirdly, (let us take) the passage from the first epistle of the Blessed Paul to the Corinthians, in which he, speaking of the building on the foundation, which is Christ, of *gold, silver, costly stones, wood, hay, stubble,* adds: *For that day shall declare it, because it is revealed in fire; and the fire itself shall prove each man's work of what sort it is. If any man's work shall abide which he built thereon, he shall receive a reward. If any man's work shall be burned, he shall suffer loss: but he himself shall be saved, yet so as through fire* (I Cor. 3:11–15). This citation, it would seem, more than any other introduces the idea of purgatorial fire; but in actual fact it more than any other refutes it.

First of all, the Divine Apostle called it not a purgatorial, but a proving (fire); then he declared that through it good and honorable works also must pass, and such, it is clear, have no need of any cleansing; then he says that those who bring evil works, after these works burn, suffer loss, whereas those who are being cleansed not only suffer no loss, but acquire even more;

then he says that this must be on "that day," namely, the day of Judgment and of the future age, whereas to suppose the existence of a purgatorial fire after that fearful Coming of the Judge and the final sentence—is this not a total absurdity? For the Scripture does not transmit to us anything of the sort, but He Himself Who will judge us says: *And these shall go away into eternal punishment, but the righteous into eternal life* (Matt. 25:46); and again: *They shall come forth: they that have done good, unto the resurrection of life, and they that have done evil, unto the resurrection of judgment* (John 5:29). Therefore, there remains no kind of intermediate place; but after He divided all those under judgment into two parts, placing some on the right and others on the left, and calling the first "sheep" and the second "goats"—He did not at all declare that there are any who are to be cleansed by that fire. It would seem that the fire of which the Apostle speaks is the same as that of which the Prophet David speaks: *Fire shall blaze before Him, and round about Him shall there be a mighty tempest* (Ps. 49:4); and again: *Fire shall go before Him, and shall burn up His enemies round about* (Ps. 96:3). Daniel the Prophet also speaks about this fire: *A stream of fire issued and came forth from before Him* (Daniel 7:10).

Since the saints do not bring with them any evil work or evil mark, this fire manifests them as even brighter, as gold tried in the fire, or as the stone amianthus, which, as it is related, when placed in fire appears as charred, but when taken out of the fire become even cleaner, as if washed with water, as were also the bodies of the Three Youths in the Babylonian furnace. Sinners, however, who bring evil with themselves, are seized as a suitable material for this fire and are immediately ignited by it, and their "work," that is, their evil disposition or activity, is burned and utterly destroyed and they are deprived of what they brought with them, that is, deprived of their burden of evil, while they themselves are "saved"—that is, will be preserved and kept forever, so that they might not be subjected to destruction together with their evil.

6. The divine Father Chrysostom also (who is called by us "the lips of Paul," just as the latter is "the lips of Christ") considers it necessary to make such an interpretation of this passage in his commentary on the Epistle (Homily 9 on First Corinthians); and Paul speaks through Chrysostom, as was made clear thanks to the vision of Proclus, his disciple and the successor of his See.* St. Chrysostom devoted a special treatise to this one passage, so that the Origenists would not quote these words of the Apostle as confirmation of their way of thought (which, it would seem, is more fitting for them than for you), and would not cause harm to the Church by introducing an end to the torment of hell and a final restoration (*apocatastasis*) of sinners. For the expression that the sinner *is saved as through fire* signifies that he will remain tormented in fire and will not be destroyed together with his evil works and evil disposition of soul.

Basil the Great also speaks of this in the "Morals," in interpreting the passage of Scripture, *the voice of the Lord Who divideth the flame of fire* (Ps. 28:7): "The fire prepared for the torment of the devil and his angels, is divided by the voice of the Lord, so that after this there might be two powers in it: one that burns, and another that illumines; the tormenting and punishing power of that fire is reserved for those worthy of

---

* It is related in the Life of St. Proclus (Nov. 20) that when St. Chrysostom was working on his commentaries on St. Paul's epistles, St. Proclus saw St. Paul himself bending over St. Chrysostom and whispering into his ear.

torment; while the illumining and enlightening power is intended for the shining of those who rejoice. Therefore the voice of the Lord Who divides and separates the flame of fire is for this: that the dark part might be a fire of torment and the unburning part a light of enjoyment" (St. Basil, Homily on Psalm 28).

And so, as may be seen, this division and separation of that fire will be when absolutely everyone will pass through it: the bright and shining works will be manifest as yet brighter, and those who bring them will become inheritors of the light and will receive that eternal reward; while those who bring bad works suitable for burning, being punished by the loss of them, will eternally remain in fire and will inherit a salvation which is worse than perdition, for this is what, strictly speaking, the word "saved" means—that the destroying power of fire will not be applied to them and they themselves be utterly destroyed. Following these Fathers, many other of our Teachers also have understood this passage in the same sense. And if anyone has interpreted it differently and understood "salvation" as "deliverance from punishment," and "going through fire" as "purgatory"—such a one, if we may so express ourselves, understands this passage in an entirely wrong way. And this is not surprising, for he is a man, and many even among the Teachers may be seen to interpret passages of Scripture in various ways, and not all of them have attained in an equal degree the precise meaning. It is not possible that one and the same text, being handed down in various interpretations, should correspond in an equal degree to all the interpretations of it; but we, selecting the most important of them and those that best correspond to church dogmas, should place the other interpretations in second place. Therefore, we shall not deviate from the above-cited interpretation of the Apostle's words, even if Augustine or Gregory the Dialogist or another of your Teachers should give such an interpretation; for such an interpretation answers less to the idea of a temporary purgatorial fire than to the teaching of Origen which, speaking of a final restoration of souls through that fire and a deliverance from torment, was forbidden and given over to anathema by the Fifth Ecumenical Council, and was definitively overthrown as a common impiety for the Church.

(In chapters 7 through 12, St. Mark answers objections raised by quotations from the works of Blessed Augustine, St. Ambrose, St. Gregory the Dialogist, St. Basil the Great, and other Fathers, showing that they have been misinterpreted or perhaps misquoted and that these Fathers actually teach the Orthodox doctrine, and if not, then their teaching is not to be accepted. Further, he points out that St. Gregory of Nyssa does not teach about "purgatory" at all, but holds the much worse error of Origen, that there will be an end to the eternal flames of hell—although it may be that these ideas were placed in his writings later by Origenists.)

13. And finally you say: "The above-mentioned truth is evident from the Divine Justice, which does not leave unpunished anything that was done amiss, and from this it necessarily follows that for those who have not undergone punishment here, and cannot pay it off either in heaven or in hell, it remains to suppose the existence of a different, a third place in which this cleansing is accomplished, thanks to which each one, becoming cleansed, is immediately led up to heavenly enjoyment."

To this we say the following, and pay heed how simple and at the same time how just this is: it is generally acknowledged that the remission of sins is at the same time also a deliverance from punishment; for the one who receives remission of them at the same time is delivered from the punishment owed for them. Remission is given in three forms and at different times: (1) during Baptism; (2) after Baptism, through conversion and sorrow and making up (for sins) by good works in the present life; and (3) after death, through prayers and good deeds and thanks to whatever else the Church does for the dead.

Thus, the first remission of sins is not at all bound up with labor; it is common to all and equal in honor, like the pouring out of light and the beholding of the sun and the changes of the seasons of the year, for this is grace alone and of us is asked nothing else but faith. But the second remission is painful, as for one who *every night washes his bed, and with tears waters his couch* (Ps. 6:5), for whom even the traces of the blows of sin are painful, who goes weeping and with contrite face and emulates the conversion of the Ninevites and the humility of Manasses, upon which there was mercy. The third remission is also painful, for it is bound up with repentance and a conscience that is contrite and suffers from insufficiency of good; however, it is not at all mixed with punishment, if it is a remission of sins: for remission and punishment can by no means exist together. Moreover, in the first and last remission of sins the grace of God has the larger part, with the cooperation of prayer, and very little is brought in by us. The middle remission, on the other hand, has little from grace, while the greater part is owing to our labor. The first remission of sins is distinguished from the last by this; that the first is a remission of all sins in an equal degree, while the last is a remission only of those sins which are not mortal and over which a person has repented in life.

Thus does the Church of God think, and when entreating for the departed the remission of sins and believing that it is granted them, it does not define as a law any kind of punishment with relation to them, knowing well that the Divine goodness in such matters conquers the idea of justice.

FROM THE SECOND HOMILY
AGAINST PURGATORIAL FIRE*

3. We affirm that neither the righteous have as yet received the fullness of their lot and that blessed condition for which they have prepared themselves here through works, nor have sinners, after death, been led away into the eternal punishment in which they shall be tormented eternally. Rather, both the one and the other must necessarily take place after the Judgment of that last day and the resurrection of all. Now, however, both the one and the other are in places proper to them: the first, in absolute repose and free, are in heaven with the angels and before God Himself, and already as if in the paradise from which Adam fell (into which the good thief entered before others) and often visit us in those temples where they are venerated, and hear those who call on them and pray for them to God, having received from Him this surpassing gift, and through their relics perform miracles, and take delight in the vision of God and the illumination sent from Him more perfectly and purely than before, when they were alive; while the second, in their turn, being confined in hell, remain *in the lowest pit, in darkness and in the shadow of death* (Ps. 87:7), as David says, and then Job: *to the land where light is as darkness* (Job 10:21–22). And the first remain in every joy and rejoicing, already expecting and only not having in their hands the Kingdom and the unutterable good things promised them; and the second, on the contrary, remain in all confinement and inconsolable suffering, like condemned men awaiting the Judge's sentence and foreseeing those torments. Neither have the first

---

* Russian text in Pogodin, pp. 118–150.

yet received the inheritance of the Kingdom and those good things *which eye hath not seen, nor ear heard, nor have entered into the heart of man* (I Cor. 2:9); nor have the second yet been given over to eternal torments nor to burning in the unquenchable fire. And this teaching we have as handed down from our Fathers in antiquity, and we can easily present it from the Divine Scriptures themselves.

10. That which certain of the saints have seen in vision and revelation regarding the future torment of the impious and sinners who are in it are certain images of future things and as it were depictions, and not what is already in fact happening now. Thus, for example, Daniel, describing that future Judgment, says: *As I looked, thrones were placed and one that was ancient of days took his seat ... and the books were opened* (Daniel 7:9-10), whereas it is clear that this in very fact has not taken place, but was revealed in the spirit beforehand to the Prophet.

19. When we examine the testimonies which you have cited from the book of Maccabees and the Gospel, speaking simply with love for the truth, we see that they do not at all contain any testimony of some kind of punishment or cleansing, but speak only of the remission of sins. You have made a certain astonishing division, saying that every sin must be understood under two aspects: (1) the offense itself which is made to God, and (2) the punishment which follows it. Of these two aspects (you teach), the offense to God, indeed, can be remitted after repentance and turning away from evil, but the liability to punishment must exist in every case; so that, on the basis of this idea, it is essential that those released from sins should all the same be subject to punishment for them.

But we allow ourselves to say that such a stating of the question contradicts clear and commonly known truths: if we do not see that a king, after he has granted an amnesty and pardon, subjects the guilty to yet more punishment, then all the more God, among Whose many characteristics love of mankind is an especially outstanding one, even though He does punish a man after a sin which he has committed, still, after He has forgiven him He immediately delivers him from punishment also. And this is natural. For if the offense to God leads to punishment, then when the guilt is forgiven and reconciliation has occurred, the very consequence of the guilt—the punishment—of necessity comes to an end.

APPENDIX II

Recent Discussion

SOME RECENT ORTHODOX RESPONSES TO THE CURRENT DISCUSSION ON LIFE AFTER DEATH

1. The Mystery of Death and the Beyond*

By Father Ambroise Fontrier
Dean of French Orthodox Parishes
of the Russian Church Outside of Russia

Radio, television, periodicals, and a book have been speaking lately (in France) about death and the beyond. Even a Greek periodical appearing in French, and supposedly Orthodox, has taken part in this chorus, publishing an article entitled: "Tell me why ... no one has ever returned!" And the author concludes: "No human knowledge can give a certain answer to this mystery of the beyond: only faith dissipates the shadows a little...." In passing, he tips his hat to the Lord, Whom he calls "the qualified ferryman ...," a ferryman who strangely recalls Charon, the pilot of hades in Greek mythology, who conducted the souls of the dead over the river Styx in his boat for the price of an obolus.

---

* Translated from the author's periodical *Catchechese Orthodoxe,* vol. VIII, no. 26, pp. 74-84.

If the author of the article in question only had the text of the Orthodox funeral service, or the services for the dead on Saturdays; if he had read the Lives of the Saints or of the Fathers of the desert—he would have been able to "give an answer to this mystery of the beyond" and edify his readers. But our "Orthodox" ecumenists and modernists, owing to their flirtation with this world for which Christ the Saviour did not wish to pray, have become the salt which has lost its savor and which is good for nothing but to be trampled underfoot, according to the infallible word of the Lord.

In order to "dissipate a little the shadows" of the editor of the Greek periodical and edify at the same time our faithful and our readers, we give here three texts on the mystery of death and the beyond.

Tr. note: The first two texts are from St. Dionysius the Areopagite and from the life of an Athonite monk, showing how an Orthodox Christian prepares for death and the separation of the soul from the body. The third text, from the life of the late Greek iconographer, Photios Kontoglou (reposed in 1965) is translated below in full. (For his biography, see The Orthodox Word, *Sept.-Oct., 1966).*

The Great Wager
Between Believers and Unbelievers

By Photios Kontoglou*

On Pascha Monday, in the evening after midnight, before lying down to sleep I went out into the little garden behind my

---

* From his book *Mystical Flowers,* Athens, 1977.

house. The sky was dark and covered with stars. I seemed to see it for the first time, and a distant psalmody seemed to descend from it. My lips murmured, very softly: "Exalt ye the Lord our God, and worship the footstool of His feet." A holy man once told me that during these hours the heavens are opened. The air exhaled a fragrance of the flowers and herbs I had planted. "Heaven and earth are filled with the glory of the Lord."

I could well have remained there alone until break of day. I was as if without a body and without any bond to the earth. But fearing that my absence would disturb those with me in the house, I returned and lay down.

Sleep had not really taken possession of me; I do not know whether I was awake or asleep, when suddenly a strange man rose up before me. He was as pale as a dead man. His eyes were as if open, and he looked at me in terror. His face was like a mask, like a mummy's. His glistening, dark yellow skin was stretched tight over his dead man's head with all its cavities. He was as if panting. In one hand he held some kind of bizarre object which I could not make out; the other hand was clutching his breast as if he were suffering.

This creature filled me with terror. I looked at him and he looked at me without speaking, as if he were waiting for me to recognize him, strange as he was. And a voice said to me: "It is so-and-so!" And I recognized him immediately. Then he opened his mouth and sighed. His voice came from far away; it came up as from a deep well.

He was in great agony, and I suffered for him. His hands, his feet, his eyes—everything showed that he was suffering. In my despair I was going to help him, but he gave me a sign with his hand to stop. He began to groan in such a way that I froze. Then he said to me: "I have not come; I have been sent. I shake without stop; I am dizzy. Pray God to have pity on me. I want to die but I cannot. Alas! Everything you told me before is true. Do you remember how, several days before my death, you came to see me and spoke about religion? There were two other friends with me, unbelievers like myself. You spoke, and they mocked. When you left, they said: 'What a pity! He is intelligent and he believes the stupid things old women believe!'

"Another time, and other times too, I told you: 'Dear Photios, save up money, or else you will die a pauper. Look at my riches, and I want more of them.' You told me then: 'Have you signed a pact with death, that you can live as many years as you want and enjoy a happy old age?'

"And I replied: 'You will see to what an age I will live! Now I am 75; I will live past a hundred. My children are free from want. My son earns a lot of money, and I have married my daughter to a rich Ethiopian. My wife and I have more money than we need. I am not like you who listen to what the priests say: "A Christian ending to our life …" and the rest. What have you to gain from a Christian ending? Better a full pocket and no worries.… Give alms? Why did your so merciful God create paupers? Why should *I* feed them? And they ask you, in order to go to Paradise, to feed idlers! Do you want to talk about Paradise? You know that I am the son of a priest and that I know well all these tricks. That those who have no brains believe them is well enough, but you who have a mind have gone astray. If you continue to live as you are doing, you will die before me, and you will be responsible for those you have led astray. As a physician I tell you and affirm that I will live a hundred and ten years.…' "

After saying all this, he turned this way and that as if he were on a grill. I heard his groans: "Ah! Ouch! Oh! Oh!" He was silent for a moment, and then continued: "This is what I said, and in a few days I was dead! I was dead, and I lost the wager! What confusion was mine, what horror! Lost, I descended into the abyss. What suffering I have had up to now, what agony! Everything you told me was true. *You have won the wager!*

"When I was in the world where you are now, I was an intellectual, I was a physician. I had learned how to speak and to be listened to, to mock religion, to discuss whatever falls under the senses. And now I see that everything I called stories, myths, paper lanterns—is true. The agony which I am experiencing now—this is what is true, this is the worm that never sleeps, this is the gnashing of teeth."

After having spoken thus, he disappeared. I still heard his groans, which gradually faded away. Sleep had begun to take possession of me, when I felt an icy hand touch me. I opened my eyes and saw him again before me. This time he was more horrible and smaller in body. He had become like a nursing infant, with a large old man's head which he was shaking.

"In a short time the day will break, and those who have sent me will come to seek me!"

"Who are they?"

He spoke some confused words which I could not make out. Then he added: "There where I am, there are also many who mock you and your faith. Now they understand that their spiritual darts have not gone beyond the cemetery. There are both those you have done good to, and those who have slandered you. The more you forgive them, the more they detest you. Man is evil. Instead of rejoicing him, kindness makes him bitter, because it makes him feel his defeat. The state of these latter is worse than mine. They cannot leave their dark prison to come and find you as I have done. They are severely tormented, lashed by the whip of God's love, as one of the Saints

218

has said.* The world is something else entirely from what we see! Our intellect shows it to us in reverse. Now we understand that our intellect was only stupid, our conversations were spiteful meanness, our joys were lies and illusions.

"You who bear God in your hearts, Whose word is Truth, the only Truth—you have won the great wager between believers and unbelievers. This wager I have lost. I tremble, I sigh, and I find no rest. In truth, *there is no repentance in hell.* Woe to those who walk as I did when I was on earth. Our flesh was drunk and mocked those who believed in God and eternal life; almost everyone applauded us. They treated you as mad, as imbeciles. And the more you accept our mockeries, the more our rage increases.

"Now I see how much the conduct of evil men grieved you. How could you bear with such patience the poisoned darts which issued from our lips which treated you as hypocrites, mockers of God, and deceivers of the people. If these evil men who are still on earth would see where I am, if only they were in my place, they would tremble for everything they are doing. I would like to appear to them and tell them to change their path, but I do not have the permission to do so, just as the rich man did not have it when he begged Abraham to send Lazarus the pauper. Lazarus was not sent, so that those who sinned might be worthy of punishment and those who went on the ways of God might be worthy of salvation.

"*He that is unrighteous, let him do unrighteousness yet more; and he that is filthy, let him be made filthy yet more. And he that is righteous, let him do righteousness yet more; and he that is holy, let him be made holy yet more*" (Apoc. 22:11).

With these words he disappeared.

---

* St. Isaac the Syrian.

Ed. note: Earlier in the book (chapter 1) we have quoted the teaching of Blessed Augustine that ordinarily it is only the saints who are able to have contact with the living, while ordinary sinners are bound in hell and cannot come out. However, it does happen, as in the present case, that God allows a soul from hell to appear to the living for some special purpose; some similar appearances are recorded in the book Eternal Mysteries Beyond the Grave. *As Blessed Augustine writes: "The dead of themselves have no power to intervene in the affairs of the living" ("Care for the Dead," ch. 16), and appear to the living only by God's special allowance. It remains true, nevertheless, that such appearances are very rare, and the vast majority of the appearances of the "dead," most notably those that occur through mediums, are the work of demons masquerading as the dead.*

2. A Return from the Dead in Contemporary Greece

By Archimandrite Cyprian
Abbot of the Monastery of
Sts. Cyprian and Justina, Fili, Greece

Herewith I am sending you an account of a person I know who died and returned to life, which I think you will find interesting as an example for your series of articles.

About four years ago, we received a call to take Holy Communion to an old lady, a widow living in a suburb of Athens. She was an old calendarist, and being almost bedridden, was unable to get to church. Though normally we do not undertake such services outside the monastery, and would direct people to a parish priest, nonetheless on this occasion I had a special feeling that I should go, and having prepared the Holy Gifts, I set out from the monastery. I found the old lady lying ill in a small and poor room; having no means of her own, she was cared for by various kind neighbors who brought her food and other necessities. I set down the Holy Gifts, and asked her if there was anything she wished to confess. She replied, "No, there is nothing on my conscience from these past years which I have not already confessed, but there is one grave sin from years ago which I would like to tell you, even though I have confessed it to many priests." I replied that if she had already confessed it, she should not do so again. But she insisted, and what she had to tell is as follows:

When she was young and newly married, some 35 years before, she became pregnant at a time when her family was in the greatest financial straits. The other members of the family pressed her to have an abortion, but she refused absolutely. Eventually, however, due to the threats of her mother-in-law, she gave in against her will, and the operation was performed. The medical supervision of the illicit operation was very primitive, with the result that she caught a serious infection, and within the space of a few days died, without being able to confess her sin.

At the moment of death, which occurred in the evening, she felt her soul part from the body in the way that is usually described; her soul remained nearby and watched the body being washed, clothed and placed in the coffin. In the morning, she followed the procession to the church, watched the funeral, and saw the coffin loaded into the hearse for transfer to the cemetery. The soul was as though flying a small height above the body.

Suddenly there appeared in the road two "deacons," as she described them, in shining white sticharia and oraria. One of them was reading a scroll. As the car approached, he held up his hand, and the car ground to a halt. The driver got out to see what was wrong with the motor, and in the meanwhile the angels started to converse. The one holding the scroll, which was clearly the record of her sins, looked up from his reading and said: "It is sad, she has a very serious sin on her list, and is bound for hell, since she did not confess it." "Yes," said the other, "but it is a pity that she should be punished, as she did not want to do it, but was forced into it by her family." "Very well," replied the first, "the only thing to do is to send her back to be able to confess her sin and repent of it."

With these words, she felt herself being drawn back into her body, for which at that moment she felt an indescribable disgust and repulsion. After a moment, she came to, and started to knock on the inside of the coffin, which had been closed. The scene that followed can be imagined.

After hearing her history, which I have set forth in brief, I gave her Holy Communion, and departed giving glory to God who had permitted me to hear it. Being a matter of confession, I cannot tell you her name, but can inform you that she is still alive. If you feel it would be edifying, you certainly have my permission to publish it.

3. The "Dead" Appear in Contemporary Moscow

By Priest Dimitry Dudko*

They say that many are complaining now, especially women: the dead are coming at night.

A woman buried her husband. Yes, she suffered a lot, she wept. She couldn't sleep.

At twelve midnight she heard someone putting a key in the door, a scraping of feet; someone came to her bed.

---

* Translated from his *Sunday Talks on the Resurrection,* St. Job Brotherhood, Montreal, 1977, pp. 63–65, 73–74, 93, 111.

"Valya, it is I."

She jumped up in fear. Yes—before her was her dead husband; a conversation began.

The next night she waited in great fear. He came the next night also.

People told her: You're dreaming. Educated people told her: You're having hallucinations because of your sufferings. Psychiatrists took her under observation....

But what is this, after all? A person is basically normal, but here there is something abnormal. Hallucinations ... But what is a hallucination? Or is it simply some kind of apparition?

Here is a daughter. Her mother died long ago; she isn't even thinking of her, and suddenly—her mother comes, at first alone, then with some kind of children.

A previously happy daughter now has become gloomy.

The daughter was taken to a hospital and treated. But treated for what?

Do we understand what this is about?

Here is a woman who is very disturbed and is thinking of killing herself. She is gloomy. Suddenly someone comes in and goes up to her.

"Vera, what are you thinking of!" A conversation begins, a good, heartfelt conversation.

The woman calms down. The woman who came goes away. After she leaves the woman comes to herself and thinks: how did she come—isn't it late? She looks at the clock—it is 2 a.m. She goes to the door—it is locked.

The next day she checks—did that woman really come to her? She had not visited those people for a long time, five years. They answer. The woman who had come in the night—has been dead for a long time. That means—she came from the other world. This woman feels good.

The first two incidents are alarming, causing fear; the last incident has a calming effect.

Unbelievers will say about both types of incidents: a hallucination, a disordered imagination....

When people don't know what to say, they say: a hallucination, imagination. But does this explain anything?

Let us give another example.

A pilot crashes, and his wife has a dream: "Give me two rubles."

The wife pays no attention; she has the same dream over and over. She begins to be alarmed. She asks: why is this happening?

Some say: pay no attention; but this doesn't calm her. Previously she had never gone to church or thought about God; but now she turns to church people. They advise her to have a pannikhida served. She doesn't know how to do it. They explain to her. She orders a pannikhida and asks: "How much does it cost?"

"Two rubles."

And so here is the meaning of the dream: "Give me two rubles."

After the pannikhida the dreams stopped.

In our time the boundaries of this world and the other world begin to become confused.* What I have related here is

---

* Compare the statement of St. Gregory the Dialogist over 1300 years ago (see above, pp. 164–165): "As the present world approaches its end, the world of eternity looms nearer.... The end of the world merges with the beginning of eternal life.... The spiritual world is moving closer to us, manifesting itself through visions and revelations." The end of this world's existence began with the coming of Christ, and sensitive souls are always seeing how the other world is "breaking into" this world ahead of time and giving "hints" of its existence.

no invention of mine, and not something recited from books; it is what has occurred in our own life, and not so long ago.

We have ceased thinking about the resurrection of the dead, and therefore the dead give us no repose....

What is death? Is there life there? As long as everything seems all right with us, we do not think about these questions. But there are cases when suddenly the boundaries of this world are torn away and a man sees something that later overturns his whole consciousness.

Perhaps some of you have read in a pre-revolutionary book how a certain person, by the name of Uekskuell, suddenly found himself in the other world; he later described all this himself.* And before this he had even been an atheist; he did not accept life after death and laughed at those who did accept it.

He saw his own body which he had left, and the people gathered around it. It seemed strange to him why they had gathered there. After all, he was not there, but here. He wanted to tell them about this, but his voice was lost in emptiness; they didn't hear him. He wanted to touch them with his hand, but his hand went right through them without touching them.

Just imagine what it would be like to be in such a situation.

We will not say what he saw, but after this vision, when returned again to his body, he abandoned all pleasures and dedicated himself to God....

Such things happen in order to bring us to our senses.

Today this isn't happening to us, but it will be.

Such people returned to life in order to finish life righteously; but will we return? God knows....

---

* Many excerpts from this book, "Unbelievable for Many but Actually a True Occurrence," are given above; see Index.

We will not read of the terrors Uekskuell experienced in trying to draw attention to himself. The world beyond the grave almost touches ours, it seems just a fraction of a millimeter away; but we don't entirely come together. And this isn't the only such incident....

I myself have heard of a man, who is still alive today, who experienced clinical death; people thought he was dead, but after his clinical death he told them everything they had said, and how they moved, in all details.

Man is not only this body, matter, dust; man is composed of body and soul. And the soul does not die like the body; it sees and knows everything....

Is there life after death or not? In the end, all this is taken on faith. That there is life there, we accept on faith; that there is no life there, we also accept on faith. But in order to say for sure, as the boy (mentioned above) says ... one must go there. And as long as we have not gone, some have faith, from which they rejoice and do good deeds; while others, just like the demons, believe and tremble. Unbelievers all tremble before the face of death, and no matter how many medicines there might be, no matter how long one might prolong earthly life, you still will not escape death. One can escape death only through faith in our Lord Jesus Christ.

Appendix III

Answer to a Critic

As the present book was being printed in serial form in *The Orthodox Word*, the editor of another Orthodox periodical began publishing a long series of attacks on the teaching of life after death set forth here (*The Tlingit Herald*, published by the St. Nectarios American Orthodox Church, Seattle, Washington; vol. 5, no. 6 and following issues). These attacks were directed, not only against the teaching of the present book, but also against the teaching set forth in the publications of Holy Trinity Monastery in Jordanville, New York (especially the issue of *Orthodox Life* of January-February, 1978, the booklet "Unbelievable for Many but Actually a True Occurrence," which appeared in *Orthodox Life* for July-August, 1976, and the anthology *Eternal Mysteries Beyond the Grave*); against the sermon of Archbishop John Maximovitch, "Life After Death," which appeared in *The Orthodox Word*, 1971, no. 4, and is reprinted above in Chapter Ten of this book; against the whole teaching of Bishop Ignatius Brianchaninov which has inspired this book; and in general against the teaching which has been set forth in so many Orthodox sources in the past several centuries and expresses the living piety of the Orthodox faithful even today.

After reading these attacks I have not found it necessary to change anything I have written here; I have only added a few paragraphs here and there to make more clear the Orthodox teaching which, I believe, is most unfairly caricatured and misinterpreted in these attacks.

There would be no purpose in making a point-by-point reply to this critic. His Patristic citations hardly ever make the points he thinks they are making, and the only reply to them is to indicate that they have been misapplied. Thus, for example: all the quotes showing that man is composed of both soul and body (7:2, p. 26, etc.)—which no one denies—say nothing whatever against the independent activity of the soul after death, which has so much evidence in its favor as to seem quite beyond "refutation" if one trusts the Orthodox sources; the many places in Scripture and in Patristic texts where death is expressed metaphorically as a "sleep" say nothing whatever of the "literal truth" of this metaphor, which has been taught by only a very few Christian teachers over the centuries and certainly is in disagreement with the Church's accepted teaching; etc. A collection of "proof texts" makes sense only if it actually *proves* an issue in dispute, not if it talks about something a little different or does not speak clearly and explicitly to the issue.

While on the one hand the critic amasses long lists of often irrelevant quotations, his more usual polemical technique is to dismiss his opponents with a sweeping statement that either has no evidence behind it at all, or else obviously contradicts a good part of the evidence. Thus, if the critic wishes to dispute the possibility of communications from people who have come back to life from the dead, he categorically declares: "These things are simply not possible" (vol. 5, no. 6, p. 25)—despite the fact that Orthodox literature contains numerous such communications; if he wants to deny that demons are seen by men after death, he proclaims: "The fathers teach no such thing" (6:12, p. 24)—despite the numerous Patristic references, for example, to the "toll-houses" encountered after death. If the critic does acknowledge the existence of evidence which disputes his point, he dismisses it with a sweeping accusation: it is all "allegories" or "moral fables" (5:6, p. 26).

The critic is also much addicted to rather cruel *ad hominem* arguments which attempt to discredit anyone who disagrees with him: "It is interesting that some people, together with the Latins, seem to think that the Scripture need not necessarily be conformed with" (6:12, p. 30)—this is said in a context where he has just "swept away" the teaching of Bishop Ignatius Brianchaninov, who, at least indirectly, is thus accused of disrespect for the Scriptures. The views of others who disagree with the critic are liable to be smeared with such unflattering epithets as "Origenistic" (6:12, p. 31) or "blasphemous" (5:6, p. 23), and the opponents themselves dismissed as having a "Platonic-Origenistic mind" or as being "under heavy Latin-Scholastic-Hellenistic influence, in a state of spiritual delusion … or simply abysmally ignorant" (6:12, p. 39).

It may already be seen, perhaps, that the polemical level of the critic in his attacks against respected Orthodox theological authorities is not very high. But because this critic, in his own way, does seem to reflect the misconceptions of some Orthodox people who are not at home in the Orthodox literature which describes life after death, it may be useful to answer some of the objections he has to the traditional Orthodox teaching on life after death.

1. The "Contradictions" of Orthodox Literature on the Soul after Death

Despite the common opinion that the Orthodox literature on life after death is "naive" and "simple," if one looks at it carefully one discovers that it is actually quite subtle and even "sophisticated." Some of it, it is true, can be read by a child on his own level—as a fascinating "story" on the same level as other incidents in the Lives of Saints (which is where some of the Orthodox after-death literature is to be found). But this material has been handed down to us by the Church not because of its "story" qualities, but precisely because it is *true;* and indeed, a chief source of this material is the ascetic treatises of the Holy Fathers, where this teaching is presented in a very sober and straightforward manner, and not at all in "story" form. Therefore, a more "sophisticated" examination of this material can also bear fruit. We have tried to do something like this in Chapter Six above, in the section called "How to Understand the Toll-Houses," where, following the explanations of St. Gregory the Dialogist and other Orthodox authorities who have examined these questions, we distinguished between the *spiritual reality* which the soul encounters after death and the *figurative or interpretative devices* which are sometimes used to express this spiritual reality. The Orthodox person who is at home in this kind of literature (often through having heard it from childhood) automatically reads it on his own level and interprets its images in accordance with his own spiritual understanding. "Bags of gold," "pyres of wood," "dwellings of gold," and such things in the other world are not interpreted by adult readers in a literal sense, and the attempt of our critic to discredit such Orthodox sources because they contain such figurative images only reveals that he does not understand how to read these sources.

Thus, many of the supposed "contradictions" in Orthodox literature concerning the other world exist in the minds of those who try to read this literature in an overly literal manner—for adults who artificially try to understand it in a childish way.

Some other "contradictions," on the other hand, are not really contradictions at all. That some saints and others whose accounts are accepted in the Church speak of their "after-death" experience and others do not is no more a "contradiction" than the fact that some saints oppose having their relics moved, while others bless such a move: this is a matter of individual need and circumstances. The critic cites the example of St. Athanasius the Resurrected of the Kiev Caves, who would say nothing of what he experienced after death, and uses this to make the categorical assertion: "Nor have such people ever told us *anything* of what took place" (7:1, p. 31; emphasis his). But the Soldier Taxiotes (Lives of Saints, March 28), St. Salvius of Albi, and many others *did* speak of their experience, and it is surely a most unscholarly and "selective" use of sources to deny their testimony. Some, like St. Salvius, at first were very hesitant to speak of this experience, but nevertheless they *did* speak of it; and this fact, far from proving that there is no such thing as experiences after death, only indicate how rich this experience is and how difficult it is to communicate it to the living.

Again, the fact that many Fathers (and the Church in general) warn against the acceptance of demonic visions (and sometimes, due to particular circumstances, they do this in very categorical terms) does not in the least "contradict" the fact that many true visions are accepted in the Church.

Often the critic in his attacks falsely applies a general Patristic statement, divorced from its context, to a particular situation which it does not fit. When St. John Chrysostom, for example, in Homily 28:3 on St. Matthew, states "nor is it possible for a soul, torn away from the body, to wander here any more," he is speaking specifically against the pagan idea that dead souls can become demons and remain indefinitely on earth; but this general truth in no way contradicts or even touches on the specific fact that, as numerous Orthodox testimonies show, many souls do indeed stay near earth for a few hours or days after death before departing to the truly "other" world. In this same passage St. Chrysostom adds that "after their departure hence our souls are led away into some place, having no more power *of themselves* to come back again"—and this likewise does not contradict the fact that, *at God's command* and for His purposes, some souls do indeed appear to the living (see the article of Photios Kontoglou above in Appendix II).

Again the fact that Christ cleared the air of the malignity of demons, as St. Athanasius the Great teaches, does not in any way deny the existence of the demonic toll-houses in the air, as the critic implies (6:8–9, p. 13); indeed, the critic himself in another place quotes the Orthodox teaching that the evil spirits which are *still* in the air cause many temptations and fantasies (6:6–7, p. 33). The Church's teaching is that whereas before our redemption by Christ, *no one* could pass through the air to heaven, the path being closed by demons, and *all men* went down to hell, now it has become *possible* for men to pass through the demons of the air, and their power now is restricted to men whose own sins convict them. In the same way, we know that even though Christ "destroyed the power of hell" (Kontakion of Pascha), any one of us can still fall into hell by rejecting salvation in Christ.

Still again, the fact that our spiritual battle against "principalities and powers" takes place in this life by no means contradicts the fact that this battle occurs also as we leave this life. The section in Chapter Six above entitled "The Toll-Houses Experienced before Death" explains the connection between these two aspects of the Orthodox unseen warfare.

That the third, ninth, and fortieth-day memorials for the dead are sometimes explained by the symbolism of the Trinity, the nine ranks of angels, and the Ascension of Christ, in no way denies the fact that these days are somehow bound up *also* with what is happening to the soul on those days (according to the "model" described above in Chapter Ten). Neither explanation is a dogma, neither "contradicts" the other; there is no need for an Orthodox Christian to deny either of them.

The undeniable fact that our fate after death depends on what we do in this life is not at all contradicted by the equally undeniable fact that prayer for the dead can alleviate their lot and even change their state, in accordance with the Orthodox teaching set forth by St. Mark of Ephesus and by the Orthodox Church in general (see above, Chapter Ten and Appendix I). The critic is so intent on finding "contradictions" in this teaching that he finds them even in one and the same Orthodox teacher, stating that St. John of Kronstadt sometimes teaches the "Patristic understanding" and sometimes the "Scholastic concept" (7:3, p. 28). St. Mark of Ephesus is also guilty of the same "contradiction"; for, while making statements on prayer for the dead which the critic thinks are "Patristic," he also teaches clearly that "the souls of the departed are delivered by prayer from confinement in hell as if from a certain prison" (see above, p. 202), which the critic regards as a "Scholastic concept," since he regards it as impossible that prayers for the dead can change their condition or obtain repose for them (7:3, p. 23).

The answer to all these and many other supposed "contradictions" which the critic thinks he has found in the Orthodox teaching on life after death is to be found in a fairer and less simple-minded reading of the Orthodox texts themselves. The Patristic and hagiographical texts do not "contradict" themselves; if we will read the Orthodox literature on life after death more deeply and thoroughly, we will find that it is not the texts that are a problem, but our own imperfect understanding of them.

2. Is there such a thing as an "out-of-body" experience (whether before or after death), or an "other world" which souls inhabit?

The critic's opinion about "out-of-body" experiences is categorical: "These things are simply not possible" (5:6, p. 25). He gives no evidence for this assertion, but only his own opinion that all the many Orthodox texts that discuss such things are "allegories" or "moral fables" (5:6, p. 26). Heaven, paradise, and hell are not "places," according to him, but only "states" (6:2, p. 23); "the soul cannot function on its own, but only by means of the body" (6:8–9, p. 22), and therefore not only can be in no "place " after death, but cannot even function *at all* (6:8–9, p. 19); "to suppose that this complex realm is yonder beyond one's repose is sheer madness" (6:6–7, p. 34).

But is it really possible that the soul in itself is nothing but "inwardness" and "repose" and has no "outward" aspect whatever, no "place" where it functions? This is surely a radical teaching for Orthodox Christianity, and, if true, would certainly require (as the critic already suggests) a radical reinterpretation and indeed revision of the Patristic and hagiographical texts which describe the soul's activities in precisely the "outward" form—as knowing, seeing, communicating, etc.

Now, it is one thing to say (as the Orthodox authorities who have examined such questions invariably say) that one must be careful not to read the Orthodox texts on the other world and life after death in too literal or earthly a manner, since that reality is in many obvious ways very different from earthly reality; but it is quite something else to "sweep away" all these texts and deny that they refer to anything *at all* in an outward way, and are nothing but "allegories" and "fables." The Orthodox literature on this subject describes it rather matter-of-factly as it appears to the person undergoing such experiences, and the Orthodox Church and faithful have always accepted these descriptions as corresponding faithfully to reality, even while making allowances for the peculiar, other-worldly nature of this reality.

It is probably no exaggeration to say that no Orthodox writer has ever been so *dogmatic* in describing the nature of this other-worldly reality as the present critic is in denying it altogether. This is not a sphere for categorical assertions. St. Paul, in describing his own spiritual experiences in the most general terms, is careful to say "whether in the body, I cannot tell; or whether out of the body, I cannot tell: God knoweth" (II Cor. 12:2). St. John Chrysostom in his interpretation of this passage shows the same caution in saying: "Were only his mind and soul caught up, while the body remained dead? Or was the body also caught up? This cannot be said for certain. If the Apostle Paul himself, who was caught up and was vouchsafed so many and such unutterable revelations, did not know this, how much less do we know it.... And if anyone should say: How is it possible to be caught up out of the body? I will ask him: How is it possible to be caught up *in* the body? The latter is even more difficult than the former, if one is to examine it according to reason and not submit oneself to faith" (Homily 26:1 on II Corinthians, in Volume 10:1 of his *Works* in Russian, Saint Petersburg, 1904, p. 690).

Similarly, St. Andrew the Fool for Christ, in describing his state during his own experience of heaven, says: "I saw myself as if without flesh, because I did not feel the flesh.... In appearance I was in the body, but I did not feel the weight of the body; I felt no natural needs for the course of the whole two weeks when I was caught up. This leads me to the thought that I was out of the body. I do not know how to say for sure; this is known to God, the Knower of hearts" (from his complete Life by Nicephorus, quoted in Bishop Ignatius, vol. III, p. 88).

Such Orthodox authorities, then—an Apostle, a great Father, a Saint of the most exalted life—all regard it as at least possible to speak of an experience of heaven as occurring "out of the body"; and it is certainly clear from their words that such experiences, whether they are "in" or "out" of the body, have something bodily and outward about them—otherwise there would be no need to speak of the "body" at all in connection with them. In this book we have tried to describe such experiences as simply as possible in the language of the Orthodox sources themselves, without attempting to give a precise definition of this state. Bishop Theophan the Recluse, in his commentary on St. Paul's statement in II Corinthians 12:2, says perhaps as much as need be said on this subject: "Within or in the depths of the world that is visible to us is hidden another world, just as real as this one—whether spiritual or finely material, God knows; what is certain is that in it the angels and saints dwell.... He (St. Paul) cannot say whether he was caught up in the body or out of the body; this, he says, God alone knows. Evidently, for us this knowledge is not necessary.... A great precision in these details is not required, and it cannot be expected that anyone should say something absolutely certain when the Apostle Paul himself is silent" (Bishop Theophan, *Commentary on the Second Epistle of the Holy Apostle Paul to the Corinthians,* Moscow, 1894, pp. 401–403).

Probably every Orthodox reader of the "other-worldly" elements in the Lives of Saints is to some extent aware that the nature of this world and these experiences is not to be precisely defined; the way they are expressed in these sources is exactly the most appropriate and accurate way they *can* be expressed in the language of this world. The attempt to dismiss these experiences as "allegories" or "fables," and to define precisely the fact that they *cannot* occur as stated, has no justification in Orthodox teaching and tradition.

3. Does the soul "sleep" after death?

The critic is so opposed to the activities of the soul in the other world, especially after death, such as are described in numerous Lives of Saints, that he ends by teaching a whole doctrine of the soul's "repose" or "slumber" after death—a device which renders all these activities simply impossible! He states: "In the Orthodox understanding, at death, the soul is held to be assigned to a state of repose by an act of the Will of God, and enter into a condition of inactivity, a sort of sleep in which it does not function, hear or see" (6:3–9, p. 19); the soul in this state "can know nothing at all, nor remember anything at all" (6:2, p. 23).

Even among the heterodox, such a doctrine of "soul-slumber" is to be found in our times only in a few of the sects which are far from historical Christianity (Jehovah's Witnesses, Seventh-Day Adventists); how astonishing it is, therefore, to find it here proclaimed so categorically as *Orthodox!* If one or two early teachers in the Church (Aphraates of Syria, St. Anastasius of Sinai), as the critic claims, did perhaps teach such a doctrine in an unambiguous way, it is abundantly clear that the Orthodox Church herself never followed them, but in its Divine services, in the works of its great Fathers, in its ascetic treatises, and in its Lives of Saints has taught so clearly that the soul is active and "awake" after death that one is justly appalled at the radicalness of the critic's teaching.

The critic himself seems to waver in his idea of what the "sleep" of the soul means, sometimes defining it in terms of an exalted "hesychast" vocabulary that somewhat softens its radicalness; but at least he is consistent in saying that the supposed "sleep" of the soul after death makes *absolutely impossible* any "outward" experiences of the soul. And as long as he continues to speak of death as a state of "inactivity" in which the soul "can know nothing at all, nor remember anything at all," it is clear that for him the word "sleep" does have a meaning that is more than metaphorical.

There would be little point in searching in the Fathers for specific "refutations" of this doctrine, for it was seldom taken seriously enough in the Church to require a specific refutation. In Chapter Ten above we have cited the teaching of St. Ambrose that the soul is "more active" when freed from the body after death, St. Abba Dorotheus' statement that the soul "remembers everything at its exit from this body more clearly and distinctly once freed from the earthliness of the body," and St. John Cassian's teaching that the soul "becomes yet more alive" after death; and similar statements could be found in many Fathers. But such citations are only a small part of the Orthodox evidence that refutes the theory of "soul-slumber." The whole Orthodox piety and practice of prayer for the dead surely presupposes that souls are "awake" in the other world and that their lot can be alleviated; the Orthodox calling on the saints in prayer, and the saints' response to this prayer, is unthinkable without the conscious activity of the saints in heaven; the immense Orthodox literature on the manifestations of saints after death cannot simply all be cast away as "fables." If the critic is right, then the Church has certainly been "wrong" for quite a few centuries.

The critic has tried to take unfair advantage of the fact that the teaching of the Orthodox Church on life after death has many elements in it that are not "precisely defined"—not because the Church does not know what it thinks on this subject, but because the reality of the other world is (to state the obvious once again) quite different from this-worldly reality and does not easily lend itself to the "dogmatic" approach the critic has taken towards it. The living contact of the saints of heaven, and sometimes of other of the dead also, with the earthly Church is known in the piety and experience of Orthodox Christians and does not need to be precisely defined; but to make this want of a "precise definition" an excuse for teaching that the souls even of the saints are in a state of "repose" that prevents any "outward" contact with men on earth, surely oversteps the bounds permissible for Orthodox Christian belief.

Among the other "after-death" experiences which the theory of "soul-slumber" does away with is one universally believed in the Church from the very beginning: the descent of the dead Christ into hell. "In the grave bodily, in hell with the soul as God, in paradise with the thief, and on the Throne with the Father and the Spirit was Thou Who fillest all things, O Christ the Infinite" (Troparion of the Hours of Pascha, used as one of the secret prayers after the Cherubic Hymn at the Divine Liturgy). The earliest generation of Christians knew without a doubt that Christ, while he was "asleep" in the tomb (as stated in the Exapostilarion of Pascha, the Kontakion of Great Saturday, etc.), *went and preached unto the spirits in prison* (hell) (I Peter 3:19). Is this also an "allegory"? The Church's tradition is also very strong that, even before this, St. John the Baptist "went rejoicing to declare to those in hell the good tidings of God having appeared in the flesh," as the troparion for the feast of his Beheading states. And what was it that the three disciples saw on the Mount of Transfiguration when they beheld Moses, if it was not his soul, which appeared in quite an "outward" manner (Matt. 17:3)? This manifestation, indeed, as it were, confirms St. Paul's hesitancy in declaring whether his own vision of heaven was "in" or "out" of the body—for Elias dwells in heaven "in" the body, having never died, while Moses is there "out of the body," his body being in the grave; but both of them appeared at Christ's Transfiguration. We earth-dwellers cannot even define the difference between these two states, but there is no need to; the simple description of such manifestations, as well as of experiences of the "dead" in the other world, evidently give us our best understanding of these matters, and there is no need for us to try to understand them in any way but the simple way the Church presents them to us.

The critic, apparently, has fallen into the very accusation he has made against others: he has taken an image, that of the "sleep" of death, which is universally accepted in the Church as a metaphor, and interpreted it in some way as a "literal truth." He often does not even notice that the very sources he quotes to support his ideas are, on the contrary, the surest *disproof* of his theory. He quotes St. Mark of Ephesus (using our translation which first appeared in *The Orthodox Word,* no. 79, p. 90) that the righteous "are in heaven with the angels before God Himself, and already as if in the paradise from which Adam fell (into which the good thief entered before others) and often visit us in those temples where they are venerated, and hear those who call on them and pray for them to God...." (6:12, p. 18). If all this (which certainly involves "outward" activity) can be done by a soul that is actually "sleeping"—that is, in "a condition of inactivity in which it does not function, hear or see" (6:8–9, p. 19)—then the theory of "soul-slumber" has no real function because it explains nothing at all, and the critic only confuses the faithful by using it.

4. Are the toll-houses "imaginary"?

The critic's greatest wrath is directed against the Orthodox ascetic teaching on the demonic toll-houses encountered by the soul after death, and one suspects that it is his desire to destroy the very concept of them that has led him into such a self-contradictory theory as that of "soul-slumber." The language he uses to describe the toll-houses is quite categorical and rather immoderate. He speaks of the "imaginary after-death toll-houses" (6:8-9, p. 18) and calls the accounts of them in Orthodox literature "wild tales" (6:8-9, p. 24) and "tales of horror well calculated to cast the soul into despair and unbelief" (7:1, p. 33); "the toll-house myth is ... utterly alien to God and His Holy Church" (7:1, p. 23). But when he tries to describe his own understanding of the toll-houses, the result is a caricature so preposterous that one cannot believe he has even read the texts in question. For him the accounts of the toll-houses "would have us believe that satan owns 'the road to God's kingdom' and can collect a tariff of those who travel on it.... The demons grant an indulgence of passage in return for the excess merits of a saint" (6:2, p. 22). The toll-houses, he thinks, describe "a wandering soul needing to be prayed to rest (as the pagans believed)"; it is an "occult concept about the journey of the soul being paid for by prayers and alms" (6:2, p. 26). He looks for "foreign influences" to explain how such a concept ever got into the Orthodox Church, and concludes (without a shred of evidence, however, apart from the same kind of vague parallels that lead anthropologists to conclude that Christianity is just another pagan "resurrection cult") that "the toll-house myth is the direct product of the oriental astrology cults which hold that all creation is not in the care of a just and loving God" (7:1, p. 23); "these toll-houses are merely an illogical mutation of these pagan myths" (6:8–9, p. 24). He finds the toll-houses to be virtually identical with the Latin doctrine of "purgatory," and states that "the difference between the purgatory myth and that of the aerial toll-houses is that the one gives God satisfaction by means of physical torment, while the other gives Him His needed satisfaction by means of mental torture" (6:12, p. 23).* The account of Theodora's passage through the toll-houses (Lives of Saints, March 26) the critic calls a "heresy-filled tale" (6:8–9, p. 24) based upon a "hallucination" (7:2, p. 14) of someone who, in Old Testament times, "would have justly been taken out and stoned" because he "was in a state of abject spiritual delusion" (6:6–7, p. 28). (Why the critic should be so angry against Theodora's account is not clear; it is only one of many similar accounts and teaches nothing different from them—so much so that I saw no need to quote it above in the chapter on the toll-houses.)

These extreme accusations are personal opinions of the critic which certainly have no evidence behind them. One wonders why he insists on making up his own interpretation of the toll-houses and refuses to understand them as the Church has always understood them; the caricature which he is railing

---

* The comparison of the toll-houses with "purgatory" is surely far-fetched. The toll-houses are part of the Orthodox ascetic teaching and have to do solely with the "testing" of a man for the sins committed by him: they give no "satisfaction" to God and their purpose is certainly not "torture." "Purgatory," on the other hand, is a legalistic Latin misinterpretation of an entirely different aspect of Orthodox eschatology—the state of the souls in hell (*after* the testing of the toll-houses) which may yet be bettered by the prayers of the Church. The Latin sources themselves give no indication that demons have any part at all in the pains of those in "purgatory."

against has never been taught in the Orthodox Church, and one is at a loss to know from what source he has taken his preposterous interpretations.

For some sixteen centuries the Fathers of the Church have spoken of the toll-houses as a part of the Orthodox ascetic teaching, the final and decisive stage of the "unseen warfare" which each Christian wages upon earth. For the same period of time numerous Lives of Saints and other Orthodox texts have described the actual experiences of Orthodox Christians, both saints and sinners, who have encountered these toll-houses after death (and sometimes before). It is obvious to all but the youngest children that the name of "toll-house" is not to be taken literally; it is a metaphor which the Eastern Fathers have thought appropriate for describing the reality which the soul encounters after death. It is also obvious to all that some of the elements in the descriptions of these toll-houses are metaphorical or figurative. The accounts themselves, however, are neither "allegories" nor "fables," but straightforward accounts of personal experiences in the most adequate language at the disposal of the teller. If the descriptions of the toll-houses seem too "vivid" for some, it is probably because they have not been aware of the actual nature of the unseen warfare waged during this life. Now too we are constantly beset by demonic tempters and accusers, but our spiritual eyes are closed and we see only the *results* of their activities—the sins into which we fall, the passions which develop in us. But after death, the eyes of the soul are open to spiritual reality and see (usually for the first time) the actual beings who have been attacking us during our lifetime.

There is no paganism, no occultism, no "oriental astrology," no "purgatory" whatever to be found in the Orthodox accounts of the toll-houses. These toll-houses teach us, rather, of the accountability of each man for his own sins, of the fact that at death there is a summing up of his success or failure in battling against sin (the Particular Judgment), and that the demons who have tempted him throughout life make their final assault upon him at the end of his life, but have power only over those who have not sufficiently fought the unseen warfare in this lifetime.

As for the literary forms in which they are expressed, the toll-houses appear alike in the Divine services of the Church (the Church's poetry), in the ascetic writings of the Fathers, and in the Lives of Saints. No Orthodox person reads any of these texts in the crudely literal way the critic has read them, but approaches them with respect and the fear of God, looking for spiritual benefit. Any spiritual father who has tried to educate his spiritual children in the age-old tradition of Orthodox piety can testify to the beneficial effect of the Orthodox sources which mention the toll-houses; indeed, the late Archbishop Andrew of Novo-Diveyevo, a widely loved and respected spiritual father, used precisely the twenty toll-houses through which Theodora is described as passing as the foundation for a very effective preparation for the sacrament of confession by his spiritual children. If there is any "disharmony" of these texts with 20th-century man, the fault lies in our pampered, permissive times, which encourage disbelief in and a lax attitude towards the truly awesome realities of the other world, and especially those of hell and judgment.

The teaching of the toll-houses in Orthodox sources has never been defined as a "dogma," belonging rather to the tradition of Orthodox piety; but this does not mean that it is something "unimportant" or something that is a matter of "personal opinion." It has been taught everywhere and at all times in the Church wherever the Orthodox ascetic tradition has been handed down. If it is a subject that has been rather outside the area of concern of many recent Orthodox theologians, this is precisely because these theologians belong first of all to the academic world and not to the ascetic tradition. Theologians of a more traditional bent, however, as well as those for whom the Orthodox ascetic tradition is a living thing, have given this subject much attention. Outside of the Russian Church, where the teaching of the toll-houses has been much discussed and defended by Bishop Ignatius Brianchaninov, Bishop Theophan the Recluse, Metropolitan Macarius of Moscow, St. John of Kronstadt, Archbishop John Maximovitch, Protopresbyter Michael Pomazansky, and numerous other teachers and theologians, it has been most emphasized in the Serbian Church, where it occupies an honored place in the *Dogmatic Theology* of the late Archimandrite Justin Popovich (vol. III). However, it has become more noticed in recent years as translations especially of Orthodox ascetical literature and the Divine services have become more available in Western languages. We will note here a few passages on the toll-houses that have appeared in English editions in the past few years and have not yet been quoted in the course of this book:

From the *Fifty Spiritual Homilies* of St. Macarius the Great, one of the basic works of Orthodox ascetic literature (A. J. Mason translation, Eastern Orthodox Books, Willits, California, 1974):

> When the soul of a man departs out of the body, a great mystery is there accomplished. If it is under the guilt of sins there come bands of devils, and angels of the left hand, and powers of darkness take over that soul, and hold it fast on their side. No one ought to be surprised at this. If, while alive and in this world, the man was subject and compliant to them, and made himself their bond-

man, how much more, when he departs out of this world, is he kept down and held fast by them (Homily 22, p. 171).

Like tax-collectors sitting in the narrow ways, and laying hold upon the passers-by, and extorting from them, so do the devils spy upon souls, and lay hold of them; and when they pass out of the body, if they are not perfectly cleansed, they do not suffer them to mount up to the mansions of heaven and to meet their Lord, and they are driven down by the devils of the air. But if whilst they are yet in the flesh, they shall with much labor and effort obtain from the Lord the grace from on high, assuredly these, together with those who through virtuous living are at rest, shall go to the Lord, as He promised.... (Homily 43, p. 274).

From the *Ladder of Divine Ascent,* another standard Orthodox ascetic text (Archimandrite Lazarus Moore translation, revised by Holy Transfiguration Monastery, Boston, 1978):

Others (of the dying) said dolefully: "Will our soul pass through the irresistible water of the spirits of the air?"—not having complete confidence, but looking to see what would happen in that rendering of accounts (Step 5, p. 60).

Indeed, the "Letter of Abba John of Raithu" that introduces the *Ladder* indicates the very purpose why such books are written:

As a ladder set up, (this book) will lead aspirants to the gates of Heaven pure and blameless, so that they may pass unhindered the spirits of wickedness, and the world-rulers of darkness, and the princes of the air (*Ibid.,* p. xlii).

From "On Watchfulness and Holiness" by St. Hesychios the Priest, in Volume I of the complete Greek *Philokalia* (Palmer-Sherrard-Ware translation, Faber and Faber, London, 1979):

> If the soul has Christ with it, it will not be disgraced by its enemies even at death, when it rises to heaven's entrance; but then, as now, it will boldly confront them. But let it not tire in calling upon the Lord Jesus Christ, the Son of God, day and night until the time of its departure from this mortal life, and He will speedily avenge it.... Indeed, He will avenge it both in this present life and after its departure from its body (#149, p. 188).
>
> The hour of death will come upon us, it will come, and we shall not escape it. May the prince of this world and of the air find our misdeeds few and petty when he comes, so that he will not have good grounds for convicting us. Otherwise we shall weep in vain (#161, p. 190).
>
> [An unwatchful man] cannot free himself from evil thoughts, words and actions, and because of these thoughts and actions he will not be able freely to pass the lords of hell when he dies (#4, p. 163).

From "On Spiritual Knowledge" by St. Diadochos of Photike:

> If we do not confess our involuntary sins as we should, we shall discover an ill-defined fear in ourselves at the hour of our death. We who love the Lord should pray that we may be without fear at that time; for if we are afraid then, we will not be able freely to pass by the rulers of the nether world. They will have as their advocate to plead against us the fear which our soul experiences because of its own wickedness. But the soul which rejoices in the love of God, at the hour of its departure, is lifted

with the angels of peace above all the hosts of darkness
(#100, p. 295).

From "Texts for the Monks in India" by St. John of
Karpathos, from the same Volume I of the new translation of
the *Philokalia:*

> When the soul leaves the body, the enemy advances
> to attack it, fiercely reviling it and accusing it of its sins in
> a harsh and terrifying manner. But if a soul enjoys the love
> of God and has faith in Him, even though in the past it
> has often been wounded by sin, it is not frightened by the
> enemy's attacks and threats. Strengthened by the Lord,
> winged by joy, filled with courage by the holy angels that
> guide it, encircled and protected by the light of faith, it
> answers the malicious devil with great boldness…. When
> the soul says all this fearlessly, the devil turns his back,
> howling aloud and unable to withstand the name of
> Christ (pp. 303–304).

From the Sunday *Octoechos,* translated by Mother Mary of
Bussy-en-Othe, in a troparion addressed to the Mother of God:

> … In the dread hour of death pluck me out from the
> midst of the accusing demons and from every punishment
> (Sunday Midnight Office, Tone 1, Canticle 7).

Some of these references, it will be noted are partial and
do not give the whole Orthodox teaching on this subject. This
is obviously because they are references to *a teaching with which
the ascetical and hymnological writers themselves and their readers
are already familiar and which they accept,* and there is no need
to "define" it or justify this teaching whenever it is mentioned.
The attempt of the critic, who has noted the existence of some
of these references, to distinguish between such experiences

which occur "before" and those which occur "after" death, and to deny the very possibility of those that occur "after" (6:12, p. 24), is quite artificial, being only a "logical deduction" from his own false teaching on the "sleep" of the soul, and has no support in the ascetic and Divine service texts themselves. The reality of demonic "testing" is one and the same, and the toll-houses are only the final phase of it, sometimes beginning at the end of this life, and sometimes only after death.

Innumerable other references to the toll-houses occur throughout Orthodox ascetic literature, Lives of Saints, and Divine services; most of these have not yet appeared in English. The critic, when he does take notice of such references, is forced to interpret them, not in accordance with the context in which they occur, but rather in accordance with his own "logical deductions" about life after death.

For example, in quoting the Prayer of St. Eustratius (Saturday Midnight Office), "May my soul not see the dark gaze of the evil demons, but may it be received by Thy bright and most radiant angels" (6:12, p. 23), the critic regards this as a proof that the soul does *not* (and *cannot*) see demons after death (this being a necessity for his theory that the soul is "sleeping" then). But it is surely clear to any unprejudiced reader that it means just the *opposite:* that the Saint prays not to see demons precisely because that is the *normal* lot of the soul after death! This is even clearer from the whole context of the Prayer of St. Eustratius, where the words which immediately precede this sentence are: "My soul is troubled and pained at its departure from my wretched and vile body. May the evil design of the adversary not overtake it and cause it to stumble in the darkness for the unknown and known sins which I have performed during this life." It is clear that the teaching of the testing by demons after death (whether or not it is given the name of "toll-houses") was familiar to St. Eustratius and forms the background and context of his prayer; and this is why Bishop Ignatius uses this prayer as an indication that this teaching was well known to the Church even at this early day (the beginning of the 4th century) (Bishop Ignatius, vol. III, pp. 140–141).

Again, the critic quotes the reply of St. Barsanuphius of Gaza to a monk who had asked him to escort him "through the air and along that way which I do not know" as though this reply is a refutation of the idea of the toll-houses. But once more, it is clear that the context both of the question and the answer is one wherein the aerial toll-houses encountered after death are accepted *as a matter of course,* and St. Barsanuphius, in wishing that Christ "make the ascent of your soul unhindered and vouchsafe you to worship the Holy Trinity with boldness, that is, as one delivered"—is only expressing part of the standard teaching on the toll-houses, which was present in the ascetic tradition of Gaza as much as in the rest of the East. (St. Barsanuphius and John, Questions and Answers, no. 145). This incident is also used by Bishop Ignatius as another of his numerous citations from Holy Fathers in defense of the teaching of the toll-houses (p. 145).

Other citations by Bishop Ignatius of ascetic Fathers who clearly teach of the toll-houses include:

> St. Abba Dorotheus of Gaza: "When the soul is insensitive it is profitable to read frequently the Divine Scripture and the sermons of the God-bearing Fathers that inspire contrition, and to remember the fearful Judgment of God, the departure of the soul from the body, and the fearful powers that are to meet it, with whose participation it performed evil in this short and miserable life" (p. 146).

St. Theognostes, another Father of the *Philokalia:* "Unutterable and unspeakable is the sweetness of the soul that departs from the body and is informed of its salvation.... Accompanied by the angel (sent for it), it goes without hindrance through the aerial spaces, not in the least disturbed by the evil spirits; joyfully and boldly it ascends to exclamations of thanksgiving to God, and comes finally to worship its Creator" (p. 147).

Evagrius of Scetis: "Come to your senses and think how you will bear your sudden departure from the body, when the threatening angels will come for you and seize you in an hour when you are not expecting it and at a time you know not! What deeds will you send before you into the air, when your enemies who are in the air begin to test you?" (pp. 148–149; *Prologue,* Oct. 27).

St. John the Almsgiver: "When the soul departs the body and begins to ascend to heaven, it is met by ranks of demons, and they subject it to many hindrances and tests. They test it in lying, slander" (etc.—a long list of sins similar to the twenty given in the life of St. Basil the New). "During the journey of the soul from earth to heaven, the holy angels themselves cannot help it; it is helped only by its own repentance, its good deeds, and most of all by almsgiving. If we do not repent of every sin here due to forgetfulness, then by almsgiving we can be delivered from the violence of the demonic toll-houses" (p. 143; *Prologue,* Dec. 19).

Another Father of the *Philokalia,* St. Peter Damascene, speaks of "the time of death, when the demons will surround my poor soul, holding the records of all the evil I have committed" (in his *Works,* Kiev Caves Lavra, 1905, p. 68).

In the Divine services, as has already been noted, there are many prayers, especially addressed to the Mother of God, which imply or directly state the ascetic teaching regarding the toll-houses. A number of these have been quoted in the course of this book. Bishop Ignatius, in quoting many more of them (from the *Octoechos,* the *Euchologion,* from prayers on the departure of the soul, from Akathists and canons to the Mother of God and various saints), concludes that "the teaching of the toll-houses is encountered as a generally known and accepted teaching throughout the Divine services of the Orthodox Church. The Church declares and reminds its children of it in order to sow in their hearts a soul-saving fear and to prepare them for a safe transition from temporal life to eternal" (vol. III, p. 149).

Typical of the references to the toll-houses in the Orthodox *Menaia* (the twelve volumes of daily services to the saints) is this troparion from the service to St. John Chrysostom (Jan. 27); it occurs in the Canon to the Most Holy Theotokos (Canticle 5), written by "John" (evidently St. John Damascene):

> Grant me to pass through the noetic satraps and the tormenting aerial legions without sorrow at the time of my departure, that I may cry joyfully to Thee, O Theotokos, Who heard the cry "Hail": Rejoice, O unashamed hope of all.

But there is no point in simply multiplying citations in Orthodox literature which show how clearly this teaching has been set forth in the Church over the centuries; Bishop Ignatius gives twenty pages of such citations, and many more could be found. But for those who do not like this teaching, it will always be possible somehow to "reinterpret" it or subject it to caricature. Still, even our critic is forced to admit the existence of at least a few of the Orthodox texts that indicate the demonic testing at death, and he defends his position that the toll-houses are "imaginary" by saying that "such visions are avoidable if we struggle in this life and repent of our sins and acquire virtues" (6:12, p. 24). *But this is the very meaning of the teaching of the toll-houses which he has caricatured and denied!* The teaching of the toll-houses is given to us precisely so that we might labor *now*, might struggle against the demons of the air *in this life*—and then our meeting with them after death will be a victory and not a defeat for us! How many ascetic strugglers has it inspired to do precisely this! But who among us can say that he has won this battle already and need not fear the demonic testing after death?

The present writer remembers well the solemn services for the repose of Archbishop John Maximovitch in 1966, culminating in the day of his funeral. All present felt they were witnessing the burial of a saint; the sadness at parting from him was swallowed up by the joy of acquiring a new heavenly intercessor. And yet several of the hierarchs present, and especially Bishop Savva of Edmonton, inspired the more fervent prayer of the people by citing the "fearful toll-houses" through which even this holy man, this miracle of God's grace in our times, had to pass. No one present thought that our prayers alone would save him from the "tests" of the demons, and no one pictured in his mind an exchange of "tolls" at some "houses" in the sky; but these appeals helped to inspire the fervent piety of the faithful, and doubtless this helped him to get through these toll-houses. The holy man's own life of good deeds and almsgiving, the intercession of the saints whom he glorified on earth, the prayer of the faithful which was actually another product of his love for them—doubtless all this, in a way known to God, and which we need not search out, helped him to repel the assaults of the dark spirits of the air. And when Bishop Savva made a special trip to San Francisco to be present at the services for the fortieth day after Archbishop John's repose, and told the faithful: "I have come to pray together with you for the repose of his soul on this significant and decisive fortieth day, the day when the place is determined where his soul will dwell until the general and terrible Judgment of God" (*Blessed John, The Chronicle of the Veneration of Archbishop John Maximovitch,* St. Herman Brotherhood, 1979, p. 20)—he was again inspiring the prayer of the faithful by citing another belief of the Orthodox teaching on life after death. Such things are seldom heard by Orthodox Christians nowadays, and therefore we should all the more treasure the contact we still have with such representatives of the Orthodox ascetic tradition.

Among Russian Orthodox Church writers, opposition to the teaching of the toll-houses has long been recognized as one of the signs of ecclesiastical "modernism." Thus, Bishop Ignatius devoted a large part of his volume on life after death to the defense of this teaching, which was already under attack in mid-19th century Russia; and incidentally, contrary to the unfounded opinion of the critic that the toll-houses themselves are accepted only by those under "Western influence," the Roman Catholic and Protestant West has no notion whatever of the toll-houses, which exist only in the Orthodox ascetic teaching, and the attack against them in the Church today is precisely from those (as in the modernist Orthodox seminaries) who are strongly "Western" in mentality and have little respect for traditional Orthodox piety.

Quite recently Protopresbyter Michael Pomazansky, perhaps the greatest living theologian of the Orthodox Church, has written an article in defense of the toll-houses, written in part as an answer to the present critic (*Orthodox Russia,* 1979, no. 7; English translation in *Nikodemos,* Summer, 1979). In this article he warns that in our contemporary non-Orthodox society there are often "questions of our Faith (which are) raised and treated from an un-Orthodox point of view by persons of other confessions, and sometimes by Orthodox Christians who no longer have a firm Orthodox foundation under their feet.... In recent years a critical approach to a whole series of our Church views has become more noticeable; these views are accused of being 'primitive,' the result of a 'naive' world view or piety, and they are characterized by such words as 'myths,' 'magic,' and the like. It is our duty to respond to such views."

And Bishop Theophan the Recluse gives perhaps the soberest and most down-to-earth answer to those who are unwilling to accept the Orthodox ascetic teaching: "No matter how absurd the idea of the toll-houses may seem to our 'wise men,' they will not escape passing through them" (see above, p. 86).

The toll-houses are not a "moral fable" made up for "simple people," as the critic believes (5:6, p. 26), they are not a "myth" or "imaginary" or a "wild tale," as he says—but a true account, handed down in the Orthodox ascetic tradition from the earliest centuries, of what awaits each of us at death.

Conclusion

The preservation of the age-old tradition of Orthodox piety in the contemporary world has become a battle against overwhelming odds. The Orthodox flocks for the most part have become so worldly that an Orthodox priest who wishes to hand down and teach this tradition is tempted to despair over the very possibility of such a task. Most priests and bishops end by following their flocks and "adapting" the tradition to the world-liness of the flocks; and thus the tradition fades and dies....

The sermons, lectures, and books of the clergy of most Orthodox jurisdictions today on the subject of life after death show that very little has been preserved of the traditional Orthodox teaching and piety. When the other world is mentioned at all, save in the most general and abstract terms, it is usually as a subject for jokes about "St. Peter" and "pearly gates" such as are often used by worldly Roman Catholic and Protestant clergy. Among many Orthodox Christians the other world has become something far away and very hazy, with which one has no living contact and about which one can say nothing very definite at all.

The suffering Church of Russia—probably due to its sufferings as much as to its innate conservatism—has preserved the traditional Orthodox attitude towards the other world much better than other Orthodox Churches today. In the free world, it is the Russian Church Outside of Russia almost alone that continues to publish the traditional Orthodox literature on this subject, continuing the tradition of the *Prologue* and other pious anthologies of old Russia, and fortunate are those Orthodox Christians who have access to this literature and can accept it in simplicity and piety, avoiding the spirit of "criticism" which leads so many, especially among converts, away from the true tradition and feeling of Orthodoxy.

It need hardly be said how "old-fashioned" the world—even the Orthodox world—regards those who publish and read such literature. It has been the chief purpose of this book to make this "old-fashioned" literature understandable and accessible to today's Orthodox Christians, who can only benefit from reading what has brought such spiritual profit to Orthodox Christian readers for many centuries.

The aim of our critic is exactly the opposite: thoroughly to discredit this literature, to dismiss it as "moral fables" or "wild tales," and to submit the Divine services and Lives of Saints to a thorough "criticism" that will expunge all such elements in them. (See, for example, his elaborate attempt to discredit the Life of St. Basil the New because it contains descriptions of the toll-houses: *Tlingit Herald*, 7:2, p. 14).

Let us give this undertaking the name it deserves: it is the work of the same *Western rationalism* which has attacked the Orthodox Church so many times in the past and has led so many to lose the true understanding and feeling of Orthodox Christianity. In the Roman Catholic and Protestant West, this attack has been thoroughly successful, and whatever Lives of Saints are left there have indeed been expunged of supernatural elements and are often considered "moral fables." While accusing all who oppose his teaching of "scholasticism," the critic proves himself to be perhaps the most "scholastic" of all: his teaching is founded not on the clear and simple texts handed down in the Church from the earliest centuries to our own, but on a series of his own "logical deductions" which require a radical reinterpretation and revision of the evident meaning of the basic Orthodox texts.

It is bad enough that the critic's tone and language are so crude, that he makes such an evil caricature of the Orthodox teaching he is attacking, and that he is so disrespectful of many venerable Orthodox teachers—the very best of those few teachers who have kept alive the Orthodox tradition of piety to our own days. Here is what he says, for example, about the sermon "Life after Death" by Archbishop John Maximovitch (see above, page 176), a holy man and great theologian of our own days: It is "a wild tale about the soul departing and being pursued and tormented by demons.... In this tale, the faithful

were told that when someone reposed, they must quickly begin
to have services said for the repose of the departed soul, since
the soul was in such desperate need of our prayers, and death
was a matter of great terror (evidently, God was unable to move
Himself to mercy or to help the pitiful soul without being
prodded or awakened by the shouts and cries of mortals). This
tale also included a patently blasphemous description of the
repose of the Most Holy Theotokos" (6:2, p. 22). Archbishop
John's name is not mentioned here, although from the description it is precisely clear what sermon the critic is referring to;
but such language shows an intolerable disrespect no matter
which Orthodox authority he might be attacking!

But what is truly tragic is that the critic, by whatever
means, is trying to deprive Orthodox Christians of that very
thing which, even without him, is already disappearing so fast
in our midst: the traditional Orthodox piety towards the other
world, revealed not only in the kind of literature we read (which
the critic is striving to discredit), but even more in our attitude
towards the dead and what we do for them. It is obvious from
the above quote that the critic, unlike Archbishop John, regards
it as unimportant to pray for the reposed immediately after
death, and indeed thinks that the soul does not need and cannot
be benefitted by our "shouts and cries"! Indeed, the critic
specifically states that "the things we ask on behalf of the
reposed are only proclamations of what they are going to receive
anyway" (7:3, p. 27) and have no effect on their eternal lot, not
seeing that by this teaching he is not only contradicting the
Holy Fathers but is also removing the chief motive which impels
people to pray for the dead at all.

How heartless to the dead! How cruel to the living! How
un-Orthodox a teaching! Surely those who pray for the dead do
not in the least understand their prayers as "magical incanta-

tions" (7:3, p. 23) or as "bribes or magical means of forcing God to be merciful" (*Ibid.,* p. 26), as the critic so cruelly states, but pray with good faith (just as in prayers for anything else) that God will indeed in His mercy grant what is asked. The "synergy" of God's will and our prayers cannot be understood by the narrow, truly worse than "scholastic" logic which the critic employs.

Those who still *live* by the traditional Orthodox sources are a dwindling minority today. What is needed are more *helps* to the understanding of this traditional piety, not an undermining and caricaturing of it and disrespect for those who teach it.

The anti-Orthodox teaching on life after death of this critic is all the more dangerous in that it appeals to a very subtle passion of contemporary mankind. The Orthodox teaching on life after death is rather severe and demands a very sober response on our part, full of the fear of God. But mankind today is very pampered and self-centered and would rather not hear of such stern realities as judgment and accountability for sins. One can be much more "comfortable" with an exalted teaching of "hesychasm" that tells us that God is not "really" as stern as the Orthodox ascetic tradition has described Him, that we "really" need have no fear of death and the judgment it brings, that if only we occupy ourselves with exalted spiritual ideas like those in the *Philokalia* (dismissing as "allegories" all the passages on the toll-houses) we will be "safe" under a "loving God" who will not demand an accounting of all our sins, even those forgotten or unrecognized.... The end of these exalted reflections is a state not far different from that of those "charismatics" and others who feel themselves already assured of salvation, or of those who follow the occult teaching that states there is nothing to fear in death.

The true Orthodox teaching on life after death, on the other hand, fills one precisely with the fear of God and the inspiration to struggle for the Kingdom of Heaven against all the unseen enemies who oppose our path. All Orthodox Christians are called to this struggle, and it is a cruel injustice to them to dilute the Orthodox teaching to make them more "comfortable." Let each one read the Orthodox texts most suited to the spiritual level at which he presently finds himself; but let no one tell him that he can dismiss as "fables" the texts he may find "uncomfortable." Fashions and opinions among men may change, but the Orthodox tradition remains ever the same, no matter how few may follow it. May we ever be its faithful children!

APPENDIX TO THE
SECOND EDITION

Dec. 7/20, 1980
[Feast of] St. Ambrose of Milan

May the blessing of the Lord be with you!

Thank you for your "open letter" of November 3 and your personal letter of November 4. I assure you that I found no reason for offense in either of them, and for me they are only the occasion for a friendly discussion of the teaching (at least one aspect of it) and the importance of two great hierarchs and theologians of 19th-century Russia—Theophan the Recluse and Ignatius Brianchaninov.

My comment on page 3* of *The Soul After Death* that Bishop Theophan was perhaps the "only rival" to Bishop Ignatius as a defender of Orthodoxy against modern errors was not meant to imply in any way that Bishop Theophan was inferior as a theologian or a Patristic scholar; I merely had Bishop Ignatius as the center of my attention there, and Bishop Theophan thereby looks a little "smaller" in that context, which of course he was not in reality. In saying, in the same place, that Bishop Theophan's defense of Orthodoxy was

---

* Page xiv–xv in the present edition.

on a less "sophisticated" level than Bishop Ignatius', I was also not implying any inferiority to Bishop Theophan, but only expressing what I believe to be the case: that Bishop Ignatius in general paid more attention to Western views and to combatting them in detail, whereas Bishop Theophan emphasized more single-mindedly the handing down of the Orthodox tradition and only incidentally touched on the Western errors regarding it. I had in mind, for example, the contrast between Bishop Ignatius' long defense and explanation of the toll-houses (which I cite on pp. 73ff* of *The Soul After Death*), and Bishop Theophan's laconic statement (the only one I know of where he criticized the Western skepticism with regard to this teaching) that "no matter how absurd the idea of the toll-houses may seem to our 'wise men,' they will not escape passing through them" (*Psalm 118,* p. 289). By speaking of the "sophisticated" level on which Bishop Ignatius wrote, I only meant to say that he was more concerned than Bishop Theophan to argue with the Western views on their own ground, while Bishop Theophan seemed more inclined to dismiss the Western views without much discussion. But perhaps this was not true in all cases.

Thus, I think that on the relative greatness of these two hierarchs there is no real disagreement between us. I certainly acknowledge Bishop Theophan's greatness as a theologian and a Patristic scholar, and my only reason for emphasizing Bishop Ignatius in *The Soul After Death* is that it was he and not Bishop Theophan who spoke in such detail against the Western errors with regard to the Orthodox teaching on life after death. I very much welcome your research on Bishop Theophan, whom I greatly respect and admire, and who unfortunately is not as

---

* Pages 64ff in the present edition.

appreciated as he should be today owing to the inclination of some people nowadays to view him rather naively as "scholastic" just because he translated some Western books or perhaps used some Western theological phrases.

Regarding the specific point of Bishop Theophan's disagreement with Bishop Ignatius' teaching: You are correct in the supposition expressed in your private letter to me that when I wrote of this disagreement on page 36* of *The Soul After Death* I had not read Bishop Theophan's booklet *Soul and Angel*, which criticizes Bishop Ignatius' teaching, and that my comments there were indeed based solely on Fr. Florovsky's small reference to it. Having since been able to obtain and read Bishop Theophan's booklet, I see that my comments there are not precise. You are, of course, correct that there was no "dispute" between the two, but only Bishop Theophan's disagreement, expressed after the death of Bishop Ignatius. The point of disagreement was also not expressed precisely (as I will discuss below). The main question you raise, however, is whether indeed this disagreement was a "minor" one, as I have stated; this question I would like to address here briefly.

Perhaps this question is only a semantic one, based on a difference of perspective in viewing the disagreement between these two theologians. Anyone reading Bishop Theophan's *Soul and Angel,* with its 200 (albeit small) pages criticizing Bishop Ignatius' teaching, and seeing the emphasis with which Bishop Theophan accused what he regarded as Bishop Ignatius' error, might be inclined to call the disagreement a "major" one. But in looking at the whole context of Bishop Ignatius' teaching on life after death, I still cannot help seeing this disagreement as a "minor" one, for the following reasons:

---

* Page 27 in the present edition.

1. Bishop Theophan, in the whole course of his criticism in *Soul and Angel,* accuses only one and the same error (or supposed error) of Bishop Ignatius: the idea that the soul and angels are bodily and only bodily in nature. Bishop Theophan himself writes: "If the new teaching had only said that angels *have* bodies, one would not have needed to argue with it; for in this case the chief, dominating side in angels would still be a rationally free spirit. But when it is said that an angel *is* a body, one must deny in it rational freedom and consciousness; for these qualities cannot belong to a body" (*Soul and Angel,* Second Edition, Moscow, 1902, p. 103). If Bishop Ignatius had indeed held such an opinion, with all the emphasis and consequences which Bishop Theophan ascribes to it, it would surely have been a serious error on his part. But even so, it would not have directly affected the rest of his teaching on life after death: angels and souls would still act in the same way and in the same "places" whether they *are* bodies or *have* bodies (or even *assume* bodies, as Bishop Theophan himself seems more inclined to believe). Bishop Theophan's criticism, thus, does not at all affect the whole system of Bishop Ignatius' teaching, but only one technical aspect of it. And even here their agreement is greater than their disagreement: both agree that there is a bodily aspect to the activities of angels, whether in this world or in the other world, and that therefore the account of their activities in the Lives of Saints and other Orthodox sources are to be accepted as true accounts and not as "metaphors" or "fantasies," as Western critics believe. Therefore, in the whole context of Bishop Ignatius' (and Bishop Theophan's) teaching on life after death, I cannot but see this disagreement as "minor."

2. I seriously question whether Bishop Ignatius actually taught the teaching which Bishop Theophan ascribes to him;

certainly, at any rate, he did not place on it the emphasis or draw the consequences from it which Bishop Theophan was most concerned to oppose. Thus, in the quotation from Bishop Theophan above, where he states that "when it is said that an angel *is* a body, one must deny in it rational freedom and consciousness"—it is clear that Bishop Theophan is only drawing the logical conclusion from what he *thinks* Bishop Ignatius believes, but nowhere can he find a quotation from Bishop Ignatius himself that he actually believes angels to be deprived of rational freedom and consciousness; certainly Bishop Ignatius did not believe this. In my own reading of Bishop Ignatius' "Homily on Death" I did not find such a teaching. I have not read his "Supplement" to this work, but I am sure that there also there will not be found the whole *emphasis and consequences* of that teaching which Bishop Theophan accuses. Without entering into the full details of the disagreement between them (which might be a major study in itself and would have, I think, no particular value for Orthodox theology or the Orthodox teaching on life after death), I suspect that the error on Bishop Ignatius' part was not in holding the precise teaching which Bishop Theophan criticizes, but (perhaps) in overemphasizing the bodily side of the angelic nature and activity (rather easy to do in combatting the overly "spiritual" emphasis of Western teachers) to the extent that he may sometimes have *seemed* to be saying that angels (and souls) *are* bodies rather than (as I think he actually meant to say) that angels and souls *have* (ethereal) bodies, or that a bodily aspect is *part* of their nature. As Bishop Theophan has said, there would be no argument between them if such was indeed his teaching, for he regards this (for example, in *Soul and Angel*, p. 139) as a permissible opinion on this complex question which has not been dogmatically defined by the Church.

All the more, then, if Bishop Theophan was even slightly mistaken as to the emphasis of Bishop Ignatius' teaching, should this disagreement be regarded as "minor" in my opinion.

3. Bishop Theophan was once specifically asked whether in the teaching of Bishop Ignatius he had found any other error, apart from the supposed teaching of the "materiality" of the soul. He replied: "No. In Bishop Ignatius there is only this error—his opinion on the nature of the soul and angels, that they are material.... In all that I have read in his books, I have noticed nothing un-Orthodox. What I have read is good" (Letter of Dec. 15, 1893, in *The Russian Monk*, Pochaev Monastery, No. 17, Sept., 1912). Thus, in the context of the whole Orthodox teaching of Bishops Ignatius and Theophan, this disagreement is truly a "minor" one.

Now to pass to a final point, concerning the aerial toll-houses encountered by the soul after death. In your open letter you quote a letter of Bishop Theophan in which he states that life after death "is a land closed to us. What happens there is not defined with precision.... As to what shall be there—we shall see when we get there." From this, as well as from the fact that Bishop Theophan does not mention the toll-houses often in his writings, you conclude that "the teaching as such, in all of its symbolism, was ... at most peripheral to his thinking," and you think I am mistaken at least in my emphasis that Bishop Theophan was a staunch defender of the Orthodox teaching of the toll-houses. To this I would reply with several points:

1. I also can recall only these two direct references in the writings of Bishop Theophan to the teaching of the toll-houses. However, these two references are sufficient to show that he did indeed hold this teaching and taught it to others, and that he was quite critical, even scornful, of those who denied it ("No

matter how absurd the idea of the toll-houses may seem to our 'wise men,' they will not escape passing through them").

2. The fact that in some of his letters when the subject of life after death is touched on, he does not mention the toll-houses, does not seem to me a necessary indication that this subject is "peripheral" to his teaching, but only that he speaks in each case to the need of his listener, and some people do not need (or are unable) to hear of the toll-houses. I have found this same thing in my own experience as a priest: With those who are ready for it, the teaching of the toll-houses is a powerful incentive to repentance and a life lived in the fear of God; but there are those for whom the teaching would be so frightening that I would not even speak of it to them until they were better prepared to accept it. A priest sometimes encounters dying people so little prepared for the other world that it would be pointless to speak to them even of hell, let alone the toll-houses, for fear of removing in them the little hope and awareness they might have of the Kingdom of Heaven; but this does not mean that hell has no part in the teaching of such a priest, or that he would not defend its reality decisively if it were attacked. Especially in our "enlightened" 20th century, many Orthodox Christians are so immature spiritually, or have been so misled by modern ideas, that they are simply incapable of accepting the idea of encounters with demons after death. Any Orthodox priest in his pastoral approach to such people must, of course, condescend to their weakness and give them the "baby food" they require until they are more prepared to accept the strong food of some of the Orthodox ascetical texts; but the Orthodox teaching on the toll-houses, handed down from the early Christian centuries, remains always the same and cannot be denied no matter how many people are incapable of understanding it.

3. Moreover, in actual fact the teaching of the toll-houses *does* appear in other works of Bishop Theophan—in his translations if not in his original works. There are numerous references to this teaching in his five-volume translation of the *Philokalia,* several of which I have cited in the text of *The Soul After Death* (pp. 80–81, 258–9, 262).* In *Unseen Warfare* also (Part Two, ch. 9), there is an exposition of the Orthodox teaching of the "examination by the prince of this age" given to everyone on his departure from the body; the word "toll-houses" does not appear there, but the text says clearly that "the most decisive battle awaits us in the hour of death," and it is obvious that the reality is the same as that which Bishop Ignatius is so concerned to defend, and which in other places Bishop Theophan does call by the name of "toll-houses."

4. The text of Bishop Theophan's *Soul and Angel* contains not one word critical of Bishop Ignatius' teaching on the toll-houses. Now in Bishop Ignatius' "Homily on Death" he states unequivocally that "the teaching of the toll-houses is the teaching of the Church" (vol. III of his works, p. 138), and goes on to justify this statement in great detail. And Bishop Theophan, in his criticism of Bishop Ignatius' teaching, states that "in the present article the new teaching of the above-mentioned brochures ["Homily on Death" and the "Supplement" to it] is examined in full detail, without leaving uncensured a single thought in them which should be censured" (*Soul and Angel*, p. 4). It is quite clear, then, since Bishop Theophan found nothing whatever to censure in Bishop Ignatius' ideas on the toll-houses, that he is in full agreement with Bishop Ignatius that "the teaching of the toll-houses is the teaching of the Church."

---

* In present edition, pp. 71–72, 247–8, 251.

5. In the very text of *Soul and Angel,* Bishop Theophan sets forth the conditions of the soul after its departure from the body in terms identical to those of Bishop Ignatius' exposition. These are precisely the conditions required for the occurrence of the encounter of the soul with demons at the toll-houses, so this quote, even though it does not directly mention the toll-houses, may be taken as an indication of Bishop Theophan's agreement with Bishop Ignatius on the nature of after-death reality, his *sole* difference with Bishop Ignatius being on the question whether the nature of angels is *only* body (which, as I stated above, I do not believe Bishop Ignatius actually taught). Here is the quote from Bishop Theophan:

"The soul, after its departure from the body, enters into the realm of spirits, where both it and the spirits are active in the same forms as are visible on earth among men: they see each other, they speak, travel, argue, act. The difference is only that there the realm is an ethereal one of subtle matter, and in them therefore everything is subtly material and ethereal. What is the direct conclusion from this? That in the world of spirits the outward form of being and of mutual relations is the same as among men on earth. But this fact does *not* speak of the bodiliness of the nature of angels, or say that their essence is only body" (*Soul and Angel,* pp. 88–89).

6. You do not disagree with me on the main point: that Bishop Theophan, like Bishop Ignatius, did hold the Orthodox teaching of the toll-houses; your only disagreement with me is on the *emphasis* the two teachers placed on it (Bishop Ignatius spoke of it more, Bishop Theophan less). I think there is a very simple explanation for this seeming difference of emphasis: It was Bishop Ignatius who felt it was necessary to write a whole treatise on the subject of life after death, where the subject of the toll-houses, being an important part of the Orthodox teach-

ing, of necessity occupies a conspicuous place; while Bishop Theophan, not having written such a treatise, mentions this subject only in passing. I would imagine (without looking through all his works to verify it) that in his other writings Bishop Ignatius mentions the toll-houses no more often than Bishop Theophan. The few references in Bishop Theophan's writings, however, do indicate that he held the teaching as firmly as Bishop Ignatius. The difference between them, then, I would say, is not what they believed or even in the force with which they expressed their belief, but in the point I mentioned at the beginning of this letter: that Bishop Ignatius was more concerned than Bishop Theophan to do close battle with the rationalistic views of the West, while Bishop Theophan handed down the Orthodox tradition with less attention to fighting specific Western errors regarding it.

In view of all this, I believe that my statement in the preface of *The Soul After Death,* that Bishop Theophan "taught the same teaching" as Bishop Ignatius, is justified: in view of the whole Orthodox teaching on life after death which they had in common, the difference between them on the one point of the "bodiliness" of the nature of the soul and angels (a difference caused, I believe, more by the polemical overemphasis of Bishop Ignatius on the "bodies" of angels than by his actually holding the teaching ascribed to him by Bishop Theophan)—is indeed "minor." With regard to the points of the teaching on life after death set forth in *The Soul After Death* (since I did not defend or even mention Bishop Ignatius' supposed teaching that souls and angels are *only* bodies), their points of agreement are close to complete. The agreement of their teaching on life after death is all the more striking when one compares it with the views of the rationalistic critics of the West who, even up to our day, deny not only the reality of the toll-houses but also the whole after-death reality which Bishops Theophan and Ignatius described in virtually identical terms, the efficacy of prayers for the dead, and so forth. Against such false views the united witness of Bishops Theophan and Ignatius to the Orthodox teaching handed down from antiquity is indeed impressive.

I should be very interested in hearing further of your research on Bishop Theophan, for whom, as I have said, I have the greatest respect. Will you be publishing an article or book on him, or any translation of his works? I myself have translated the first part of *The Path to Salvation,* which is now appearing serially in the newspaper *Orthodox America.*

With love in Christ,
Unworthy Hieromonk Seraphim

P.S. I do not know how "open" your letter to me was, or to whom it was sent. I am sending copies of my reply only to a few people who are closely interested in this subject.

Fr. Seraphim in blessed repose, two days after his death.

About the Author

FATHER SERAPHIM was born Eugene Dennis Rose on August 13, 1934, in San Diego, California. His father Frank was of Dutch and French ancestry, while his mother Esther's family was from Norway. Esther was a Protestant, and Frank, although he had grown up as a Roman Catholic, became a Protestant for the sake of his wife. Frank worked at several occupations, owning a candy store for a while, then working for General Motors, and finally taking a job as a janitor at a sports stadium.

Eugene graduated from San Diego High School in 1952 at the top of his class. He was regarded by his parents, teachers and peers as a young "genius" destined for a brilliant career in science or mathematics. By the time he entered Pomona College in southern California, however, such earthly pursuits seemed to him unimportant beside a new, all-consuming passion: to *know,* to understand reality in the highest sense. Feeling estranged from the society around him, he rebelled against its superficiality and materialism, and rejected the Protestant religion in which he had been raised. His search for Truth led first through Western philosophy and then through a study of the wisdom of the Orient, for which he learned the Chinese language, both ancient and modern.

Having graduated from Pomona College in 1956 with a bachelor's degree in Oriental Languages, Eugene enrolled in the Academy of Asian Studies in San Francisco, and studied under its Dean, Dr. Alan Watts. At the same Academy, he found a true representative of the Chinese tradition, a philosopher named Gi-ming Shien. Eugene went to various Eastern temples and helped Gi-ming to translate the *Tao Teh Ching* from the ancient Chinese characters. In 1957 he became a student of the University of California, Berkeley, where he received his master's degree in Oriental Languages in 1961.

The wisdom of the pre-Christian philosophers, as profound as it was, left Eugene unfulfilled, and he was in despair at not knowing why. From Gi-ming, and also from the writings of the French metaphysician René Guénon, he had learned the value of adhering to the traditional, *orthodox* form of a religion, whatever that religion might be. Unable to find the end of his search in the traditional Eastern religions he had already experienced, he went one day to see the orthodox, Eastern form of the religion he had known as a child—Christianity. Describing this moment many years later, he wrote:

"For years in my studies I was satisfied with being 'above all traditions' but somehow faithful to them…. When I visited an Orthodox church, it was only in order to view another 'tradition'—knowing that Guénon (or one of his disciples) had described Orthodoxy as being the most authentic of the Christian traditions.

"However, when I entered an Orthodox church for the first time (a Russian church in San Francisco) something happened to me that I had not experienced in any Buddhist or other Eastern temple; something in my heart said that this was 'home,' that all my search was over. I didn't really know what this meant, because the service was quite strange to me, and in a foreign language. I began to attend Orthodox services more frequently, gradually learning the language and customs, but still keeping all my basic Guénonian ideas about all the authentic spiritual traditions.

274

"With my exposure to Orthodoxy and to Orthodox people, however, a new idea began to enter my awareness: that Truth was not just an abstract idea, sought and known by the mind, but was something personal—even a Person—sought and loved by the heart. And that is how I met Christ."

Eugene was received into the Orthodox Church on the Sunday of the Prodigal Son, February 25, 1962, in the Mother of God "Joy of All Who Sorrow" Russian Orthodox Cathedral in San Francisco. On receiving the Holy Mysteries for the first time he felt a heavenly, Divine taste in his mouth which lasted for over a week. "I have been reborn in the Lord," he later wrote to a friend, "... and I have known in Him such joy as I never believed possible while I was living according to the world."

In San Francisco Eugene became a disciple of Archbishop John Maximovitch (canonized in 1994 as St. John of Shanghai and San Francisco): a hierarch known the world over as a miracle-worker, clairvoyant elder, ascetic, "fool for Christ," father of orphans, and deliverer of the oppressed. With this unearthly man as his guide, Eugene entered into what he was later to call the indefinable "savor" or "fragrance" of Orthodoxy, into the essence and heart of unadulterated, otherworldly Christianity.

Seeing potential greatness in the young Eugene, Archbishop John made special efforts to prepare him for a life of service in the Church. He began a series of theological classes in San Francisco, which Eugene attended diligently. Eugene graduated from this course at the head of his class, even though all the lectures were delivered in Russian and Eugene was the only American Orthodox convert in the class.

Eugene wanted to dedicate the rest of his life to bringing the Truth of Holy Orthodoxy to his contemporaries. Together with a young Russian, Gleb Podmoshensky, he started a missionary Brotherhood dedicated to one of the original Orthodox missionaries who had come from Russia to America: the holy miracle-worker Fr. Herman of Alaska (†1836).

In 1964 the brothers opened an Orthodox bookstore in San Francisco and began to publish a magazine, *The Orthodox Word,* printing each issue on a simple letterpress. All of these undertakings were begun with the blessing and encouragement of Archbishop John Maximovitch.

After the death of Archbishop John in 1966, the brothers began to search for land in the wilderness of northern California, where they could continue to print *The Orthodox Word* and at the same time enter into the experience of the Orthodox ascetics ("desert-dwellers") throughout the ages. Archbishop John had blessed this step as well, for not long before his death he had told Eugene that he believed the brothers would establish a missionary monastery in northern California.

In 1969 Eugene and Gleb moved to a secluded mountainside ("Noble Ridge") near the small town of Platina, California, bringing all their printing equipment with them. A year later, the Brotherhood's patron, Fr. Herman of Alaska, was canonized by the Orthodox Church, thus becoming America's first canonized saint. The brothers helped to prepare for the canonization by publishing material on St. Herman's life and miracles, and by writing and printing the Church service to him.

On October 27, 1970, the brothers were tonsured as monks by Archbishop Anthony Medvedev of Western America and San Francisco (†2000), of the Russian Orthodox Church Outside of Russia. At their tonsure, Eugene was named after the Russian ascetic St. Seraphim of Sarov, Gleb was given the name of St. Herman of Alaska, and the new monastery was also named after St. Herman. Fr. Seraphim's "elder from the mantle" at his tonsure was the humble Archimandrite Spyridon

Efimov (†1984). Fr. Spyridon had been a disciple of Archbishop John and, like his teacher, had received the gift of clairvoyance from God. In succeeding years, Fr. Spyridon visited the monks whenever he could, giving valuable spiritual counsel and helping to set the new St. Herman of Alaska Monastery on a secure spiritual footing.

Fathers Seraphim and Herman also looked for spiritual guidance from Bishop Nektary Kontzevitch of Seattle (†1983), a disciple of Elder Nektary of Optina Monastery in Russia. Bishop Nektary loved to visit the new monastery in northern California, which reminded him of the forest monasteries in Holy Russia. "In Platina," he wrote in a letter, "the spirit of Optina dwells." At the same time he warned the monks not to fall into pride. "Don't think that anything you have is by your own efforts or merit," he told them. "It's a gift of God!"

In the bosom of God's nature, Fr. Seraphim's spirit began to soar. He built for himself a small cabin in the forest, and there immersed himself in prayer and the God-inspired writings of the Holy Fathers. Through gradual inward purification, through ascetic struggle and unseen warfare, he began to acquire the mind and heart, the way of thinking and feeling of these ancient teachers and visionaries. Although he had a deep bond with nature and animals and cherished every day he could stay on Noble Ridge, he felt himself to be only a pilgrim on this earth and was consciously preparing himself for the life beyond. Several miraculous instances were witnessed of how he received guidance and help from the other world, especially from his reposed spiritual father, Archbishop John.

From his mountain refuge, Fr. Seraphim produced an outpouring of books and magazines which served to place traditional wisdom in a modern context. He wrote, translated, typeset, printed, and sent them out all over the world, where their full significance would be seen only after his death. Never idle for a moment, he was driven to make the fullness of Truth available to rootless, fragmented modern man—while there was still time. Beholding the rise of unbelief and anti-Christianity in the world, he would say, "It's later than you think! Hasten, therefore, to do the work of God."

As new brothers joined the monastic community in Platina, Fr. Seraphim served as their spiritual guide. Daily they would unburden their hearts to him, and he would uplift them with words of counsel, supplemented with Patristic writings that he translated especially for them.

Fr. Seraphim was ordained a deacon on January 2, 1977; and he was ordained to the priesthood on the Sunday of the Myrrhbearing Women, April 24, 1977. Both ordinations were performed by the aforementioned Bishop Nektary of Seattle.

In spite of Fr. Seraphim's love for wilderness solitude and his retiring, philosophical disposition, his last years were spent in ever-increasing pastoral activity—in sprirual conversations with monastery pilgrims, in informal talks and public lectures at the monastery and elsewhere, and in celebrating services at missionary parishes that the monastery had helped to establish. He was deeply loved by his spiritual children for his simple wisdom and his ability to understand human suffering. Some were surprised to find that this man, who was so uncompromising when it came to writing about spiritual deceptions which could lead people astray, was at the same time so compassionate when it came to dealing with the individual, fallen person.

A brief and sudden illness took Fr. Seraphim from this earth on September 2, 1982. He was only forty-eight years old. His last days were filled with intense prayer, as people gathered from far and wide to be at his bedside in the hospital. Unable to speak behind a respirator mask, he looked to heaven and prayed with tears as he prepared his soul for the future life.

In his coffin in the humble monastery church, Fr. Seraphim's face took on an expression of unearthly tranquility, testifying to the peace he had found with God. He was so radiant—literally golden—that children could hardly be drawn away from his coffin. The mystery of death and the life beyond, which he had pondered for most of his intellectual life, was now a mystery to him no more. Miracles began to be recorded of his help from the other world to his spiritual children.

During Fr. Seraphim's lifetime, his books were known to a relatively small number of people, primarily in English-speaking countries. In the two decades following his death, however, his writings have had a worldwide impact. Translated into many languages—Russian, Greek, Serbian, Romanian, Bulgarian, Georgian, French, Latvian, Polish, Italian, Chinese, and Malayalam (South Indian)—they have changed countless lives with their sobering truth. In Russia and other Eastern European countries during the Communist suppression of spiritual literature, his books *Orthodoxy and the Religion of the Future* and *The Soul After Death* were secretly distributed in the form of typewritten manuscripts, becoming known to millions. With the cessation of religious persecution, his books and articles were published in those countries in mass quantities, and have been on sale everywhere. When American Orthodox Christians go to Orthodox churches and monasteries in Eastern Europe, the first question they are often asked is, "Did you know Fr. Seraphim Rose?" In more recent years, Fr. Seraphim has become widely revered in among Orthodox Christians in Greece, through Greek translations of his life and works.

Besides the two books just mentioned, Fr. Seraphim's published works include *God's Revelation to the Human Heart; Heavenly Realm; Genesis, Creation and Early Man; Nihilism;* and *The Place of Blessed Augustine in the Orthodox Church.* All of these books were published by the St. Herman Brotherhood after Fr. Seraphim's repose, along with his one-thousand-page biography, *Father Seraphim Rose: His Life and Works.* The Brotherhood is currently preparing for publication other books by Fr. Seraphim, including his collected lectures.

Orthodox Christians in Russia and other Orthodox countries of Eastern Europe have seen this American from southern California, Fr. Seraphim, as pivotal to the restoration of traditional spiritual principles in their homelands—lands that had been ravaged by decades of enforced godlessness. It is time now for more of his fellow Americans—who face rising godlessness in their own homeland—to hear his message and be awakened to the eternal Truth for which he lived and died.

—Hieromonk Damascene
St. Herman of Alaska Monastery
Platina, California

Bibliography

ORTHODOX SOURCES (IN ENGLISH)

Adamnan, St., *Life of St. Columba*, tr. by Wentworth Huyshe, London, George Routledge and Sons, Ltd., 1939.

Ambrose, St., "Death as a Good," in *Seven Exegetical Works*, tr. by Michael P. McHugh, The Fathers of the Church, vol. 65, Catholic University of America Press, 1972.

—— "On Belief in the Resurrection," in Nicene and Post-Nicene Fathers, Second Series, vol. 10, Eerdmans Publishing Co., Grand Rapids, Mich., 1969.

Anonymous Monk of Whitby, *The Earliest Life of Gregory the Great*, tr. by Bertram Colgrave, University of Kansas Press, Lawrence, Kansas, 1968.

Athanasius the Great, St., *Life of St. Anthony the Great*, Eastern Orthodox Books, Willits, Calif., 1976.

Augustine, Blessed, "Care for the Dead," in *Treatises on Marriage and Other Subjects*, The Fathers of the Church, vol. 27, New York, 1955.

—— *The City of God*, Modern Library ed., New York, 1955.

—— "The Divination of Demons," in *Treatises on Marriage and Other Subject*, New York, 1955.

Basil the Great, St., *Exegetical Homilies*, The Fathers of the Church, vol. 46, Catholic University of America Press, 1963.

Bede, Venerable, *A History of the English Church and People*, tr. by Leo Sherley-Price, Penguin Books, Baltimore, 1968.

Boniface, St., *The Letters of Saint Boniface*, tr. by Ephraim Emerton, Octagon Books (Farrar, Straus, and Giroux), New York, 1973.

Cavarnos, Constantine, *The Future Life according to Orthodox Teaching*, Center for Traditionalist Orthodox Studies, Etna, Calif., 1985.

Cyril of Jerusalem, St., *Catechetical Lectures*, Nicene and Post-Nicene Fathers, Second Series, vol. 7, Eerdmans Publishing Co., Grand

Rapids, Mich., 1973.

Chrysostom, St. John, *Homilies on St. Matthew,* Nicene and Post-Nicene Fathers, Eerdmans Publishing Co., Grand Rapids, Mich., 1973.

Climacus, St. John, *Ladder of Divine Ascent,* tr. by Archimandrite Lazarus Moore, Eastern Orthodox Books, Willits, Calif., 1977.

—— *Ladder of Divine Ascent,* revised ed. by Holy Transfiguration Monastery, Boston, 1979.

Damascene, St. John, *Exact Exposition of the Orthodox Faith,* The Fathers of the Church, vol. 37, New York, 1958.

The Departure of the Soul according to the Teaching of the Orthodox Church, St. Poimen's Greek Orthodox Brotherhood, Phoenix, Ariz., 2016 (forthcoming).

Dorotheus of Gaza, St. Abba, *Discourses and Sayings,* tr. by Eric P. Wheeler, Cistercian Publications, Kalamazoo, Mich., 1977.

Fastre, J. A. M., S.J., tr., *The Acts of the Early Martyrs,* Fifth Series, Philadelphia, 1878.

Gregory the Great (the Dialogist), St., *Dialogues,* Fathers of the Church, vol. 39, New York, 1959.

—— *Morals on the Book of Job,* Oxford, John Henry Parker, 1844.

Gregory of Nyssa, St., "On the Soul and the Resurrection," in Nicene and Post-Nicene Fathers, Second Series, vol. 5, Eerdmans Publishing Co., Grand Rapids, Mich., 1972.

Hierotheos (Vlachos), Metropolitan of Nafpaktos, *Life After Death,* Birth of the Theotokos Monastery, Levadia, Greece, 1996.

John (Maximovitch), Archbishop, "Life after Death," in *The Orthodox Word,* 1971, no. 4.

Larchet, Jean-Claude, *Life after Death according to the Orthodox Tradition,* Orthodox Research Institute, Rollinsford, New Hampshire, 2012.

The Lenten Triodion, tr. by Mother Mary and Archimandrite Kallistos Ware, Faber and Faber, London, 1977.

Lives of Saints:

Sts. Cyprian and Justina, in *The Orthodox Word,* 1976, no. 5.

Bibliography

St. Salvius of Albi, in *The Orthodox Word,* 1977, no. 5.

Sts. Timothy and Maura, in *Orthodox Life,* May-June, 1978.

Macarius the Great, St., *Fifty Spiritual Homilies,* tr. by A.J. Mason, Eastern Orthodox Books, Willits, Calif., 1974.

Mitrophan, Monk, *How Our Departed Ones Live, and How We Shall Live after Death,* vol. 1, tr. by Archpriest John Shaw, published by Archpriest Stefan Pavlenko, Burlingame, Calif., 2005.

Octoechos, Sunday, tr. by Mother Mary, Bussy-en-Othe, France, n.d.

Orthodox Life (texts on life after death), 1978, no. 1.

Panteleimon, Archimandrite, comp., *Eternal Mysteries beyond the Grave,* Holy Trinity Monastery, Jordanville, N.Y., 1968. Reprint, 2012.

The Philokalia, vol. 1, tr. by Palmer, Sherrard, and Ware, Faber and Faber, London, 1979.

Savva, Bishop of Edmonton, *Blessed John: The Chronicle of the Veneration of Archbishop John Maximovitch,* St. Herman of Alaska Brotherhood, Platina, Calif., 1979.

The Sayings of the Desert Fathers, tr. by Benedicta Ward, A. R. Mowbray & Co., London, 1975.

Sederholm, Fr. Clement, *Elder Leonid of Optina,* St. Herman of Alaska Brotherhood, Platina, Calif., 1990. Reprint, 2002.

Seraphim of Sarov, St., *Little Russian Philokalia,* vol. 1: *St. Seraphim of Sarov,* St. Herman of Alaska Brotherhood, Platina, Calif., 1978. Reprint, 2008.

—— *The Spiritual Instructions of St. Seraphim of Sarov,* St. Herman of Alaska Brotherhood, Platina, Calif., 1978.

Symeon the New Theologian, St., *The Sin of Adam,* St. Herman of Alaska Brotherhood, Platina, Calif., 1979. Reprinted as *The First-Created Man,* 1994.

Uekskuell, K., "Unbelievable for Many but Actually a True Occurrence," in *Orthodox Life,* July-August, 1976.

Vasilios (Bakogiannis), Archimandrite, *After Death,* Tertios Publications, Katerini, Greece, 1995.

Vassiliadis, Nikolaos P., *The Mystery of Death,* The Orthodox Brotherhood of Theologians "The Savior," Athens, Greece, 1993.

Znosko, Vladimir, *Hieroschemamonk Feofil* (Theophilus of Kiev), tr. by Lev Puhalo and Vassily Novakshonoff, Holy Trinity Monastery, Jordanville, N.Y., 1970.

ORTHODOX SOURCES (IN RUSSIAN AND SLAVONIC)

Athanasia Logacheva, Life of a Nun, in *Soul-Profiting Reading*, June, 1902.

Avraam (Reidman), Schema-archimandrite, comp., *The Path of the Soul after Death*, "Palomnik," Moscow, 2007.

Barsanuphius and John, Sts., *Guidance in Spiritual Life (in Questions and Answers)*, Moscow, 1855.

Basil the Great, St., *Complete Works*, Soikin ed., St. Petersburg, 1911.

Brianchaninov, Bishop Ignatius, *Collected Works*, vol. 3, Tuzov ed., St. Petersburg, 1883.

Cassian, St. John, *Conferences*, tr. by Bishop Peter, Moscow, 1892.

Chrysostom, St. John, *Collected Works*, vol. 10:1, St. Petersburg, 1904.

Dudko, Priest Dimitry, *Sunday Talks on the Resurrection*, St. Job Brotherhood, Montreal, 1977.

Ephraim the Syrian, St., *Collected Works*, vol. 3, Moscow, 1882.

Euchologion (Book of Needs), Moscow, Synodal Printshop, 1902 (reprinted by Holy Trinity Monastery, Jordanville, N.Y., 1961), Part I.

Florovsky, Rev. Georges, *Ways of Russian Theology*, Paris, 1937.

Gregory the Great (the Dialogist), St., *Homilies on the Gospels*, tr. by Hieromonk Clement Sederholm, St. Petersburg, 1860.

Gregory the Theologian, St., *Complete Works*, Soikin ed., St. Petersburg, 1911.

Lenten Triodion (Slavonic), Vienna, 1855.

Lives of Saints (according to St. Demetrius of Rostov), Moscow, Synodal Printshop, 1902.

St. Andrew the Fool for Christ of Constantinople (Oct. 2).

St. Basil the New (March 26).

Sts. Cyprian and Justina (Oct. 2).

St. Mark of Thrace (April 5).

St. Niphon of Constantia (Dec. 23).

St. Patricius of Prussa (May 19).

St. Perpetua (Feb. 1).

St. Proclus (Nov. 20).

Taxiotes the Soldier (March 28).

Sts. Timothy and Maura (May 3).

Macarius, Metropolitan of Moscow, *Orthodox Dogmatic Theology*, vol. 2, St. Petersburg, 1883.

Mark of Ephesus, St., First and Second Homilies on Purgatorial Fire, in Archimandrite Amvrossy Pogodin, *St. Mark of Ephesus and the Union of Florence*, Holy Trinity Monastery, Jordanville, N.Y., 1963.

Mitrophan, Monk, *How Our Departed Ones Live, and How We Shall Live after Death*, vol. 1, St. Petersburg, 1897.

Octoechos (Slavonic), Vienna, 1855.

Sederholm, Hieromonk Clement, *Optina Elder Leonid*, St. Herman of Alaska Brotherhood, Platina, Calif., 1976.

Theophan the Recluse, Bishop, *Commentary on the Second Epistle of the Holy Apostle Paul to the Corinthians*, Moscow, 1894.

—— *The One-Hundred-Eighteenth Psalm* (Interpretation), Moscow, 1891 (reprinted by Holy Trinity Monastery, Jordanville, N.Y., 1976).

—— Letter to a Dying Woman, in *Soul-Profiting Reading*, August, 1894.

ORTHODOX SOURCES (IN GREEK)

Cavarnos, Constantine, *The Future Life According to Orthodox Teaching*, Ekdoseis "Orthodoxou Typou," Athens, Greece, 1984.

Hierotheos (Vlachos), Metropolitan of Nafpaktos, *Life After Death*, Nativity of the Theotokos Monastery, Levadia, Greece, 1995.

Livanos, Christos Constantine, *Do the Toll-Houses Exist?* Hellenic Orthodox Apostolic Brotherhood "St. Athanasios the Great,"

Toronto, Canada, 1998.

Vasilios (Bakogiannis), Archimandrite, *After Death,* Tertios Publications, Katerini, Greece, 1994.

Vassiliadis, Nikolaos P., *The Mystery of Death,* The Orthodox Brotherhood of Theologians "The Savior," Athens, Greece, 1993.

ORTHODOX SOURCES (IN SERBIAN)

Justin (Popovich), Archimandrite, *The Orthodox Philosophy of Truth: The Dogmatics of the Orthodox Church,* vol. 3, Belgrade, 1978.

"AFTER-DEATH" BOOKS;
WRITINGS ON OCCULTISM AND SPIRITISM

Apuleius, *The Golden Ass,* tr. by Robert Graves, Farrar, Straus and Young, New York, 1951.

Barrett, Sir William, *Death-Bed Visions,* Methuen, London, 1926.

Blackmore, Simon A., S.J., *Spiritism: Facts and Frauds,* Benziger Brothers, New York, 1924.

Budge, E. A. Wallis, tr., *The (Egyptian) Book of the Dead,* Bell Publishing Co., New York, 1960.

Crookall, Robert, *Out-of-the-Body Experiences,* The Citadel Press, Secaucus, N.J., 1970.

Eliade, M., *Shamanism,* Routledge & Kegan Paul, London, 1961.

Evans-Wentz, W.Y., ed., *The Tibetan Book of the Dead,* Oxford University Press, Oxford, 1960.

Fiore, Charles and Landsburg, Alan, *Death Encounters,* Bantam Books, New York, 1979.

Ford, Arthur, *The Life Beyond Death,* G. P. Putnam's Sons, New York, 1971.

Fortune, Dion, *Through the Gates of Death,* Samuel Weiser Inc., New York, 1977.

Green, Celia, *Out-of-the-Body Experiences,* Ballantine Books, New York, 1975.

Greenhous, Herbert B., *The Astral Journey,* Avon Books, New York, 1976.

Grof, Stanislav and Halifax, Joan, *The Human Encounter with Death,* E. P. Dutton, New York, 1977.

Hill, J. Arthur, *Spiritualism, Its History, Phenomena, and Doctrine,* George H. Doran Co., New York, 1919.

Holzer, Hans, *Beyond This Life,* Pinnacle Books, Los Angeles, 1977.

Hynek, J. Allen and Vallee, Jacques, *The Edge of Reality,* Henry Regnery Co., Chicago, 1975.

Jung, C. G., *The Interpretation of Nature and the Psyche,* Routledge & Kegan Paul, London, 1955.

Kubler-Ross, Elizabeth, "Death Does not Exist," in *The Co-Evolution Quarterly,* Summer, 1977.

—— *On Death and Dying,* Macmillan Publishing Co., New York, 1969.

—— Articles on:
　Kemf, Elizabeth, in *East-West Journal,* March, 1978.
　Kronisch, Lennie, in *Yoga Journal,* September-October, 1976.
　Laughingbird, Gaea, in *Berkeley Monthly,* June, 1978.
　Pearre, James, in the *San Francisco Sunday Examiner and Chronicle,* Nov. 14, 1976.
　San Diego Union, Sept. 2, 1979.

Loehr, Franklin, *Diary after Death,* Pillar Books, New York, 1976.

Matson, Archie, *Afterlife: Reports from the Threshold of Death,* Harper & Row, New York, 1977.

Monroe, Robert A., *Journeys Out of the Body,* Anchor Books (Doubleday), Garden City, New York, 1977.

Moody, Raymond A., Jr., *Life after Life,* Mockingbird Books, Atlanta, 1975.

—— *Reflections on Life after Life,* A Bantam-Mockingbird Book, 1977.

Muldoon, Sylvan and Carrington, Hereward, *The Phenomena of Astral Projection,* Samuel Weiser, New York, 1972.

Osis, Karl, and Haroldsson, Erlendur, *At the Hour of Death,* Avon Books, New York, 1977.

Powell, A. E., *The Astral Body,* Theosophical Publishing House,

Wheaton, Ill., 1972.

Psychics, by the Editors of *Psychic Magazine,* Harper & Row, New York, 1972.

Sherman, Harold, *You Live after Death,* Fawcett Books, New York, 1972.

Smith, Susy, *Life is Forever,* G. P. Putnam's Sons, New York, 1974.

—— *Out-of-Body Experiences,* Dell Publishing Co., New York, 1969.

Spraggett, Allen, *The Case for Immortality,* New American Library, New York, 1974.

Swedenborg, Emanuel, *Heaven and Hell,* tr. by George F. Dole, Swedenborg Foundation, Inc., New York, 1976.

Trobridge, George, *Swedenborg: Life and Teaching,* Swedenborg Foundation, New York, 1978.

Van Dusen, Wilson, *The Presence of Other Worlds,* Harper & Row, New York, 1973.

Walker, Benjamin, *Beyond the Body: The Human Double and the Astral Plane,* Routledge & Kegan Paul, London, 1974.

Weiss, Jess E., *The Vestibule,* Pocket Books, New York, 1977.

Wheeler, David R., *Journey to the Other Side,* Ace Books, New York, 1977.

ATTEMPTS AT CHRISTIAN APPROACHES AND EVALUATIONS— MOSTLY EVANGELICAL PROTESTANT

Baker, H. A. *Visions Beyond the Veil,* Whitaker House, Monroeville, Pa., 1973.

Brooke, Tal, *The Other Side of Death,* Tyndale House, Wheaton, Ill., 1979.

Eby, Richard E., *Caught Up into Paradise,* private printing, c. 1978.

Ernest, Victor H., *I Talked with Spirits,* Tyndale House, Wheaton, Ill., 1975.

Faust, Floyd, *Life Death Life,* The Upper Room, Nashville, Tenn., 1977.

BIBLIOGRAPHY

Ford, Marvin, *On the Other Side,* Logos International, Plainfield, N.J., 1978.

Graham, Billy, *Angels, God's Secret Messengers,* Doubleday, New York, 1975.

Levitt, Zola, and Weldon, John, *Is There Life after Death?* Harvest House Publishers, Irvine, Calif., 1977.

Lewis, C. S., *Miracles,* The Macmillan Co., New York, 1967.

Lindsay, Hal, *Life after Death,* Christ for the Nations, Dallas, Texas, 1977.

Malz, Betty, *My Glimpse of Eternity,* Chosen Books, Waco, Texas, 1977.

Myers, John, ed., *Voices from the Edge of Eternity,* Spire Books, Old Tappan, N.J., 1973.

Peale, Norman Vincent, *The Power of Positive Thinking,* Prentice-Hall, Inc., New York, 1953.

Rawlings, Maurice, *Beyond Death's Door,* Thomas Nelson, Inc., Nashville, 1978.

Ritchie, George C., Jr., *Return from Tomorrow,* Chosen Books, Waco, Texas, 1978.

Sandberg, Anne, *Seeing the Invisible: What Happens after You Die?* Logos International, Plainfield, N.J., 1977.

Swihart, Phillip J., *The Edge of Death,* Inter-Varsity Press, Downers Grove, Ill., 1978.

Wilkerson, Ralph, *Beyond and Back,* Melodyland Publishers, Anaheim, Calif., 1977.

Winter, David, *Hereafter: What Happens after Death?* Harold Shaw Publishers, Wheaton, Ill., 1977.

RUSSIAN EDITIONS OF *THE SOUL AFTER DEATH*

Dusha posle smerti (The Soul After Death), samizdat, Moscow, 1984.

Dusha posle smerti, Moscow, 1991.

Dusha posle smerti, joint publication of the editorial staff of "Skete" and the Stavropol regional committee of the Red Cross Society, Moscow, 1992.

BIBLIOGRAPHY

Dusha posle smerti, "Glagol," St. Petersburg, 1994.

Dusha posle smerti. Moscow: Sretensky Monastery, 1997, 2007.

Prinosheniye pravoslavnogo amerikantsa. Sbornik trudov ottsa Serafima Platinskogo (An offering of a contemporary American: the collected works of Fr. Seraphim of Platina) [includes *The Soul After Death*], Valaam Society of America—Russian Mission, Moscow, 1998, 2001.

Dusha posle smerti, "Palomnik," Moscow, 2003, 2005.

Dusha posle smerti, Kievo-Pechersky Lavra, Kiev, 2006.

THE SOUL AFTER DEATH IN OTHER LANGUAGES

L'Ame après la mort (The Soul After Death, in French), Orthodox Monastery of the Archangel Michael, Lavardac, France, 1999.

L'Anima dopo la morte (in Italian), Servitum-Interlogos, Sotto il Monte and Schio, Italy, 1999.

Dusha posle smrti (in Serbian), "Svetigora," Cetinije, Yugoslavia, 1995.

Dusha posle smrti (in Serbian), "Srpski Sion," Sremski Karlovci, Yugoslavia, 1995.

Dushata sled smertta (in Bulgarian), Pravoslaven kosher, Trnovo, Bulgaria, n.d.

Marana Shesham? (in Malayalam [south Indian]), Mar Baselius Foundation, Prakkanam, India, 2000.

Ē Psukhē meta ton thanato (in Greek), Myriobiblios, Athens, 2003.

Die Seele nach dem Tod (in German), Russisches Orthodoxes Kloster des Hl. Hiob von Pocaev (Russian Orthodox Monastery of St. Job of Pochaev), Munich, Germany, 2000.

Sufletul după moarte (in Romanian), Protos. Teodosie Paraschiv, Bucharest, Romania, 1994.

Sufletul după moarte (in Romanian), Editura Anastasia, Bucharest, Romania, 1996, 2002.

Sufletul după moarte (in Romanian), Editura Tehnopress, Iaşi, Romania, 2003.

Index

INDEX

Ezekiel, Prophet, on resurrection, 126

Faustus of Lerins, St., on the relative "materiality" of the soul, 28
Felix the Confessor, St., appearance from the dead of, 17
"flashbacks" of life, 20, 33, 46, 84
Florovsky, Fr. Georges, 263
  Ways of Russian Theology by, 27
Fontrier, Fr. Ambroise, 214
Ford, Arthur, 164, 166

Garrett, Dr. Larry, on hypnotism, 124
Germanus of Capua, St., the ascent to heaven of, 131
Graham, Billy, on angels after death, 84
Gregory of Nyssa, St.
  against reincarnation, 126
  on the soul after death, 209
Gregory of Tours, St., on the experience of St. Salvius of Albi, 33, 135
Gregory the Great, the Dialogist, Pope of Rome, St.
  on angels, 130
  on clairvoyance, 118
  on demons, 35
  on heaven, 130
  interpretations of after-death experiences of, 17, 67–68
  on the meeting of others after death, 13–14
  misinterpretation of, 208–9
  prayers for the dead of, 190–92
  the prayer for Emperor Trajan of, 192, 203

on the soul after death, 3, 165, 196, 201
on the spiritual world, 224n, 230
on toll-houses, 72
on visions, 14–15, 17, 146, 164–65, 191
Gregory the Sinaite, St., on spiritual discernment, 61
Gregory the Theologian, St., on angels, 25

"hades," 103, 108
hallucinations, 2, 11, 13, 19, 47, 50, 101, 120, 223–24, 242
Hastings, Dr. Arthur C., on hypnotism, 123
heaven, 6, 12, 16–17, 24–25, 28, 32, 42–43, 45–46, 48–49, 55, 64–66, 71, 74–75, 83, 88, 92–93, 95–96, 98–99, 102, 104, 108–9, 111, 114–16, 121–22, 126, 128–35, 138–44, 148, 152–53, 166, 169–70, 172, 175, 194, 197, 209, 211, 216, 232, 234, 238–40, 246–47, 251, 260, 267
hell, 6, 14, 35–38, 43, 49, 65, 68, 76, 87–88, 92–96, 102, 104, 108, 111–12, 114–15, 121, 123, 126, 128–33, 145–49, 152–53, 160, 166, 172, 175, 186–87, 190, 194, 197–98, 200, 207, 209, 211, 219–20, 222, 232–34, 239–40, 242, 244, 247, 267
Herman of Alaska, St., ascent to heaven of, 131
Hesychios, St., on the hour of death, 72, 247

SAINT HERMAN OF ALASKA BROTHERHOOD

Since 1965, the St. Herman of Alaska Brotherhood has been publishing Orthodox Christian books and magazines.

View our catalog, featuring over fifty titles, and order online, at www.sainthermanmonastery.com

You can also write us for a free printout of our catalog:

St. Herman of Alaska Brotherhood
P. O. Box 70
Platina, CA 96076
USA